SCHOOL BUSINESS ADMINISTRATION
A PLANNING APPROACH

SCHOOL BUSINESS ADMINISTRATION
A PLANNING APPROACH

I. CARL CANDOLI
Superintendent of Schools
Lansing, Michigan

WALTER G. HACK
The Ohio State University

JOHN R. RAY
University of Tennessee at Knoxville

DEWEY H. STOLLAR
University of Tennessee at Knoxville

Allyn and Bacon, Inc. Boston

Library of Congress Catalog Card Number: 73–76583

Printed in the United States of America

To our wives:
        Joan, Barbara, Nancy, and Lois

CONTENTS

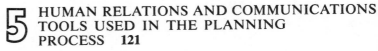

PREFACE

The function of school business administration is becoming more visible on the American educational scene. School business has been known as big business since the turn of the century, and its magnitude today is greater than ever. It is becoming increasingly visible as the competition for the public sector dollar grows more intense and educational priorities are no longer taken for granted.

Public education has been caught in the crunch of the taxpayers' revolt. Because of its heavy dependence on revenue from local property taxes, it has become particularly vulnerable to voter disenchantment with heavy tax burdens. The *Serrano* decision in California has carried ominous implications of further financial problems, and these have accentuated public and professional demands for knowing how present resources are being expended and what results are accruing from them. The burden of educational accountability weighs heavily on the shoulders of the school business administrator.

His position is becoming more sensitive because of the nature of new demands for accountability. Not only do new demands accrue to him because he has a technical specialization in the accounting function, but also because he is expected to possess the conceptual tools to aid or give leadership to the administrative team as a system-wide accountability program is developed. Specifically, the school business administrator is expected to assume his conventional responsibilities but additionally provide the management input into the system so it can make plausible management cost-benefit decisions, and in turn present this information in understandable form to local policy makers, and eventually to the public.

It is from this newly emerging responsibility that the thrust for this book is developed. The school business administrator's position is one where specific planning skills become crucial. He must plan as he assesses, designs, and implements the basic administrative program responsibilities under his jurisdiction. He must also plan with many others in order to know the educational program for children and youth—that program which serves as the end of his activity. He must also plan with many others to determine how best to coordinate his activities with those other specialists who serve the educational program. He must plan in order to provide the best and most useful information to other specialists to upgrade the decisions made in other administrative units of the school system. Thus, the school business administrator must be an effective planner within his own unit, and he must be an expert planner as he coordinates his work with other units to develop a complementary system working toward the goal of an increasingly effective school system.

In order to provide some guidance to the student interested in the field, the authors decided that these two concepts needed to be presented in a developmental sequence. The book, as a consequence, has been written in four parts. Part I considers the role and the setting of school business administration. The context is woven with the threads of historical perspectives as well as the emerging problems of public education in today's complex and dynamic society. Emphasis is given to the increased professionalization of the school business administrator's role as a member of the superintendency team.

Part II is developed from several important conceptual tools which are needed by school business administrators as they address the tasks of their increasingly crucial role. These include conceptual tools relating to the legal and judicial context, the management sciences, human relations and communication, and the processing of data.

The many tasks indigenous to school business administration make up Part III. In this segment of the book the tasks and promising conceptual and technical approaches are described in ways applicable to a wide range of school systems. Consideration is given to budgeting; personnel administration; accounting, auditing, and reporting; purchasing; maintenance and operation; insurance; transportation and food services; and capital outlay.

Part IV is composed of a single chapter—Chapter 15. The function of this final chapter is to draw together the three preceding parts and suggest an overview of the job and a perspective of the person in the school business administrator's position. It is designed to assist the student in making a decision as to whether he has the professional perspective and point of view necessary to perform as a school business administrator in a planning-oriented context.

The book clearly espouses a fundamental point of view of the authors; i.e., the way the school business administrator works and relates to pupils, teachers, fellow administrators, parents and community co-workers is a major determinant of the success he will enjoy. Thus, primary emphasis is given to this view. The technical skills of the school business administrator are not depreciated, however. It is recognized that one must have and use them, but no attempt is made to describe fully the range and depth of these kinds of skills. Instead, general skills are suggested in Part III as approaches to the tasks which are spelled out. Higher levels of specific skill development are left to further courses in the preparation programs of school business administrators and other structured field-related activities such as supervised field experiences and internships.

The authors are grateful to their friends and colleagues of the Lansing, Michigan Public Schools, The Ohio State University, and the University of Tennessee. Since there is "nothing new under the sun," we can only conclude that any knowledge and appreciation of the planning and team approach of educational administration which we have developed must have come to us from the interest, inspiration, and support which they have afforded us.

I. C. C.
W. G. H.
J. R. R.
D. H. S.

THE ROLE AND SETTING OF SCHOOL BUSINESS ADMINISTRATION

School business administration is probably more visible today than it has ever been. This is true in terms of visibility in the eyes of the education profession as well as in the eyes of the general public as a whole. The financial "crunch"; the calls for accountability; equal educational opportunity; reordering priorities; increasing productivity; the search for program and fiscal alternatives; and the taxpayers' revolt have placed demands on the school business administrator for explicating and defending his procedures and processes, as well as developing and adopting activities which can deliver the needed services as perceived by the given public.

Segments of the education profession likewise hold expectations for the behavior of the school business administrator. These segments, which are likewise under pressure from the public and their professional peers, look to the school business administrator to complement their efforts to meet the challenges of the day. These groups want the school business administrator to communicate educational needs, to provide more supportive services, to respond to more individualized needs, and provide the "software" necessary to upgrade business-oriented decisions in their own areas of responsibility.

The two chapters in Part I deal with the role and setting of school business administration. These are seen as an integral part of and embedded in general school administration. The case is made that the role of the school business administrator is discrete but interactive with the superintendency.

In order to understand the contemporary role and setting, and to think in terms of a more responsive future posture for the school business administrator, one must understand the evolution of both the general superintendency and the school business administrator, and how these separate roles have interacted. The authors take the position that the emerging relationship between the function of the superintendency and that of school business administration can be characterized by the "superintendency team" concept, and that planning is a powerful unifying force in this concept.

THE EMERGING PLANNING ROLE OF SCHOOL BUSINESS ADMINISTRATION

PLANNING: ITS RELEVANCY TO EDUCATION

One of the phenomena of the latter half of the twentieth century has been the rapid rise of the influence of the planner. The legitimization of the planning function, first in the military, later in business and industry, and most recently in municipal government and educational systems, has served to awaken the nation to the urgent need for utilizing planning processes as a first step in the orderly development of long-range guidelines for planned program implementation.

The continuing evolution of educational systems from small, fragmented, ineffective organizations numbering over 100,000 nationally to much larger, centrally controlled, but inefficient overlapping bureaucracies has forced a recognition of the business administration function as an integral part of the operation of the modern educational system. At the same time, as the thousands of consolidations of small units were taking place, new expanded school systems were beginning to realize the difficulty and enormity of the business function. The growth of the central business office has been an attempt to respond to the pressures for adequate business procedure application to the administration of the educational enterprise. This educational enterprise often commands the largest single budget in a community. Indeed, the expenditures for public education in the United States have grown to an estimated forty billion dollars annually and projections indicate continued growth.

From the early development of school business administration through the very recent past, the focus of the business office has been largely on day-to-day operations of the school system. True, there have been attempts to perform planning activities but these have been largely short-range efforts and have all too often been virtually extracurricular attempts by concerned individuals to determine directions and implications of certain actions. There is little in the literature or in field practice to suggest that any great effort has been expended in the orderly, systematic, coordinated creation of alternative plans for school districts to use as guidelines for future actions. This paucity in planning is best reflected in the manner in which many school systems have had to adopt "crash" programs to achieve certain goals and in the way accumulated pressures have led to several dislocations in educational programs.

Particularly acute has been the planning void in the utilization of modern technology. The technological explosion has, in effect, created a cultural gap in the sense that second-, third-, and even fourth-generation technological devices, i.e., computers, have been developed while educational organizations were still trying to master the first-generation equipment. The increasing tempo of development has forced an awareness of the planning needs that exist.

Scientific-technological progress has provided the tools with which to mechanize the business function in our educational systems and has forced an awakening of the need to develop planning procedures. The gathering, sorting, storing, and interpreting of data which once required inordinate amounts of energy, time, and resources has now become almost a by-product of sophisticated business equipment and procedures utilized by most educational systems. The time is already at hand when organizations are in danger of being overwhelmed by the deluge of data, most of which is irrelevant or at the least unusable by the system. This is not because these data are not accurate or true but because of a lack of sophistication in the application of planning procedures. Most school systems now have the means to generate tons of statistical summaries ranging from demographic to financial to personnel kinds of information. The difficulty arises when school system personnel attempt to utilize these data for long-range planning or specific task assignments. Quite often, because of the naïveté with which those tasks are approached, the data become quite worthless and one often hears the phrase "garbage in, garbage out" concerning the use of exotic machines for the production of specific answers to irrelevant questions. It would seem that most educational systems are suffering from a technological gap resulting from the wide disparity between the capacity of machines invented to assist man in the performance of routine, mechanizable tasks and the ability of man to assimilate this sometimes awesome capacity for the betterment of the system. It's as though man is still attempting to steer a horse and buggy suddenly moving at the speed of sound. It is terrifying, yet one cannot let go of the reins for fear of certain death.

Recent events in American society have served to focus increased attention on the importance of planning to the educational system. And because the questions of resource identification, collection, and allocation ultimately determine educational direction, the business administrator of the school system has had to assume a greatly expanded planning role. Among the forces that have highlighted the planning needs of school business administrators are included:

1. Increased size of school districts.
    It is no longer possible to consider a school system as one that includes one or two schools. Rather it's a natural trend for school systems to become larger and more diverse, causing the business function to become significant in a greater variety of activities.
2. Expansion of school system responsibility.
    Gone is the time when the educational system concerned itself only with the three R's. Modern systems are engaged in all sorts of endeavors including service functions (hot lunch and transportation), social functions (desegregation, cocurricular activities), psychological functions (special education, therapy, programs for the emotionally disturbed, etc.), sociological functions (programs for disadvantaged pupils and adults, community programs, etc.), recreational and leisure time functions (adult education, evening activities, after-school activities, etc.), and such other programs creative personnel can conceive.
3. Changing educational aspirations.
    Recognition is growing that formal education for all citizens is crucial to success in our modern technological society. Edu-

cation has become a "cradle-to-grave" concern, and the school systems have had to devise educational programs for clients ranging from preschool or early childhood to golden or retirement age.

4. Increased costs of educational services.

   Professional personnel and other school system personnel have learned the negotiations game from labor. Educational personnel will no longer accept whatever wages are offered them, and as a result the past decade has seen a dramatic increase in educational expenditures. This factor, coupled with natural increases due to the inflationary spiral, has seriously curtailed the amount of discretionary resources available to the school systems. Projections indicate that these pressures will continue to mount as teacher and other groups become still better organized and as the other costs continue to increase.

5. Civil rights movement.

   The minority groups in the United States are realizing that one of the main avenues to upward social and economic mobility lies in better educational programs. Therefore, strong pressures are being exerted by minority groups to force educational systems to design educational programs aimed at providing certain skills for minority group people. The demands for educational services being sounded have severely strained both the creative ability and the resources of many school systems.

6. The technological and knowledge explosions.

   Technology has dramatically and irrevocably altered the structure of our society. In travel we've moved from the concept of around the world in eighty days to around the world in eighty minutes. In production we've almost eliminated the common and unskilled laborer. In communications we've developed the ability to transmit visual images all over the world and universe. The discovery of new knowledge has assumed geometric progression, with the total body of knowledge doubling every five years. While our society now has the capacity to eradicate hunger and poverty from the world, in fact we are polluting the land, water, body, and air. All that is needed is the will to solve these human-technical problems. We are in grave danger of eliminating all mankind by permitting the wrong kind of planning to proceed. We can explore space and yet have not willed that the problems of the city, of air and water pollution, of hunger, of poverty, and of racial discrimination be resolved. As technology continues to provide the means to many other material satisfactions, educational systems will have to provide the means to the successful use of technology.

As a result of the many pressures impinging on the educational system, the planning function is rapidly assuming a top priority with school administrators. Our world has moved from a state of sporadic and infrequent change to one of continuous change. Where school business administrators could once predict future expenditures on the basis of past experience, it now becomes necessary to identify and project the effect of many variables when attempting to identify long-range needs. Solutions that were once unilateral have become multilateral with planning efforts directed at the provision of a series of alternatives that recognize as many variables as can be identified. The school business administrator-planner has become a most important member of the chief school administrator's planning team. He not only must concern himself with the day-to-day fiscal and management operations of the school system but must energetically pursue long- and short-range planning efforts. In addition to the normal tasks assigned the business administrator, he must now cultivate an expertise in such areas as demography, city planning, economic cycles and trends, communications, and negotiations. It is a safe statement to suggest that, particularly in the larger systems, the school business administrator should spend the greatest portion of his time in the development of long- and short-range plans. This does not mean that the day-to-day tasks of school operation are not important, for they are of prime responsibility. It does mean that those tasks can and should be standardized and mechanized to permit a channeling of time and energy into the more creative activity of planning.

There was a time when the chief task of the school business administrator was to build a budget that balanced the income and expenditures. Then, using the budget statement as a "bible," the business administrator became a control agent making sure that the system operated within the prescribed limits for the particular year. Budget cycles were largely repeats with some adjustments for growth, program additions, and inflation. The traditional role of the business administrator was similar to that of the policeman. He served as the chief control officer of the school system and, depending upon his ability to relate to people, inspired a range of emotions from acceptance as a necessary evil to pure hatred. The office of the school business administrator is usually where the buck stops and he and his office become the favorite whipping boys for most of the system's ills. This can no longer be the primary role of the school business administrator, for society is simply changing much too quickly to allow one person or one office to dominate so completely. Decisions affecting what happens in a school or in a classroom cannot be made at the central office. Professional educators will no longer allow someone far removed from the scene of the action to dictate to them. Principals and teachers are demanding the right to determine where and when resources can best be used. They are also demanding a partnership role in the development of priorities for allocation of resources. Still another voice is being heard more loudly. This is the growing insistence of the clients to be included, to have some say in what is happening in their schools. And since they provide a large portion of the fiscal resource, they have a very real vested interest and must be encouraged to join in.

This rapidly changing pattern of behavior on the part of school boards, personnel, students, and patrons strongly suggests a real change in the role of the school business administrator. While the control function will always be an important and crucial component of the office, decisions as to priority will involve many other people.

The changing role of the school business administrator will include such planning activities as the development of alternative strategies for identifying resources to permit totally different kinds of educational programs to operate in the future. The school business administrator must be able to project the impact of societal change which leads to educational modifications. He must be able to predict the composition of the school clientele in the future and utilize this to develop alternative schemes for resolving the educational needs. He not only must realize whether present resources are adequate but must devise means for gathering and allocating new resources in the future. A good knowledge of the economic forces at work, along with an ability to accurately predict future economic potential, will be most important.

The era of planning into which we are now entering will demand far greater capacity to conceive, to conceptualize, to negotiate, and to compromise on the part of the school business administrator. At the same time, it will provide a great opportunity to create, to affect, and to participate in a uniquely American invention—our public school system.

OTHER MODELS

There are examples of the planning function that have been developed in other sectors of our society. As we consider the development of appropriate educational planning designs, a brief examination of how the planning role has evolved in different organizations will provide some basis for exploratory efforts in educational systems and more particularly in the field of educational business administration.

Military

The planning role is not a new one. All great military commanders of history were brilliant planners. The logistics of moving men and supplies demanded careful attention to astute planning. Military strategy is, in effect, the creation of a plan of action which carefully identifies as many variables as can be anticipated and then prepares alternative actions based upon these variables. The brilliant commander plans beyond the immediate confrontation in order to predict future confrontations. Napoleon was finally defeated because of an error in planning; his supply lines were overextended and could not service his armies. The great allied victories in World War II were blueprinted long beforehand in the war game rooms of Allied planning headquarters. The gathering of resources for the Normandy invasion long preceded the actual fact. Not only were plans developed and rehearsed, but contingency plans were carefully laid in the event that original plans had to be scrapped.

The military has long recognized the importance of carefully conceived long- and short-range plans. Personnel and resources are identified for this function. Field or operational line personnel are clearly defined, as are staff or planning personnel. Sophisticated educational programs have been developed by the military to train planning staff. Persons with planning potential are identified early in their careers and are slowly introduced and nurtured into the planning activities. The most outstanding military personnel are those who perform the planning role.

The staggering proportions of a military effort with the myriad of concomitant activities needing coordination necessitate a carefully conceived plan. For every man engaged in battle in World War II, there were some nine or ten military personnel engaged in support/supply activities. The coordination of these millions of men to ensure attainment of military goals was the result of superb planning. Yet the military realized that to have such a large proportion of personnel devoted to support duty meant the severe restriction of alternative uses of a huge resource.

Therefore, the military planners began to devise ways of reducing the force needed to support the fighting man. By using and further refining technological breakthroughs, this need for support forces has been cut at least in half without any loss in effectiveness. In fact, the evidence is that the supply and support operations have become even more efficient. By developing machines to do most of the routine tasks, by using mechanical high-speed carriers to move troops and supplies, by computerizing many of the clerical tasks, and by creating planning staffs, the military has succeeded in realizing significant improvements in the conduct of defense affairs.

Most recently, the Planning Programming Budgeting System devised and developed for military use has still further enabled more efficient use of resources. Planning Programming Budgeting has attempted to rid the military establishment of waste and duplication. That it has not completely succeeded is due more to human failings and political manuevering than to the Planning Programming Budgeting System itself. Through the use of systems analysis, the many components needed to attain certain goals and objectives can be clearly identified. These components can be further refined into subcomponents and then carefully coordinated into a time-line sequence leading to the final desired outcome. Subtasks can be properly weighted and assigned resource and time inputs for completion. The military has become more proficient in the use of Planning Programming Budgeting techniques for the completion of particular missions.

The Planning Programming Budgeting System, with its emphasis on program support for particular function or program regardless of where the program operates, introduces an exciting dimension to fiscal planning. As an example, the food service needs of the various branches of the military can be resolved cooperatively with the focal point being the feeding of men in the most reasonable, efficient way without duplicating effort up and down the line. Similarly, other supply and service problems can be studied and resolved to minimize differences and maximize efficiency. At the same time, special program needs can be identified and planned for as the total effort proceeds.

The planning model created by the military must be classed as a highly centralized model with subunit planning possible in relation to common military goals. Because of a fairly restricted type of purpose (national defense), centralized control is fairly easily accomplished, and diverging, competing units are not too common.

The Business-Industrial Model

Planning in business and industry is considerably different from planning in the military. While goals of corporate structures are quite similar in that a prime concern is the profit motive, products and materials are so diverse, so totally different, that planning details vary considerably from one firm to another. Yet, the concept of planning is similar throughout.

Corporate level staff rarely engage in the day-to-day operations of production. Rather, the main thrust of top level administration is geared to the formulation of long-range plans for the organization. Out of these long-range efforts come short-range directions leading to the accomplishment of long-range goals. Considerable effort is expended in the prediction of future markets, in projecting future production schedules, in influencing client tastes, in assessing the changing nature of the American society. In this age of diversification, corporations are engaged in many unrelated activities designed to provide a cushion for planning errors or the introduction of still unforeseen variables into the mix. True, most corporate bodies can and do relate these diverse segments when program planning permits, but usually the member firms of a corporate body are quite free to operate within the set parameters of policy.

Business and industry have, with some success, been able to resolve the centralization-decentralization dichotomy by centralizing certain functions that are best centralized and decentralizing other functions. Although this issue will continue to plague all organizations, business and industry seem to have been most effective in resolving these issues.

Figure 1.1 reflects a typical industrial pattern of organization. Following this figure to logical conclusions, the appropriate planning efforts are performed at various levels. Long-range goals for the corporation are established at the Board of Directors level. Decisions about probable markets and products needed are made there. Decisions on corporate emphasis and resource allocation are part of long-range planning. Increasingly, pressures other than the profit motive are being felt and addressed. If, for example, companies A, B, and C manufactured cars, and companies D and E

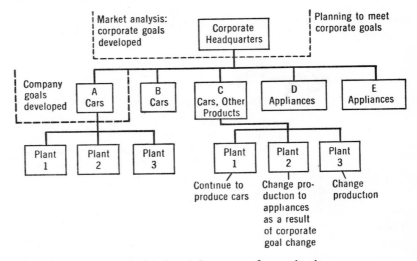

FIGURE 1.1 Typical industrial pattern of organization.

were producers of appliances; decisions at the corporate level could increase or decrease the car production of company C or even change it to the production of a different product. If the planning effort indicated a reduction in the need of cars ten years hence but a sharp increase in the market for freezers, company C might become a producer of freezers. More probably company C might become a parts producer of common parts for all of the other companies in order to streamline the total operation of the corporation. The point is that the central planners (corporation executives) determine what role each company shall have on the basis of long-range plans, which include goal statements and projections of performance needed to attain goals.

An important part of the planning function in any organization is the capacity to evaluate performance in terms of objectives and goals. It's perhaps easier to evaluate in business and industry, for if a certain production level is identified as a goal, say one million cars, and if the company produces only nine hundred thousand cars, a production goal is not met. Reasons for failure may be varied ranging from poor to unrealistic expectations to poor management and facilities. However, on the basis of data available, corporate planners can either effect changes that will increase production or decrease expectations. It's entirely possible that because of prevailing conditions the profit motive will be better realized by a nine hundred thousand-car production than with the production of one million automobiles. All of these variables are analyzed and used to adjust plans for future years.

It's most important to realize that planning is not a one-time activity but that it must be considered a continuing effort. Conditions change, demands and tastes change, inputs vary, and as a result plans must be able to be changed. Long-range plans are really direction setters and should be in constant review and refinement to reflect most recent input data. This ability to plan has made American business and industry the most productive the world has ever known.

An Education Model

Operationally, most educational systems move from crisis to crisis with the chief school administrator and his cabinet-level staff bouncing from one trauma to another like puppets on a string. The school business administrator is often forced by unforeseen emergencies to juggle budget and resource allocations in order to enable the system to survive.

Since mere survival is not enough and does not by any stretch of the imagination imply a viable, vibrant, effective educational system, careful consideration of alternative models is appropriate for professional educators. Any such model must provide the framework within which the educator can, with confidence, predict success for the educational system. At the very least, the model(s) should allow the educator to foresee where possible breakdowns might occur.

Taking a cue from business and the military, educational systems simply must devote time and resources to the planning function in order to ensure realistic, relevant goal formulation and program implementation. Unless educational plans are developed and followed, already scarce resources are going to be tragically inadequate and often misused by the system(s) — misused because of a multiplicity of overlapping functions that could lead to duplication of program effort on the part of staff.

Most school systems have very fine philosophical statements of goals and objectives that are usually reproduced on page one of staff handbooks and public relations materials. These statements are often well conceived and the result of many hours of staff time and effort. Unfortunately, very few school systems have been able to translate philosophical jargon into measurable, attainable, definitive goal statements. One of the continuing tasks in education is the struggle to develop goal statements in clear, concise, understandable language that will allow translation of these statements into educational programs to be implemented by the school system. Financial planning and resource procurement and allocation based upon clear goals and projected educational programs to meet these goals will provide for making the key decisions and the rationale upon which each is based. The identification and articulation of long- and short-range goals is the single most important outcome of the planning function in any school system.

Educational planning is a relatively new concept being utilized in many of the more sophisticated school systems of the country. Originally introduced as a result of planning experiences and models utilized in the military, the planning role is rapidly being developed to resolve educational problems with a set of uniquely educational tools. Thus the Planning Programming Budgeting System has been refined to the Planning Programming Budgeting Evaluation System or PPBES. Continuing efforts by selected school systems and the Association of School Business Officials are aimed at providing a viable, pertinent, understandable PPBES approach to education.

The development of an educational model to carry on the planning function must rest on the validity of several assumptions. These include:

1. The planning role must be separated from the operational role so that resources are available to carry out the planning task, because those charged with planning obligations cannot devote the time and energy needed to the operational duties of the system. (This will be expanded upon in subsequent sections.)
2. Planning encompasses the total system and its needs, not only the planning of facilities or any other segment.
3. The diversity of skills needed to mount a planning function is a "team" effort and not a one-person show.
4. Resources needed for planning are crucial to its success and are a continuing part of any budget.

Ideally then, the educational system should create a planning cadre that would address itself to the planning function. This staff would undertake all planning activities for the system ranging from the establishment of educational goals; the development of educational programs reflecting the goals; the identification of resources needed to implement programs; the allocation of physical and human resources in implementations, and finally the evaluation process so necessary to continued plan development. At the very least, the superintendent of schools would be readily available to the planning staff for consultation and direction. Most preferably, the superintendent would be the chief planner and would actively participate in the planning, particularly at the decision level. Key members of any planning team would be the financial planner, the curriculum planner, the facilities planner, and the evaluations specialist. Decisions as to programs, facilities, organization, resources, and time would be the task of the planning team. The school system would operate its educational programs on the basis of desired outcomes as identified and codified by the planning effort. Changes, modifications, and alternatives would all be the responsibility of the planning staff, as would be evaluation of program effectiveness. Decisions as to continuation of programs, shifts in emphasis, initiation of new and different programs, priorities in the application of resources, and allocations would be planning tasks.

Because the foregoing implies a staff of such size that is not realistically or physically possible for the many, many smaller school systems, alternatives must be devised. One alternative, again dependent upon the size of the system, would be to establish a one-person planning office whose main task would be the generalized planning role and the coordination of total systems planning. This office would then draw on specialized personnel in other divisions of the school system for input into the development of a total plan. This means that persons in various components of the school system, i.e., the business office, the curriculum office, and so forth, would have to be provided with sufficient resources to enable the channeling of some time and effort into the planning process.

Another alternative presently utilized by many systems, particularly in the development of facility plans, would be to contract with either private consulting firms or university planning teams for the development of educational plans. While this method of planning does provide a school system with a set of master plans for implementation, it is not without some danger. First, while the objectivity used by the outside consultant is a real strength, lack of complete knowledge of a school system could be a weakness. Second, although the outside agency has great expertise in the planning process, the increased planning capacity of the local school system must be a main objective to ensure continued success. Third, there is great danger in accepting a master plan based on present data and then following it blindly without giving consideration to changing variables and their effects on the plan.

A third alternative, not yet explored, would be for groups of districts to pool their planning resources and to share the services of a planning staff. This would not only provide smaller districts with planning services, but would also tend to encourage cooperative efforts in certain curriculum areas not feasible for the very small district.

In the opinion of the authors, some combination of the preceding alternatives is most desirable. The educational system must develop a planning capacity of its own and should call on specialists from the field to supplement and complement its own staff. In this way, expert advice on particular problems can be made available while at the same time local personnel can give continuity to the planning process.

Of course, the least desirable way of carrying on the planning function is to expect existing staff to attempt to plan while at the same time resolving all existent operational decisions entrusted to them. While this is most common, it is not the most efficient and productive use of human resources.

Recognizing that the pressures of time and limited resources often determine the scope of the planning effort, the authors urge that a firm commitment be made to the planning function in every system.

THE PLANNING ROLE

Long-Range Planning

An obvious bias of the authors is the continued emphasis on the need for systematic, coordinated planning, both long and short range. Mouthing this generality is somewhat analogous to declaring a bias for country and motherhood unless an attempt is made to define just what planning is, how it's accomplished, and what its payoff is to the educational system.

In considering long-range planning, care must be taken to

clarify what is meant by long range. In terms of time span, long range is generally considered to be anything in excess of fifteen to twenty-five years. Many authors talk of planning in terms of long range (twenty years or over), middle range (ten to twenty years), and short range (five to ten years). Others would emphasize short range as including one to five years, middle range a span of five to fifteen years and long range anything beyond fifteen years. For purposes of this discussion, we have chosen to identify long-range planning as that which forces the planning group to consider alternatives not presently utilized and to develop approaches not yet a part of the educational system. This could mean, in terms of time, any period in the future that, given present planning capability, can be projected or hypothesized. This rather tenuous description is given because of our strong conviction that a very real danger inherent in attempting to plan in the long range is that the "plan" becomes the rigid perimeter beyond which the system cannot operate. It is hoped that the foregoing can serve to emphasize that planning is a continuing activity, one that forces consideration of changing variables, and that the mark of nobility of any plan is its ability to adjust and adapt to changing situations. Therefore, it is inadvisable to place any rigid time span on such effort, but rather it is necessary to suggest that long-range planning is a constant activity to be undergone by any organization. This does not mean that such efforts are completely discarded as new understandings and resources are introduced, but rather that new inputs are utilized to refine and clarify planning efforts.

We are increasingly aware that educational systems can no longer operate as closed systems but that the educational system is an open system with real concern for an intercourse with exogenous forces. Closed systems are most unstable in the long run, for they lack the capacity to sense changes in the surrounding environment which have very real implications for the effectiveness of the system. There it becomes crucial that all planning efforts recognize exogenous factors and that the planners make a concerted effort to identify and subsume as many of these forces as can be located. In addition, the capacity to interact with still other forces must be considered as an integral part of long-range planning.

As an attempt at simplification, let us draw an analogy that is easily understood. Assume that the reader lives on the East Coast and that his long-range goal is to move to the West Coast.

As planning proceeds for the move, the reader attempts to search out all possible alternatives. These may include:

1. Various modes of travel, i.e., rail, bus, air, and private car.
2. Time involved in each mode of travel.
3. Cost of each.
4. Convenience of each.

Finally, after careful consideration of all factors identified the reader decides that because he will need his auto in his new location, and because he has ten days before reporting to his new position, it would be most practical and rewarding to drive west. After a week of travel, with side trips to visit friends, the reader finds himself in Kansas when his car breaks down. Best estimates indicate that the major repairs needed will take two days and will probably cost more than is warranted as an expenditure on his car. Because of the time deadline for arriving on the West Coast, the reader decides to sell his car and to fly for the rest of the journey. He thus arrives in good time to begin his new position.

The foregoing illustrates a long-range plan (moving west) that was fully implemented by making adjustments as variables changed and as the time elapsed. While educational planning is not that simple, the logistics of long-range planning are very similar to the analogy. Future educational goals are formulated, all possible alternatives are identified and evaluated. Then, on the basis of best possible judgment, implementation is initiated with necessary adjustments and changes made along the way. As is very apparent, the formulation of goals is the crucial task in long-range planning. Goal statements provided in clear, concise, measurable terms are not easily produced. Yet before any real attempt can be made at long-range planning, precise, understandable goal statements are a necessity. Without such statements, planning is a futile exercise because the planner has no idea of the direction to be developed. It is therefore most crucial that the planning team carefully and diligently conceive a well-ordered, viable set of educational goals that are realistic in terms of the clientele to be served.

Short-Range Planning

After the long-range parameters have been established, the immediate concerns of the school system must be addressed. Such short-range concerns can and do vary from problems of facility overcrowding to optimum deployment of staff. As the many immediate problems are studied for resolution, great care must be taken to relate short-term solutions to long-range objectives.

As an example, if the long-range goal of the educational system is to change from a K8-4 organization to a K5-3-4 organization, and if immediate facility needs indicate a severe shortage of elementary spaces, it would be foolish to plan and construct a K-8 building when the construction of grades six through eight facilities would hasten the implementation of the long-range educational goal. The provision of 6th and 8th grade facilities would enable the freeing of space for elementary pupils by removing 6th to 8th grade pupils from existing buildings.

Similarly, if long-range plans call for the development of a differentiated staffing pattern, short-range efforts to test a variety of staffing models will provide a sound basis for eventual implementation.

Short-range planning must not only resolve immediate concerns but must also provide the avenue for long-range plan realization. Thus, short-range efforts must be conceived so that they will provide the flexibility and adaptability to serve differing purposes. Using the prior example of the planning of the sixth- to eighth-grade middle school, if long-range demographic projections indicate that the area will need a high school facility fifteen years hence and that pre-high school enrollments will fall considerably by that time, then good planning practice will dictate that the sixth to eighth-grade facility be planned for easy conversion to other use.

Short-range plans are especially crucial to the financial well-being of the educational system. The financial planner, working with program planners, can effectively project educational costs over the short term. These predicted budget figures are a basis for sound judgments to be made by the planning staff. Decisions on tax levy requests to be submitted to the electorate are predicated on such information. Efforts to gather state and federal support for education can also be initiated as a result of short-range planning. Priorities are more easily established when cost-benefit analysis is made of program plans with the most effective programs highest in priority.

Short-range planning provides information as to kinds and numbers of staff needed to provide educational services. It allows the planning team to test various staffing models to determine the best pattern to follow. It also gives some indication of particular emphasis needed to fill potentially difficult assignments.

While it is crucial for short-range efforts to recognize and move toward long-range goals, a concomitant obligation of short-range planning is the adaptation of the long-range plan to include changing variables as these changes occur. In this manner changes in demography can be incorporated into the evolving long-range plan.

It is the conviction of the authors that as a series of short-range plans is implemented the long-range plans will be sufficiently altered so that the passage of time will cause increased sophistication and expectation in terms of the long-range plan. This is considered by many to be the concept of continuous planning, for the long-range plan is never fully implemented but is continually changed to reflect new challenges, needs, and goals.

A CASE STUDY: RELEVANCY OF PLANNING TO SCHOOL BUSINESS ADMINISTRATION

The decision by one of the nation's largest school systems to create a planning staff and to decentralize the operations of the school district into a series of smaller, semi-autonomous systems required strenuous planning efforts on the part of the school business administration staff. Because the system had previously operated as a centrally controlled and administered bureaucracy, all business and operational decisions had been made at the central headquarters of the educational system. At the recommendation of the superintendent, the board of education approved the creation of a series of subunits, each servicing several thousand students and each having the capacity to render day-to-day educational decisions. Central headquarters suddenly changed from a control agency to a support and planning agency.

The business division had to plan its own demise as an entity because its role had been dramatically changed. Where it had once been directly responsive to one man, the superintendent, it now had to interact with and respond to a number of area and district superintendents. In addition, selected personnel had to assume the role of economic planning staff for the total educational system. While certain questions will continuously be very difficult to resolve, the primary issue for the school business division became one of determining which functions could and/or should be decentralized, which should remain centralized, and what personnel were to perform the planning role for the system.

Preliminary decisions were made to continue the automated payroll, bookkeeping, accounting, and related functions centrally. At the same time, decisions were made on dispersal to the various subdistricts of specialized business office staff, i.e., purchasing personnel, administrative personnel, clerical and support personnel. These decisions reflect an effort to continue the multitude of routinized operations requiring sophisticated data processing capacity and highly specialized staff at a central location to ensure the most efficient use of very costly equipment and personnel. At the same time the various subunits would be provided with a sufficient staff with which to develop a capacity to react to local needs and situations as these needs are identified. While many routine types of tasks, i.e., certain purchases, payroll, accounting, and so forth, are best accomplished on a large-scale or centralized basis, other tasks, i.e., specialized purchasing, identification of unique needs, allocation of resources, etc., are best done on a decentralized base.

The creation of a central planning cabinet and staff called for a redefinition of many roles that existing personnel performed. While the school system had historically been heavily centralized with one man, the superintendent, making most of the decisions, it now became a series of subschool districts with many operating decisions to be made by the subdistrict administrator. Because of the size of this particular school district, the business functions were divided among several cabinet-level personnel. Thus, there were various departments including data processing, accounting operations, plant planning, purchasing, curriculum, personnel, human relations, vocational education, administration, etc., each headed by assistant or associate superintendents with appropriate staffs that included business applications. A table of organization of the original model appears in figure 1.2.

In the traditional scheme, all the administrative personnel were line personnel and made decisions affecting the total system. The district administrators had little power and merely served as buffers between school personnel (principals) and the central office. Because of its very size and scope, the ability of the school district to react to unique needs and to respond to individual members of the school community became extremely restricted,

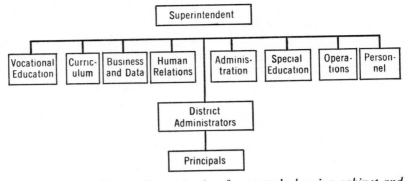

FIGURE 1.2 Table of organization for central planning cabinet and staff.

if not nonexistent. The various cabinet-level personnel, because of the severe pressures of system-wide responsibility, had to develop district-wide approaches to the solution of educational problems. Thus, allocation of teachers and other human resources were on a teacher-pupil formula devised for the total system. The business division worked from the formula to allocate resources for materials, supplies, and equipment. Purchasing became a highly specialized activity with centrally established criteria as to types and amounts of supplies and equipment provided a particular school or classroom. While the extreme centralization of all facets of the educational system allowed for and encouraged a very high degree of efficiency in use of resources and also enabled the development of a very effective system of school operations, events of the 1960s led to increasing discontent on the part of clients, particularly those persons representing the increasing minority group population of the city. Educational needs, once relatively stable and confined to basic education, became much broader and very complex. Diversity of population creates diversity of educational needs which must be translated into diversity of educational programming. As the demography of the city changed and as it became increasingly clear that the school system also had to change in order to perform its role in an effective manner, the need to establish both a creative, planning capacity as well as the means to more closely relate to the individual client assumed the highest priority.

The decision to decentralize was the result of several years of careful study and planning. It was reinforced by the realization that unless a planned decentralization was forthcoming, events unfolding in other metropolitan centers would give emphasis and support to a continued breakdown in communications between the system and its constituents and lead to efforts to decentralize the system through external pressures. Careful study of events in other cities and of the developing demands of clients locally led to several criteria under which decentralization is proceeding. Among these are:

1. The setting of overall educational and social policy as the responsibility of the Board of Education. This responsibility cannot be decentralized.

2. The data needed to establish educational policy and goals are provided through the efforts of the central planning staff.

3. Day-to-day operational decisions must be made quickly and efficiently as close to the source of need as possible.

4. The subunits of the school system should have all necessary support and operational staff assigned to the local subunit and not have to work through central headquarters to arrive at decisions.

5. Local communities can and should be involved through the mechanism of advisory councils established at every school and at every subdistrict and area.

6. The selection of professional personnel is best accomplished at the local level, therefore each subdistrict must develop the personnel function.

7. Certain tasks, i.e., data processing, resource gathering, payroll, personnel record processing, etc., are best accomplished on a central base and performed as a service to the subdistricts.

8. Broad educational planning, while done at the central staff level, will allow for certain subdistrict and school unit decisions on programs necessary to meet local needs.

9. Decentralization in and of itself is no panacea; rather it is the result of well-planned reallocation of the decision-making power in order to increase the quality and effectiveness of the total system.

10. Planning must be an ongoing activity of all decentralized units. These subdistricts must have ready access to the expertise available at the central headquarters to assist in particular planning tasks.

As the decentralization effort proceeded, many new variables were being identified and problems previously unrecognized were demanding attention. As an example, the purchasing of classroom furniture has always been done in carload lots with exact specifications and sizing determined centrally. Now, because of new programs that required unique and different types of furniture, it was no longer possible to purchase the same item for use throughout the entire system. In order to continue to realize volume-buying savings, the purchasing of new furniture was to be coordinated by the central office with exact specifications supplied by the subdistrict and area business staffs.

As another example, while primary resource allocations were still being made from the central office on the basis of enrollments, the possibility of district and area superintendents reallocating resources for their own unit on the basis of local needs and priorities was recognized. In addition, it was possible for subdistricts to submit proposals for specific programs for funding above and beyond the basic allotments. This change alone demanded that local districts develop the capacity to plan, to innovate, and to create in order to continue to progress.

Granted, the decentralization process took some time to implement and the capacity to effectively plan was and is still in the embryo stage, the total school system was nevertheless aware that things were happening and that the process of change had been initiated. The question now was could sufficient, meaningful progress be made quickly enough to forestall the many critics of change and supporters of the status quo? In the words of the superintendent, "We were rapidly being sunk by our own incapacity to react quickly and effectively to changing educational needs because tradition had so tightly bound us to a very rigid and immobile organizational structure. We simply had to break out of these bounds in order to survive."

It is the opinion of the authors that educational planning is not only crucial to success, but, even more important, it is the key to survival for our educational systems.

THE APPLICABILITY OF PLANNING

Planning is a normal activity for most rational people. Few persons go through life reacting emotionally and haphazardly to the changing situations one confronts on a daily basis. Rather, most people set particular goals and objectives and then work toward these goals. For example, the young person who decides to make his way as an engineer plans his academic experiences so that he can achieve his career ambition. Young families plan for the future by developing family goals in terms of children, housing, education, leisure, and so on. The homemaker utilizes great planning expertise in determining menus, schedules, priorities, budget allocations, and so forth.

As has been proven, business, industry, and the military have all developed planning capacity in order to realize goals more efficiently. While the basic purposes of these agencies are considerably different from that of the educational system, the results of their experiences can be of great value to education in the development of planning procedures.

The Team Approach

As our educational systems have grown and become more complex, and as the sphere of influence of education has assumed expanded importance, the myriad of duties and roles for educational leaders have multiplied tremendously. It has simply become impossible for one person or one office to grasp the multitude of tasks and facts needed to plan effectively for education.

Past educational experience has shown that the need to administer more effectively and efficiently the increasingly complex and diverse school systems has led to growing specialization of administrative tasks. Today, among the larger school systems of the country, administrative and teaching specialization abounds. Even subareas within major task areas require added emphasis. Thus the business function finds personnel concerned with purchasing (or even specific types of purchasing), accounting, operations, transportation, data processing, and so on as areas of specialization. The coordination of these many efforts rests with the chief business officer of the school district. In like fashion, curricular efforts are specialized as are personnel duties and other tasks necessary to the success of the school system.

The planning role is assuming the same general growth pattern. While it is still premature to project future planning staff positions, it is quite probable that there will be a variety of specific skill areas provided by a variety of persons in order to accomplish the planning tasks.

Present planning seems to emphasize the facilities aspect

largely to the exclusion of other areas. However, the more sophisticated school systems are becoming aware of serious voids in their planning structures and are initiating the gathering of planning teams. As educational leadership has become a team effort with different people leading diverse tasks, so must planning evolve into a team approach. Educational planning clearly must address itself to school system goals and long- and short-range efforts to meet these goals. Included as input for total school system planning must be the following areas:

1. Curriculum or program planning
2. Facilities or housing planning
3. Economic or business planning
4. Staff or personnel planning
5. Administrative or organization planning
6. Evaluation

In addition, technical processes and skills to gather and interpret demographic data, to relate to the planning efforts of other agencies, to understand and relate to emerging social forces, to actively involve staff, students, and community, and to develop clear, concise plans for general consumption are important to the planning process.

Obviously, one person cannot hope to acquire all of the aforementioned skills personally but rather must work cooperatively with many specialists to provide the total input needed. Therefore, the development of the planning team will be of even greater importance in the coming decades.

The Service Approach

Planning per se is a most important role in the total operation of the school system. Decisions as to type, scope, quantity, and quality of education are the result of planning efforts. Viable alternative solutions to problems can be formulated and tested prior to reaching the decision stage. Thus, planning properly conceived and implemented is a very vital service to the operation of a school system.

The planning function is not a line function of the educational system but rather a staff function. As a service to the ongoing program and operational staff, the planning effort addresses long-

and short-term needs of the system and prepares alternative solutions for consideration.

Operations personnel have neither time nor energy to engage in extensive planning. It is also debatable whether operational personnel have the kinds of skills so necessary to educational planning. However, operational personnel do have problems, need program direction, and must be supported and assisted in their efforts. This then becomes a primary task of the planning staff: the support of line personnel, the identification of alternative solutions to pressing problems, the development of coordinated long- and short-range plans, and the capacity to function as a service arm of the school system.

This role is of sufficient importance to require that the planning function be completely removed from the day-to-day operations of the school system.

Central Office Approach

Because of the particular and unique nature of the planning process with the wide variety of diverse skills and inputs required, the logical home for the planning staff is the central office. This does not mean that a planning team isolates itself from the reality of the educational system, but that planning staff and resources are gathered and housed in one location in order to better serve the various components of the school system.

The economics of utilizing scarce resources most efficiently clearly indicates the folly of trying to establish several planning offices in the typical school system. Since total system planning is a primary task of the planning office, and since the coordination of all educational efforts is a function of central office personnel, the provision of planning services from a central office is in keeping with other central office duties.

In addition to total planning, the planning division of the school system must serve the other units of the system by providing certain ad hoc planning services as they are requested. Gathering and translating local demographic data, evaluating particular program ideas, resolving unique facility problems, assisting in stimulating community participation, and providing specific data are all legitimate types of tasks expected of the planning team. These and others are important to the success of local units and hence to the total system.

It is most important that all planning personnel remember that planning is a means to an end and not an end in itself. If the product of planning effort does not assist in improving the program of education for students, then it is time, effort, and resource wasted and should not be done. Obviously, the authors adopt the point of view that sound educational planning is essential and vital to any school system.

SUMMARY

Chapter 1 presents a summary of the emerging planning role of school business administration. Rationale is developed to indicate the development of the planning function in education, and examples of planning activities in other segments of our society are presented, i.e., the military and the business sectors.

Attention is called to the changing nature of school systems and the strong implications for a changing role on the part of the school business administrator. The need for administrative team effort with the business administrator, a key member of the team, is emphasized.

A planning model for educational institutions is developed with specific attention given to the role of the school business administrator. Incorporated in the education model are alternative possibilities for consideration.

Definitions of long- and short-range planning efforts are presented along with a case study of a major school system's effort to develop planning capacity.

The chapter concludes by presenting specific planning needs and by suggesting avenues leading to implementation of the planning process.

SUGGESTED ACTIVITIES

1. Identify a major decision related to school business administration in a school system, then trace the planning activities (or lack of them) that went into the decision. Try to identify and describe the several planning activities.

2. Ascertain through interview or observation the several most important problem areas in a school system. Identify those

which have implications for planning in the school business administration function. Select one or more of these problem areas and suggest what kind of planning is required of the school business administrator.

3. Identify a general social issue, decision, or movement that has made a major impact on the planning function of the school business administrator in a given school system. Describe how this phenomenon has influenced the function, and how the school business administrator might plan to accommodate such unexpected influences.

4. What evidence can be found that some use is made of the military, business-industrial, and educational models in the planning function of the school business administration operations of a modern school system?

5. Describe some of the areas of common interest shared among planners from education, civil government, business and industry, and voluntary organizations (clubs, churches, etc.).

SUGGESTED READINGS

Beebe, C. E. *Planning and the Educational Administrator.* New York: United Nations Institute for Educational Planning, 1967.

Cotton, John F., and Hatry, Harry P. *Program Planning for State, County, City.* Washington, D.C.: State-Local Finances Project of the George Washington University, 1967.

Furse, Bernard S., and Wright, Lyle O. *Comprehensive Planning in State Education Agencies.* Salt Lake City: Utah State Board of Education, 1968.

Hack, Walter G., et al. *Educational Futurism 1985.* Berkeley, Calif.: McCutchan Publishing Corporation, 1971.

Likert, Rensis. *New Patterns of Management.* New York: McGraw-Hill Book Company, 1951.

McGregor, D. *The Human Side of Enterprise.* New York: McGraw-Hill Book Company, 1960.

Morphet, Edgar L., and Jesser, David L., eds. *Emerging Designs for Education.* New York: Citation Press, 1968.

Morphet, Edgar L., and Ryan, Charles O., eds. *Planning and Effecting Needed Changes in Education.* New York: Citation Press, 1967.

Pfeiffer, John. *New Look at Education.* New York: Odyssey Press, 1968.

THE CONTEXT AND DEVELOPMENT OF SCHOOL BUSINESS ADMINISTRATION

A planning function appropriate to the needs of contemporary American schools was described in Chapter 1. In the present chapter the authors draw the focus a bit tighter and address themselves to the role of the school business administrator in the context of the planning function of educational administration in general. Since school business administration is an integral part of general educational administration and the school superintendency, many of the role antecedents of the former area of specialization are drawn from these latter fields. Thus, the chapter deals with the evolution of the superintendency and the relatively recent emphasis on the superintendency team concept. Out of this context one can trace the genesis and growth of school business as a discrete function in educational administration. The role of the school business administrator is described in terms of his tasks; the processes he employs; the relationships he has with other members of the administrative, professional, and service staffs; and the functions he performs in contributing to the achievement of the school systems' educational objectives.

EVOLUTION OF THE SUPERINTENDENCY

Despite the fact that some aspects of this role of the school business administrator emerged before the role of the superintendency, the current role of the former is and will continue to be identified with that of the superintendent of schools.

The position of superintendent of schools is of relatively recent origin in the institution of public education. Early prototype positions were developed in Buffalo and Louisville in 1839 and in Cleveland in 1841. Generally speaking, these positions tended to be related to "superintendence of instruction," and matters of budget, fiscal affairs, and business administration were handled by board members, board committees, or chief fiscal officers (usually laymen) who reported directly to the board of education or its counterpart. Thus, the traditions of local control, Jacksonian democracy, and skepticism of professionals effectively separated educational program considerations from those of school financing and business.

The American society has always had a changing and dynamic nature. Social demands have stimulated social innovation and invention. As the American population grew and prospered, heavy demands were placed on the simplistic educational system originally designed for the frontier and agrarian society. Industrialization and concomitant urbanization concentrated the population, increased the variety and intensity of skills demanded for job entry, and required schools to assume broader community and social service functions. The waves of immigrants arriving on American shores during the second half of the nineteenth century forced the schools to accept the role of an "acculturation agent." Increasing educational requirements and the modest knowledge explosions of the day resulted in broadening and deepening the educational programs. All of the above changes in the nature of the educational program in turn resulted in vast expansions in the revenues and expenditures required for public education. In comparison to other private and public sector expenditures, school expenditures appeared to increase in geometric proportion to population growth. In the age of "big business," public education had clearly emerged as one of the giants.

Because of the rapid expansion and the changing character of the educational program, many of the finance and business

TABLE 2.1. The magnitude of American education

Estimated School Age Population (July, 1971)	52,266,000
Public School Enrollment (Fall, 1971)	46,168,540
Number of Basic Administrative Units (1971–72)	16,920
Total Instructional Staff in Local Public Schools (October, 1970)	2,349,049
Total Non-Instructional Staff in Local Public Schools (October, 1970)	1,001,705
Estimated Public School Revenue Receipts (1971–72)	$46,633,454,452
Estimated Current Expenditures for Public Elementary and Secondary Schools (1971–72)	$39,600,072,382

SOURCE: Calculated from *Ranking of the States, 1972* (Washington: Research Division, National Education Association, 1972). Copyright © 1972 by the National Education Association. Used with permission.

functions of school boardmen were gradually delegated to the superintendent of schools. However, vestiges of lay control of the school still remain in the forms of fiscal officers, treasurers, and comptrollers reporting directly to the boards of education. Often these positions carry with them state mandated functions, e.g., approving purchases or contracts, encumbering funds to satisfy these obligations, accounting for a school district's receipts and expenditures to state officials, and so forth.

The role of the superintendent has demonstrated variability all through the years because of changing patterns of school district size. In the middle and late 1800s the number of superintendencies grew significantly. Most of these were situated in relatively small communities. As population increased and became concentrated in urban industrial centers, the number of large school districts grew proportionately faster than that of small districts. The current trend reflects a decreasing number of small school districts and at the same time a growing number and growing size of urban school districts.

In complex urban and suburban school districts one observes a wide range of situational variables that bear on the role of the superintendent. Frequently the "size" of the job is not directly related to the size of the community (population-wise) or the number of pupils enrolled. Instead, the complexity of the job is determined by the number and variety of elements in the program, the amount of effort needed to design and implement programs, and other community demands placed on the educational administrator. Thus, the nature of the superintendency and the role expectations are at the same time both dynamic and idiosyncratic. These are constantly changing and are reflective of the unique setting in which they occur.

Conceptual Settings of the Superintendency

Despite the quicksilver character of the superintendency as it has evolved over the years, several conceptualizations have been developed to describe and analyze educational administration in general, and these can be applied to the position of the superintendent.

Administrative Process Setting

Scholars with various points of view have sought to analyze administrative activity. Fayol from industrial management,[1] Gulick from public administration,[2] and Jesse Sears from education[3] identified and described what is now known as the administrative process. A concept implied in a yearbook published by the American Association of School Administrators,[4] seems to be a most relevant description of this process as it might characterize the superintendency. The five crucial activities of the school administrator were described as:

1. *Planning* or the attempt to control the future in the direction of the desired goals through decisions made on the basis of careful estimates of the probable consequences of possible courses of action.
2. *Allocation* or the procurement and allotment of human and material resources in accordance with the operating plan.
3. *Stimulation* or motivation of behavior in terms of the desired outcomes.

[1] Henri Fayol. *General and Industrial Management* (London: Sir Isaac Pitman and Sons. Ltd., 1949). p. xi.
[2] Luther Gulick and L. Urwick. eds.. *Papers on the Science of Administration* (New York: Institute of Public Administration. 1937). p. 13.
[3] Jesse B. Sears. *The Nature of the Administrative Process* (New York: McGraw-Hill Book Company. 1950).
[4] American Association of School Administrators. *Staff Relations in School Administration* (Washington. D.C.: The Association. 1955). chapter 1.

superintendent, the practice of naming assistant superintendents responsible for one or more of the task areas has become well established, especially in large city school systems. Thus a large system might have a general superintendent, and assistant superintendents in charge of curriculum, pupil services, staff personnel, and business and financial affairs. The following section deals with one such area of specialization.

THE CHARACTER AND DEVELOPMENT OF
SCHOOL BUSINESS ADMINISTRATION

As one component of the superintendency, school business administration has followed the evolution of the superintendency, but also has had its own unique emphases. The earliest manifestation of school business administration occurred outside what might be termed the professional administrative position of the time. It was observed that in the earliest superintendency, business and fiscal affairs were typically handled by school committees, board members, or chief fiscal officers (usually laymen) reporting directly to the board of education. This precedent, set in New Jersey, Pennsylvania, and Ohio was adopted in varying degrees by many other states. As a result, the concept of multiple control was well accepted in school business administration in the latter part of the nineteenth century. The vestiges of it are still apparent. The essence of multiple control is more than one administrator reporting directly to the policy-making body. In this instance, both the superintendent and the business official report to the board of education, and the board itself must coordinate the efforts of educational programming with those of fiscal and business programs.

The concept of unit control is in direct contrast to that of multiple control. In a situation of unitary control, a single administrator has responsibility for the implementation of educational policy as well as fiscal and business policy. A board can then evaluate the performance of the total administrative effort without having to sort out where responsibility is to be fixed between (or among) the administrators reporting to it.

Frederick W. Hill in his Special Committee Report to the Association of School Business Officials identified several milestones in the history of the school business administrator.[7] The nearly complete lay control of school business affairs was challenged in 1841 when the Cleveland, Ohio city council appointed an "Acting Manager" of schools with responsibilities in several business affairs areas. Other cities followed suit and established these positions even before city superintendents were appointed.

By the end of the nineteenth century and the beginning of the twentieth century professionally trained business administrators were employed by boards of education. These frequently were business-oriented administrators serving in a multiple control organization.

In the early years of the present century considerable interest was generated in "professionalizing" this area of administration. Professor N. L. Englehart, Sr., of Teachers College, Columbia University was influential in identifying school business administration as a specialized area of general school administration and in designing preparation programs for it.

Professionalization among school business administrators has had a second side. As early as 1910 the National Association of Public School Business Officials was formed and later became the Association of School Business Officials of the United States and Canada (ASBO). This organization has been devoted to upgrading the performance and professionalism of school business officials. It embraces both education-oriented and business-oriented professionals in the field.

State law regarding certification for school business administrators remains unclear in most states. Since historical precedent provided for laymen rather than professionally trained administrators to serve as fiscal and business administrators, most states have not designated specific training or experience requirements for such individuals. In a presentation at the fifty-fourth annual meeting of the Association of School Business Officials, William E. Endicott reviewed progress on state certification for these administrators.[8] In 1965 six states had such certificates. By 1968 three additional states had established certification and several others either provided (but did not require) it or were in the process of studying such provisions.

[7] Association of School Business Officials. *The School Business Official* (Evanston. Ill.: The Association. 1960). pp. 10–13.

[8] Association of School Business Officials of the United States and Canada. *Proceedings, Fifty-fourth Annual Meeting* (Evanston. Ill.: The Association. 1968). pp. 243–49.

Endicott observed a major retardant in the movement toward establishment of certification standards.

> It is interesting to note that the 1966 survey indicated that the Association [*sic*] in three other states were at that time actively pushing for certification. However reports from the field and the State Education Departments now show that the effort was made and failed. Generally in each case it has been the inability to obtain agreement between the educationally trained School Business Administrator and the Business Administrator who has come out of industry or commerce to agree upon higher standards and/or save harmless clauses.[9]

In the discussion in an earlier part of the present chapter, it was observed that the school business administration function is an integral part of the superintendency. However, because of the variability of size of school systems, the complexity of educational programs, historical precedent, and state law, there is a considerable variation in the nature of the position which includes the business administration function. In relatively large cities the position is frequently designated as assistant superintendent in charge of business. Other titles cited are director of business affairs, associate superintendent for business services, director of administrative services, and administrative assistant.

As there is variation in titles, there is also variation in tasks performed. Tasks that generally fall in the domain of school business administration are frequently distributed among the superintendent, the school business administrator, and the fiscal officer appointed by the school board. Thus, surveys in the field are not particularly helpful in determining what business administrators do, or should do.

The ASBO has identified major areas of responsibility for school business administrators, and these appear to be the most representative of those positions entailing the business administration function in schools. These responsibilities are:

1. Budgeting and financial planning
2. Purchasing and supply management
3. Plant planning and construction
4. School-community relations
5. Personnel management

[9] ASBO. *Proceedings, Fifty-fourth Annual Meeting.* p. 248.

   6. In-service training
   7. Operation and maintenance of plant
   8. Transportation
   9. Food services
  10. Accounting and reporting
  11. Office management[10]

From the above tasks, it is apparent that the school business administrator works in very critical areas, that he is the delegate of the superintendent in several of the latter's important task areas, and that the nature of the business administrator's tasks requires a close working relationship with the superintendency.

THE SCHOOL BUSINESS ADMINISTRATOR AS A MEMBER OF THE SUPERINTENDENCY TEAM

Up to this point a case has been built for perceiving the school business administration function as a vital and integral part of the superintendency. In the following paragraphs the authors propose to describe the responsibilities and behaviors as well as the relationships of the business administrator in this context.

Responsibilities of the School Business Administrator

Ample evidence has been cited to substantiate both the varied and dynamic character of the school business administrator's position. Responsibilities that accrue to this person reflect the same features. It appears that these variations are related to the maturation and acceptance of the role as a professional position in school systems. Furthermore, the levels of role maturation seem to follow Katz's taxonomy of skills of an effective administrator.[11] Katz developed the idea that the tasks of an administrator could be analyzed in terms of technical, human, and conceptual skill areas.[12]

The initial level of skills required in the school business administrator is technical in nature. Skills related to performance

[10] ASBO, *The School Business Administrator* (Evanston, Ill.: The Association, 1960), pp. 16–18.
[11] Robert L. Katz, "Skills of an Effective Administrator," *Harvard Business Review*, 33, no. 1 (Jan.-Feb. 1955), pp. 33–42.
[12] Katz, "Skills of an Effective Administrator," pp. 33–42.

in the several tasks are required and demanded. The school business administrator performs in skill areas of budget development, purchasing, accounting, warehousing, building maintenance and operation, facility planning and construction, and transportation and food services. At this role level he performs a relatively discrete function. He serves as a specialist in his own area of competence. He applies his specialized knowledge to responsibilities and problems assigned to him by the superintendent.

In the technically oriented role level the school business administrator serves as a second set of hands for the superintendent. He acts for the superintendent in business affairs and exercises influence over others in the system as a delegate of authority.

The second level of skills which reflects increased professional maturation of the position is that of human relations. At this level the school business administrator is a specialist among specialists. His task is not only technical, but it is also to relate his responsibilities and skills to others in the system. He no longer is the second set of hands of the superintendent; he no longer is exclusively the agent of the superintendent but instead is a coordinate administrator who directly relates his function with those of the other administrators.

At this level the school business administrator spells out the business implications of group and individual administrators' proposals and decisions. He is advisory to the board, the superintendent, the central office, and the principals.

The third and highest level of maturation of the role of the school business administrator is reflected in what Katz identifies as conceptual skill. The dominant feature of this role level is participation in planning and policy development and execution. It is important to note the necessity of planning as a vehicle to achieve appropriate policy development and execution. Without the ultimate policy goals, planning is an empty concept. Such responsibilities clearly demand well-developed conceptual skills, and hence this role level might be characterized by this term.

When the school business administrator's role is perceived as being primarily conceptual in orientation, he provides more than consultant help to coordinate administrators. He becomes an active planning member on the superintendency team. As a planner, he lends his own unique creativity and expertise to the team. He creates, structures, leads, and participates in planning for the school business administration function, and relates this planning to the several other structures developed by his fellow administrators. He indeed becomes a planner among planners. As a result of this relationship, the school business administrator is involved in long-range curriculum planning, and is not merely informed of his technical responsibilities accruing from a new program. He is involved in long-range staff personnel development programs rather than being told he must plan to increase the personnel budget by 30 percent in five years. He is involved in planning long-range pupil personnel programs rather than being given the responsibility of setting up shuttle bus service among the several school sites during the school day.

The Organizational Context of the Superintendency Team

The notion of the superintendency team was probably well established in practice before it attained much visibility in the literature. As implied in the previous sections, teams may be drawn together on many different bases. A superintendent who assumes primary or nearly complete responsibility for planning might surround himself by very competent and dedicated technicians and his organization would then appear to be "lean, efficient, and well directed." In one sense this is analogous to a general and his army, a quarterback (or coach) and his team, and so forth. Thus, one must look beyond the mere existence of a team. Instead, the organizational context within which a team operates must be considered.

Fench and Wilson articulated a more enlightened and more contemporary view of the superintendency team. They observe:

> The term "superintendent" is gradually taking on a new connotation. Historically the term brought to mind the image of a person; now it is beginning to symbolize a process. It is becoming a function rather than an individual, a collective noun instead of a title. The new meaning is confirming the prediction that the management of a school system as a one-man operation is rapidly fading except in the very small districts; and the very small district is fading, too. The word "superintendency" describes the aggregate overseeing and leading of a school system's operations.[13]

---

[13] Edwin A. Fench and Robert E. Wilson. *The Superintendency Team* (Columbus. O.: Charles E. Merrill Books. Inc.. 1965). p. 3.

Fench and Wilson described their concept of the superintendency team by articulating seven principles of operation:

1. The board of education must declare educational objectives in formally adopted policies.
2. The duties of each administrator must be defined in detail and made known to all school personnel.
3. Each assistant should be empowered with authority to decide and act within his jurisdiction.
4. Responsibilities for an assistant's acts and decisions cannot be delegated.
5. Building principals are responsible for everything that happens within their buildings during school hours.
6. The nature of public education places an obligation on the superintendent to administer schools in a democratic spirit.
7. Adequate provisions must be made for lateral communication among the "middle managers."[14]

The team structure suggested by these writers reflects an acceptance of the bureaucratic model. In recent years there has been considerable criticism of the use of the bureaucratic model for designing administrative organizations for school systems. Morphet, Johns, and Reller observed that although many writers have identified and described its defects, none has advocated its complete abandonment.[15] They recognized the bureaucratic character of educational organizations and articulated the assumptions underlying the bureaucratic concept:

1. Leadership is confined to those holding positions in the power echelon.
2. Good human relations are necessary in order that followers accept decisions of superordinates.
3. Authority and power can be delegated, but responsibility cannot be shared.
4. Final responsibility for all matters is placed in the administrator at the top of the power echelon.
5. The individual finds security in a climate in which the superordinates protect the interests of subordinates in the organization.

[14] Fench and Wilson, *The Superintendency Team*, pp. 49–58.
[15] Edgar L. Morphet, R. L. Johns, and Theodore L. Reller. *Educational Organization and Administration: Concepts, Practices, and Issues* (Englewood Cliffs, N.J.: Prentice-Hall, Inc., 1967), pp. 52–53.

6. Unity of purpose is secured through loyalty to the superordinate.
7. The image of the executive is that of a superman.
8. Maximum production is attained in a climate of competition and pressure.
9. The line-and-staff plan of organization should be utilized to formulate goals, policies, and programs, as well as to execute policies and programs.
10. Authority is the right and privilege of a person holding a hierarchical position.
11. The individual in the organization is expendable.
12. Evaluation is the prerogative of superordinates.[16]

In supporting the critics of the bureaucratic model Morphet and his colleagues took the position that there are severe limitations in bureaucracies, but no single superior alternative has been developed. Consequently, efforts should be made to improve the relationships between the individual and the bureaucratic structure. The modification they developed was identified as the emerging pluralistic collegial concept. In contrast to the bureaucratic model, these three authors developed a parallel list of assumptions underlying the emerging pluralistic collegial concept:

1. Leadership is not confined to those holding status positions in the power echelon.
2. Good human relations are essential to group production and to meet the needs of individual members of the group.
3. Responsibility, as well as power and authority, can be shared.
4. Those affected by a program or policy should share in decision making with respect to that program or policy.
5. The individual finds security in a dynamic climate in which he shares responsibility for decision making.
6. Unity of purpose is secured through consensus and group loyalty.
7. Maximum production is attained in a threat-free climate.
8. The line and staff organization should be used exclusively for the purpose of dividing labor and implementing policies and programs developed by the total group affected.

---

[16] Morphet et al., *Educational Administration*, pp. 102–104.

9. The situation and not the position determines the right and privilege to exercise authority.
10. The individual in the organization is not expendable.
11. Evaluation is a group responsibility.[17]

The present authors support the point of view that, given today's circumstances, it is advisable to modify the bureaucratic model in designing organizational structures for the administration of public education. When applying this notion to the superintendency team, the authors propose a concept which also varies from that which was articulated by Fench and Wilson.

The major organizational characteristics of this superintendency team concept are those of recognizing and mobilizing the inputs of all cabinet-level administrators in both (1) planning and making decisions and (2) implementing the decisions. This is in contradistinction to the division of labor, specialization, and isolation that has characterized traditional central office staffs. Translated into a conventional table of organization, the concept is depicted in figure 2.1.

Operational characteristics of this superintendency team concept may be summarized as follows:

1. Major task areas or functions are "covered" by administrative specialists at the assistant superintendent level. These functions are designed to provide services to principals and teachers, and thus enable them to concentrate on instruction.
2. The superintendent acts as the team leader with the major responsibility of initiating the structure for group decision making and coordinating the work of the several specialists.
3. Team members act in both line and staff relationships in their areas of specialization.
   a. A team member acts in a line relationship over his own unit and over the school principals in his own area of jurisdiction.
   b. A team member acts in a staff relationship to the superintendent and coordinate team members.
   c. Principals report to individual members of the superintendency team according to their several areas of jurisdiction; all team members evaluate the principals and the final evaluation is made by the superintendent.
   d. Principals are accountable to the superintendency team.

[17] Morphet et al., *Educational Administration*, pp. 107–109.

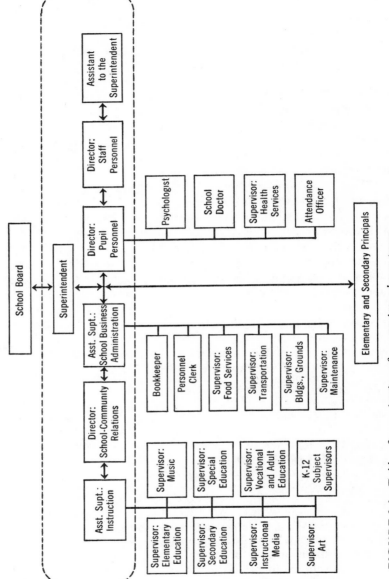

FIGURE 2.1 Table of organization of a superintendency team.

Role of the School Business Administrator on the Team

In one sense, all the preceding sections of this chapter have been a prologue to a description of the role of the school business administrator in a planning context. The content of the several sections suggests major dimensions of the role. These include the school business administrator as (a) a general administrator, (b) an administrative specialist, (c) a member of the superintendency team, and (d) a planner on that team.

As a general administrator the school business administrator employs those processes which have long been associated with and common to this activity. He plans, decides, programs, stimulates, coordinates, and appraises.

The position of school business administrator is one which calls for expertise in the specific area of the business affairs in the administration of schools. Therefore, the above processes are employed and applied to specific tasks within the general area of business affairs. These tasks include budgeting, purchasing, plant planning and construction, school-community relations, personnel management, operation and maintenance of plant, transportation, food services, accounting and reporting, and office management.

The overall objective of school business administration is to contribute to the development and implementation of those general policies and administrative decisions which provide the most effective and efficient management of business affairs in a school system in order to optimize the reaching of its educational goals. The objective is clearly implementative, that is, maximum utilization of fiscal and physical resources in the attainment of educational goals.

The school business administrator does not work in isolation. He must relate to many individuals, offices, and groups in order to reach his objectives of implementing educational goals through the appropriate administration of the school system's business affairs. The structure of these relationships is best provided by the superintendency team. It is important that he relate his unique skills and responsibilities to administrative problems and policy questions which are identified and defined by the broadly based administrative team. He must provide consultative help in pointing out the business implications of policies and decisions, and conversely, he must be provided with the other task area implications of the "business" policies and decisions to which he contributes.

The office of school business administration should have a close working relationship with building principals. The superintendency team idea calls for both line and staff relationships with these administrators in the field. The business administrator performs as a line officer in that principals are directly responsible to him for business affairs conducted in their individual school units. He also serves as an advisor in terms of establishing appropriate business procedures and as he provides technical assistance to principals as they carry out their responsibilities in the business affairs area.

Since the superintendency team concept accommodates a relatively wide diffusion of decision-making responsibilities, the business administrator is obliged to provide information and consultation to other groups. Among these are the board of education and/or specific board committees, teacher groups, community groups, and the community at large.

The school business administrator as a member of the superintendency team can enhance his own planning capability. The very nature of the interaction within the team and the relationships he has with principals, teachers, and others requires a comprehensive planning orientation. Instead of a splintered, diffused, and sometimes unrelated set of administrative tasks, an open and participative decision-making process requires a well-defined and well-executed planning process.

SUMMARY

The school business administration function is an integral part of the superintendency. Even though, in one sense, it developed prior to and separate from the superintendency, it has now become a vital part of it. The position of school business administration carries with it the crucial elements of the administrative process as it relates to the superintendency, and its major substantive aspects are vital to the ongoing functioning of the superintendency. Thus, one can conclude that the interaction between the superintendency and the school business administrator requires a close and vital relationship. It is the authors' contention that this can be best accomplished in the superintendency team concept.

This concept is developed around the notion that planning a total educational program requires free input and interaction among specialists whose specific responsibilities are limited and unique but whose ultimate responsibility—the education of children and youth—is common. Thus, the school business administrator participates in general planning as well as planning in school business affairs; he reacts to and points out business implications of other policy and technical proposals; and lastly, he is responsible for his specific business administration tasks.

SUGGESTED ACTIVITIES

1. Interview administrators in small, medium, and large school systems. Identify where and with whom most of the responsibility for school business administration lies. Try to draw generalizations as to the comparative structures.

2. Identify a group of decisions that relate to school business administration and analyze them to determine what implications these decisions might have for other school administration task areas.

3. Discuss the pros and cons of restricting school business administrators' positions to those who have taught and have had appropriate educational administrative positions.

4. Describe an example where the principal should be able to influence:

   a. the planning functions of the school business administrator and

   b. the operational responsibility of the school business administrator.

SUGGESTED READINGS

American Association of School Administrators. *Profiles of the Administrative Team.* Washington, D.C.: The Association, 1971.

Association of School Business Officials. *The School Business Administrator.* Evanston, Ill.: The Association, 1960.

Campbell, Roald F., Cunningham, Luvern L., and McPhee, Roderick F. *The Organization and Control of American Schools.* Columbus, O.: Charles E. Merrill Books, Inc., 1965.

Davis, Donald E., and Nickerson, Neal C. *Critical Issues in School Personnel Administration.* Chicago: Rand McNally & Company, 1968.

Hill, Frederick W., and Colmey, James W. *School Business Administration in the Smaller Community.* Minneapolis: T. S. Denison & Company, Inc., 1964.

Jordan, K. Forbis. *School Business Administration.* New York: The Ronald Press Company, 1969.

Miner, John B. *The School Administrator and Organizational Character.* Eugene, Ore.: The Center for the Advanced Study of Educational Administration, University of Oregon, 1967.

Roe, William H. *School Business Management.* New York: McGraw-Hill Book Company, Inc., 1961.

PLANNING TOOLS AND PROCESSES FOR SCHOOL BUSINESS ADMINISTRATION

Before a generalized concept of role can be played out in the execution of the specific tasks which are incumbent upon that role, it is helpful to consider how the role is to be played. It was noted in Chapter 2 that the school business function is derived from and hence is an integral part of the superintendency. Administrative processes described in that chapter are indigenous to both the superintendent and school business administrator roles.

The authors contend that several sets of conceptual tools are useful to the business administrator as he applies the administrative process in the accomplishment of the several tasks. Since these conceptual tools are used in nearly all of the tasks, they are treated as a discrete perspective in Part II rather than being thoroughly explicated in each of the several task area chapters which constitute Part III.

The first of the conceptual tool chapters deals with legislative and judicial tools. The way the school business administrator behaves as he functions within his role is markedly influenced by the constraints of law and its interpretation. Chapter 3 describes the general legislative and judicial context as well as relating specific concepts which must be considered as the school business administrator executes his responsibilities.

The management sciences, despite the controversy regarding the extent to which they are applied to educational administration, have contributed an important perspective to the administration of any complex organization. Chapter 4 includes a description of those concepts which appear to be most relevant to the work of the school business administrator. Since some kind of management — good or bad — exists, it is important to include a description and application of these concepts as they provide for an ordered, systematic, and "conceptually clean" description of practices that otherwise might be derived from "common sense," tradition, or hunch by the individual administrator in his own unique setting.

Since the stuff that holds an organization together is the interaction of people, the authors maintain that human relations and communications skills are of paramount importance. In nearly every task, the school business administrator must relate to others — subordinates, superordinates, community people, pupils, and hosts of others. Thus, the theme of relating and communicating is a constant thread in the fabric of his administration. Chapter 5 describes the nature of these tools and suggests some guidelines as to their application in selected administrative tasks in the school business field. From these generalizations and specific applications, it is assumed that other more extensive and intensive applications will become apparent to the practicing administrator.

The last of the major conceptual tools discussed is that of data processing — or information systems — tools. In order for the school business administrator to be an efficient and effective decision maker, he must gather, store, process, and disseminate information. The nature and variety of this data is so diverse and its application is so varied that one requires a systematic way of perceiving it. Chapter 6 provides an elementary conceptualization of an information system, and then describes some specific processes and techniques which are closely related to the work of the school business administrator. Because of the rapid public acceptance of data processing in the private sector, many school systems are under pressure to adopt these techniques which are frequently not fully understood by school personnel, board members, or the general public. Thus, it is essential that the basic concepts be understood by all school personnel — and especially the school business administration — in order to not only use the tool effectively, but also to avoid costly mistakes brought about by actions of inadequately informed people.

LEGISLATIVE AND JUDICIAL TOOLS USED IN THE PLANNING PROCESS

In both the literature and practice of school business administration it is well accepted that these administrators must possess and act from a knowledge of law as it applies to their professional field of activity. However, in the past the context of this action has often appeared to be "know school law sufficiently well to keep out of trouble." The authors maintain that this limited concept of school law for the business administrator is inadequate as he plays a key role in the planning process employed in the school system.

The legal perspective adopted by the school business administrator in the latter context must be a more dynamic, aggressive, and proactive one than that so prevalent in the past. The relationship between the legal setting of a school system and its planning function is a crucial one. Purposeful, comprehensive, and meaningful planning which is designed to really make a difference in the quality of educational services offered to a community must be carried out in an environment of law. This setting must be both well understood and used as an important input in the planning process. It goes without saying, of course, that this context is an important consideration for administrators of curriculum, personnel, and many other school system programs as well as those of the business administrators. Our attention, however, will be limited to the latter as he uses legal and judicial tools in executing his unique responsibilities.

As the school business administrator plans for and carries out his responsibility, he must act in the knowledge that he not only has certain legal constraints, but also that he can exercise or call on given authority and powers. In the past much attention was given to the former. Frequently, business administrators were noted for their ability to know and be able to cite scores of laws, opinions, findings, and cases, and use these to convince any superintendent, principal, or teacher that his request could not be met or was clearly illegal. Many boards and superintendents depended on the business administrator to keep the district out of trouble by knowing and respecting all the constraints.

At the same time, however, school systems and their administrators possess or have access to considerable authority and power which can be legitimately used to achieve the goals of the educational program. However, in the past these powers were not always fully exercised and so school systems and their administrators tended to be conforming and reactive. In the planning context, an understanding of law can assist administrators in finding new and creative approaches to their tasks.

With the compounding of social problems, the demand for change and innovation has made very clear the necessity of planning. It is the authors' contention that adequate planning in school business administration, which is necessary in effecting appropriate change and innovation in education programs, does indeed require the utilization of legal authority and powers inherent in or available to the position of the school business administrator. These seem to fall into three areas of utilization.

First, he must avail himself of the knowledge of the legal setting in terms of legal constraints, fiscal controls, and legal procedures.

Secondly, the school business administrator must recognize his own limitations in interpreting the law and so should utilize legal counsel. In some states the city attorney has the responsibility of providing legal counsel to the city school district; many states have enacted permissive legislation to enable school districts to retain an attorney, and nearly all states permit boards of education to obtain legal opinion on specialized functions such as issuing school bonds or entering into construction contracts. One should also use the offices of the state's attorney or attorney general to obtain current opinion on knotty legal questions within the state.

A third area of application of legislative and judicial tools in the planning function of the school business administrator is that of adopting a legal orientation as to the powers and authority exerted within the several levels of government, and the relationships among these levels. In a simplistic model, one can accept the notion that authority should accompany responsibility, and that authority is implemented through the exercise of power. Thus, in knowing where responsibility lies, one can begin to ascertain where and what kind of authority and exercise of power is appropriate. Such an orientation provides one with a base for concluding legal generalities. Thus, one is not dependent on only specific statutory law or the state education code, but instead has a legal *gestalt* into which the specific laws and legal problems fit.

LEGAL SETTING FOR SCHOOL BUSINESS ADMINISTRATION

Much professional literature has already been produced which provides a comprehensive description of the allocation of responsibility, authority, and power among levels of government in regard to public education.[1] However, only a brief summary of generalizations from that body of knowledge will follow in order to provide an orientation of the legal setting of school business administration.

Federal Responsibility and Authority

Newton Edwards characterizes the American scheme of government as a type of federalism, since there is a division of powers between the central government and the several constituent states.[2] Through the instrument of the United States Constitution, a federal government was created by virtue of the states delegating powers to the central government. As a result, it has only those powers which the states either expressly or by implication delegated to it; all other powers are reserved to the states.

[1] Newton Edwards, *The Courts and the Public Schools* (Chicago: University of Chicago Press, 1955).

[2] Edwards, *Courts and Public Schools*, p. 1.

Since no specific reference is made to education in the Constitution, federal government powers in education must be derived from implied powers. To date, the general welfare clause has been the primary source for federal government involvement in public education. With the relationship between national welfare and education becoming more and more visible and crucial during the past decade, it follows that federal involvement in education has become both commonplace and substantial. Recent examples of national welfare concerns which prompted educational legislation take the form of the National Defense Education Act of 1958, the Vocational Education Act of 1963, and the Elementary and Secondary Education Act of 1965.

The above mentioned positive responses of the federal government to educational concerns are not the only educational influences exerted by the federal government. The Constitution also limits the exercise of power of the several states. Classical examples of federal limitations on the laws of state are the McCollum case in Illinois involving the constitutionality of released time for religious instruction[3] and more recently the case involving racial segregation in public school systems.[4]

State Responsibility and Authority

Since authority over matters of public education was not delegated to the federal government, it was reserved to the states. As a reserved power, states are plenary in power in these matters —subject, of course, to the limitations mentioned above in connection with the federal authority. Newton Edwards stated:

> The primary function of the public school, in legal theory at least, is not to confer benefits on the individual as such, the school exists as a state institution because the very existence of civil society demands it. The education of youth is a matter of such vital importance to the democratic state and to the public weal that the state may do much, may go very far indeed, by way of limiting the control of the parent over the education of his child.[5]

School districts, as creatures of the state, have no original

---

[3] McCollum v. Board of Education, 333 U.S. 203 (1948).

[4] Brown v. Board of Education, 347 U.S. 483 (1954).

[5] Edwards, *Courts and Public Schools*, p. 24.

powers, but only those delegated to them by the state. The state (usually through legislative action) has the authority to modify or abolish school districts and change the powers delegated to them. It has been held that "School districts are state organizations: their school personnel are state employees, and their school buildings are state property."[6]

Responsibility for public education in a state may be thought to originate in the legislature. It is here that basic educational policy is created and where financial systems, appropriations, and controls are enacted. However, with education growing in complexity and magnitude, many legislatures have created state boards of education and charged them with the responsibility of developing specific education policy complementary to the basic policy enacted by the state legislature.

In most states the executive responsibility in matters of education is delegated to a state superintendent for public schools (or a comparable officer). This official is frequently appointed by the state board of education, although the practices of popular election or appointment by the governor or the legislature are used in some states. The superintendent and his staff—usually termed the state department of education—have the responsibility of implementing the policies developed by the legislature and the state board of education.

The judicial function in public education at the state level is split. State school legislation is subject to interpretation by the state court system, but the state board of education holds quasi-judicial power insofar as it maintains an evaluative function over the whole state school system.

This type of structure of educational governance at the state level exerts a unique influence on the school business official in the local school district. He is a state official, the incumbent in a position approved (and often certificated) by a state agency. He must work within general and specific educational policies created by the legislature and state board of education, and administered, supervised, and evaluated by a state superintendent and state department of education. As a result, the business administrator must know the character of these policies and regulations; he must monitor the development, modification, and interpretation of them;

---

[6] Robert J. Simpson, *Education and the Law in Ohio* (Cincinnati: The W. H. Anderson Company, 1968), p. 1.

and perhaps most importantly, he must know and appreciate the processes employed in order that he can effectively intervene in their genesis and development. This requires a state leadership role for the local school district business administrator. He must assume a responsibility for providing his expertise in state policy formulation. The rationale for this dimension of the local school district business administrator's role is predicated on the principle that those who are affected by a policy should have a voice in its development. Planning for involvement is crucial if this approach is to be taken.

A second type of state level influence on the school business administrator is that exerted by agencies of general rather than educational governance. Although educational appropriations and the mechanisms for allocation are specifically designed for the public schools of a state, frequently they are administered, monitored, and evaluated by general government offices. Thus, school business administrators must be familiar with state government accounting and auditing procedures and requirements. Certain state level procedures for purchasing, issuing of bonds, employment of civil service personnel, and so forth, must be followed in public school systems since they are state agencies.

In judicial matters, the school business administrator of the local school system is bound by rulings of the state courts. However, it is also important that he is familiar with the opinions of the state's attorney or attorney general as these constitute valuable (but not infallible) directions of possible, subsequent court action.

State Responsibility and Authority Delegated to Local School Districts

In all states with the exception of Hawaii considerable responsibility and authority in the conduct of public education is delegated by the state to local school systems. In general, states create the educational programs and local school districts operate them. These processes are predicated on the concept that the state is plenary. Thus it delegates to school districts of its own creation the authority to operate these programs.

Several distinctions in this act of delegation should be made explicit. First, states discriminate in the nature of the powers they delegate. When subordinate bodies for governance are established, they are classified in one of two ways:

1. Municipal corporations—Local units of government such as cities incorporated primarily to regulate and administer their own concerns.

2. Quasi-corporations—Political or civil divisions of the state such as school districts created primarily to serve as an instrumentality of the state and to carry out functions of the state. Thus, school districts do not have "home rule" powers frequently delegated to cities and other units of municipal government.

A second distinction, within the context of the first, is that the powers delegated to school districts are not of the same order. Instead there are three categories:

1. Mandated powers—States will frequently mandate that all school systems must do certain things. For example, state law might require that all school districts provide free transportation to students living more than two miles from their school.

2. Permissive powers—In order to accommodate variations in educational programs required in different school systems, states enact permissive legislation. This allows but does not require a school system to offer a given program. For example, school districts may provide free transportation (without state subsidy) to all children in the school system regardless of home-to-school distances.

3. Prohibitions—This third element is not a power in the same sense as the two above; however, it relates to what schools may not do. Frequently states spell out prohibitions in no uncertain terms. For example, school districts may not be permitted to use the district's buses to transport student spectators to a football game.

In essence, when states delegate powers to school districts, the state limits the action of the system to what it *must* do, what it *may* do, and spells out what it *may not* do. The school system is severely restricted and thus holds no plenary power.

A third distinction of powers granted to school districts by the state is related to administrative powers of the local school boards or administrators. There appear to be two classifications:

1. Discretionary powers—Powers delegated to an authority which must be carried out by it. For example, the state provides that a board of education can employ teachers. However, this power cannot be delegated to a superintendent or principal, it must be exercised only by the board of education.

2. Ministerial powers—Powers delegated to an authority which may in turn be delegated to a subordinate body. For example, the state permits boards of education to purchase educational supplies within certain limitations. The board, in turn delegates this (with additional limitations) to the school business administrator.

It is imperative that all school administrators know the process and the substance of delegation of responsibility and authority within their own states and localities. This is important not only in knowing what is "legal," but also is necessary in developing and expanding the planning role.

Local School District Responsibility and Authority

From the foregoing it is apparent that the nature of local school district responsibility and authority is essentially implementive. The tradition of local control of education grew strong over the years. However, it must be recognized that only recently have states vigorously exercised their authority. States have enacted a great deal of permissive legislation and many local districts (especially those with sufficient school revenue) have often gone far beyond the mandatory programs spelled out by the state.

The most important exercise of local district authority is found in the local policies developed to carry out the state policies. In this way the local district executes a state policy as a quasi-corporation of the state. However, to implement the policy fully, administrative machinery must often be established. Thus, in the local district, power (or decision making) is exercised on several levels. These have been spelled out by a publication of the University of the State of New York:

Policy—expresses the philosophy of the board of education and answers the question, "Why?" (e.g. Why do we transport school children in our district?) This policy is established by the board after giving due consideration to the known wishes of the people of the district and to the counsel of the chief school officer and his staff. Such action is said to be at the legislative decision level.

Bylaws—express the "local law" within the framework prescribed by state law and other mandates. They answer the question "What?" (e.g. What transportation will be provided in our district?) Since bylaws prescribe the functions to be preformed, it is logical to assign administrative responsibility within their framework. Bylaws are established by the board after due consideration for the wishes of the people of the district and the counsel of the chief school officer and his staff. This action is also at the legislative decision level.

Rules and Regulations — express the methods by which policies and bylaws are to be carried out. They answer the question, "How?" (e.g. How will transportation be carried out in this district?) They constitute the administrative plan and are developed by the chief school officer with the help of his staff. This phase of work is at the administrative decision level. (Since rules and regulations must be consistent with policies and bylaws, they should be approved by the board and recorded in the board minutes.)

Procedures — express the operational details for carrying on the program. They answer the question, "Details?" (e.g. How does a child who normally rides bus route #1 arrange to ride bus route #2 to his grandmother's house?) These procedural matters rest at the operational decision level and may be readily changed as conditions demand. The board and higher administrative levels need not be concerned with them. Accepting the concept of decision levels defined above, the steps in policy development become apparent. The board of education must first establish its philosophy (policy); it must next determine what services are to be provided (bylaws). It then becomes the duty of the chief school administrator and his staff to work out the administrative details (rules and regulations). The methods of application are left for decision by those who actually operate the program (procedures).[7]

The school business administrator must have an adequate understanding of policy, bylaws, rules and regulations, and procedures in his school system. But he must not stop there; he must also be aware of the relationships between these several levels of decision making. This is important in order to provide comprehensiveness in decision making to ensure that appropriate follow-up steps will be taken and to avoid incomplete or "short-circuit" actions which do not produce desired results. It is also important to ensure that appropriate persons are involved in the making of decisions at a given level. It is obvious that a board of education should not specify rules and regulations or procedures, and a business administrator should not take it upon himself to create a policy.

---

[7]The University of the State of New York, *School Business Management Handbook 1, Responsibility* (Albany, N.Y.: The University, 1955), pp. 48–49.

LEGAL TOOLS IN SCHOOL BUSINESS ADMINISTRATION PLANNING

Legislation, judicial decisions, and administrative procedures evolving from the three levels of government all provide specific legal tools which may or must be used by the school business administrator. In the previous section exhortations were made for a thorough understanding of these tools. In Part III of the text, the several chapters pertaining to the task areas of school business administration, further reference will be made to specific legal aspects of each area. The purpose of the present section is to provide an overview of some of the most important legal concepts, which are general in nature and apply to many if not most of the several task areas.

Minutes of the Board of Education

State statutes determine whether it is obligatory for a board of education to maintain records and what must be included in the records. However, the official records of the board are ordinarily *prima facie* evidence of its actions. Minutes of a board may be corrected and supplemented.

Contractual Authority

Since school districts are agencies of the state charged with carrying out state functions, it follows that they must be provided authority to do so. State statutes provide limited contractual authority to school districts. Although patterns of limitations vary among states, restrictions usually include requirements that contracts be made by designated agents at legal board meetings, that contracts be written to include specified data, that contracts exceeding a given amount be awarded after competitive bidding, and that a specified indebtedness ceiling be respected.

Common essential elements in all contracts are said to include: "(1) legal capacity on the part of the contracting parties; (2) mutual assent of the contracting parties to the terms of the contract, or what is commonly known as a 'meeting of the minds'; (3) a valid consideration; (4) rights and liabilities sufficiently definite to be enforceable; and (5) an agreement of such a nature as not to be prohibited by the statutes or the common law."[8]

Because contractual authority of school districts is determined only by state statute, boards of education and their agents frequently enter into contracts which exceed their authority. These contracts, termed *ultra vires,* are generally unenforceable and thus there can be no recovery of any amount for the vendor or other party to the contract. It is a case of "let the vendor beware."

In a case of an invalid contract which otherwise is within the authority of a board of education, the district may have an obligation to make a reasonable settlement (*quantum meruit*) with the second party. This recovery is based on the principle that it is unjust or inequitable to permit one party to be enriched at the expense of another.

Frequently, invalid contracts are consumated by an agent of the board who does not have the authority to obligate the school district. A principle of law provides that the district for whom the agent has acted may subsequently ratify the unauthorized act of its agent. However, such ratification can take place only if the contract was legal in all other respects.

If a contract is *malum in se* (tainted with bad faith or fraud) and violates public policy, it is considered utterly void and the courts will do nothing with it. Both parties are left without recourse.

Competitive Bids

Although there is no uniformity among all states regarding the requirement of competitive bidding, nearly all school districts throughout the country use this procedure in some form. Boards may use competitive bidding at their own discretion if it is not mandated by law. If a board so elects, it is then obligated to clearly state in any advertisement that bids are to be competitive, and thus the district binds itself to accept the lowest responsible bid. If the advertisement merely invites bids, the board is not obligated to accept any of the bids. Thus, if in its advertisement a board offers to accept the lowest bid, it must do so unless substantial reasons are given for the rejection.

If competitive bidding is used, it is necessary to provide "a

[8] Edwards, *Courts and Public Schools,* p. 200.

common standard" on which the bids are to be based. Failure to do so eliminates the basis of real competitive bidding. Thus, rather definitive plans and specifications must be provided to prospective bidders in order to enable them to ascertain a precise bid on a specifically designated job. This practice incorporates an enlightened business principle as well as a legal requirement.

Boards of education may solicit alternate bids on essentially the same work. In essence, several rather than one bid are requested, and the board exercises its discretion in selecting the lowest responsible bidder on the best alternative. Contractors are free to submit bids on any or all of the separate alternatives and thus compete freely.

Many states require competitive bidding and further specify that the contract be awarded to "the lowest responsible bidder." It has been held that this does not require the board to accept the lowest dollar bid. Instead, the board can exercise its discretion in determining which bidder is most responsible and how this is equated with the dollar bid. Boards, in exercising this discretion, must act in good faith, must not act capriciously, and must conduct appropriate investigation to enable them to make a decision based on substantial facts.

Often a board in its advertisement for competitive bids declares its intention to award the contract to the lowest responsible bidder, but subsequently finds none of the bids acceptable. It has been held that despite the original declaration, a board may reject all bids, but the board in doing so must indicate substantial reasons for doing so. This is another illustration of the board's exercise of discretion with justification.

When the board accepts the bid of a contractor, it has been held (1) that the contractor must be notified, (2) that a definite offer must be submitted to him, and (3) that there must be a definite acceptance by him. This is contrary to the popular belief that the board merely has to extend a contract to the contractor.

The law protects contractors who, in the process of submitting bids, make errors in their bids. The general principle is that of not permitting one of the parties to profit by the mistake of another. Thus, the contractor may withdraw his erroneous bid and he is not obligated to enter into a contract with the school district.

In like fashion, boards of education may make slight or superficial alterations in the specifications once a contract is let. The degree of change, however, must be such which does not substantially alter the character of the building or item and thus destroy the equity of competitive bidding on the original specifications.

School Monies

A considerable portion of the responsibilities borne by the school business administrator is that devoted to money management. Fiscal matters in his office include gathering, holding, investing, and expending monies.

School monies themselves are classified in several ways. The most generic classification is by function. Income monies are designated as revenue or nonrevenue. Nonrevenue monies are those which do not add to the assets of the school system. These typically are monies derived from bond issues (which must be eventually repaid), monies derived from the sale of school property (and so the form of the asset is changed but not increased), or monies derived from loans (which must be repaid). Revenue monies are those which add to the assets of the school system and include taxes, transfer payments or subventions, gifts, fines, fees, tuitions, etc.

The body of school law reflects the statutory constraints imposed on the business administrator as he husbands the financial resources of the school system.

Nonrevenue Sources of School Monies

In most states, nonrevenue monies are subject to rather explicit control in their gathering, holding, and expending. The issuance of school bonds is subject to state-mandated procedures that usually require a specified board resolution, hearing or public notice, and popular vote. States also exercise quantitative controls on the amount of indebtedness a district can assume (usually a proportion of the district's assessed valuation of taxable property). Other similar controls are those related to the types of bonds issued, terms and maturity schedules, and maximum allowable interest rates. States also specify appropriate uses of the bond issue. Generally accepted uses are those of the acquisition and improvement of land, construction of new or additions to existing buildings, remodeling of existing buildings, and the purchase and installation of equipment for the types of capital outlay projects.

State statutes governing the floating of loans most often specify the purpose as borrowing against anticipated revenues for operating expenses during the current fiscal year. Many states limit those loans to the current fiscal year as local school taxes are usually levied on a year-to-year basis. This also sets up a quantitative limitation as school systems cannot borrow beyond the actual amount of taxes which are anticipated for the given year.

The sale of school district property imposes fewer specific controls on boards and administrators, but several generalized limitations are apparent. Procedures for these sales are often specified, e.g., public notice, sealed bids, etc., are required. The disposition of monies obtained is sometimes prescribed in order to eliminate the diversion of revenues into purposes for which they were not intended. For example, some states specify that proceeds from the sale of school buildings be added to the school building fund and be used only for these purposes.

Revenue Sources of School Monies

Most of the financial resources for which the business administrator is responsible are classified as revenues. The following discussion identifies the major revenue sources and briefly describes major legal constraints attendant to the administration of each classification.

The majority of school systems derive a considerable amount of revenue from state sources. However, since most states have a program of state assistance to local school systems which includes some kind of equalization factor, the proportion of state revenues usually has an approximately inverse relationship to local taxing ability. Thus, state transfer payments (or subventions) to local districts tend to be variable grants and as such frequently incorporate complex patterns of controls. These controls are usually spelled out in terms of conditions for eligibility. For example, in order to qualify, school systems frequently must employ teachers of certain qualifications, in a fixed proportion to pupil enrollment, and pay specified salary levels. The systems must maintain minimum program standards to be eligible for state financial assistance and frequently must levy a local school tax at a mandated level.

Local school tax revenue is the single largest source of revenue in school systems in the majority of states. As stated in several contexts in the present chapter, local school tax law is determined by the state, and local boards and administrators execute state policy at the local level. Within the context of state policy, local school boards usually have the responsibility of developing school system budgets which, in turn, determine directly or indirectly the local school tax levy to be applied for the given fiscal year. Thus, school business administrators usually find themselves deeply involved in an interacting web of decisions involving program-budget-tax questions and relationships.

Revenue made available to school systems from the federal government has been largely categorical in nature and therefore designed for and used in well-defined and specific educational programs. The several programs described as "titles" under the National Defense Education Act, the Vocational Education Act, and the Elementary and Secondary Education Act set forth both specific programs to be implemented and specific criteria to be met by eligible school systems. Frequently local systems must provide "matching" monies in order to qualify for federal program monies. Since these programs are optional many alternative decisions must be made. The school business administrator must be knowledgeable of the federal programs so he will be able to provide his input into "cost-benefit" analysis of the alternative programs to determine both appropriate participation and a prediction of long-term consequences.

School systems are recipients of revenue from many sources other than the state, local, and federal governments. School boards collect tuition payments from nonresident students, fees charged to students, typically from "unusual" programs requiring special materials in the given class. Student fines, gifts, and the like are also considered as revenue. These revenues usually account for a very small proportion of revenues and are often unpredictable in amount. However, the school business administrator must be aware of the law permitting and the conditions prerequisite to their collection.

Although the investment of school funds is seldom a large item, state law usually spells out definitive procedures for it. Because of high public visibility of this concern and the vulnerability of any public official to charges of graft, the school business administrator must be aware of the law in this matter. Inactive funds from current operating budgets or from bond issues often may be invested in government notes and other low-risk securities. Interest on these investments must be added to certain funds, according to many state statutes.

Control Systems for School Fiscal Policy

The discretionary power of local school boards and hence the school business administrator is severely limited. As indicated in the first section of this chapter, the state through the exercise of its plenary power specifies general policies, then delegates to the state those powers which must be exercised at the local level to implement the state's educational program. In terms of fiscal policy, the state usually specifies the nature of local taxes, procedures that local school boards may use to levy taxes, and quantitative limitations. The state also specifies other sources of revenue that may be obtained and used, as well as how these revenues may be expended.

The budgetary function in school systems is a crucial one, and it lies at the heart of state fiscal policy for schools. As will be seen in the later chapter on budgeting, this process is used to determine not only the amount to be expended in a given area or account, but also to determine the total amount of revenue needed to support the program. Because of the cruciality of the latter decision, states usually set up precise procedures to ensure adequate decision making at appropriate levels. Budgeting authority dichotomizes school systems into two groups:

1. Fiscally dependent systems—those in which school boards must get budgets approved by another local governmental body, e.g., a city council.
2. Fiscally independent systems—those in which the school board can act (within state controls) without approval from other local bodies.

Administrator responsibility in accounting, auditing, and reporting is also limited. Usually a state-specified accounting system is mandated to provide uniform reporting and controls. Common definitions of revenue and expenditure areas are mandated. Frequently state-specified or administered auditing procedures are employed to monitor the accounting function in the states' school systems.

State law frequently spells out control procedures in regard to transferring monies within and between state-specified funds. Most states have some explicit provision for carrying balances from the end of one fiscal year to the succeeding one.

Several areas of fiscal policy and money management seem to "hit the headlines" nearly every year in one part of the country or another. One of the most visible problem areas is that of the gathering and use of "extra curricular" monies. Some years ago most states considered the administration of such monies as beyond the jurisdiction of legislatures. However, in more recent years states have required school boards and administrators to carry out fiscal control procedures when handling these funds in much the same way as when administering monies generated from school taxes.

Frequently, local school systems will carry relatively large balances of funds which are in excess of the amount needed for month-to-month expenses. As a result, legislation has been enacted (or judicial opinion has found the implied power) to enable boards to invest these "inactive" funds. The law typically specifies the conditions under which these monies may be invested, and the appropriate kind of investment. The preceding discussion on investments as a source of revenue suggested several kinds of applicable fiscal controls.

From this very brief review of state-mandated fiscal control systems, and the description of several key legal concepts running through most state legislation, it is apparent that school business administrators may use these as decision-making tools. The basic legislative tool can serve as a base of understanding the legal requirements. It can also assist the administrator in finding the pertinent legislation in the state education or school code. A third function of the legislative and judicial tool might be that of an analytic device to assist the business administrator in evaluating the present legislation. Through such an analytic process the administrator might then formulate more appropriate and viable legal provisions and thus exert professional leadership in upgrading public education in his state.

SUMMARY

Because schools are agencies of the state, a school business administrator must be knowledgeable in legislative and judicial matters that involve public education. He must have a generalized knowledge and appreciation of the legal bases in order to see the *gestalt* and thereby relate specific legal principles to the total legal concept. The derivation of legal power to enact educational policy, the exercise of plenary power by the states, and the delegation of power by the state to local school boards are among the fundamental legal concepts underlying the governance of public schools.

Since school business administrators are typically given responsibilities of executing local school district policies, it is necessary for them to know the policy-making structure and how they can relate administrative procedures to such policy. The chapter covers several specific conceptual tools which the school business administrator uses. These include the minutes of the board of education—the legal voice of the board; contractual authority—the power and constraints on contractual obligations; competitive bids—the procedures and principles necessary to protect the school system and satisfy the law; school monies—to protect the resources of the school system and use them as intended; control systems for school fiscal policy—those fiscal controls designed to provide fiscal accountability.

It is the authors' contention that these legal and judicial concepts underlie nearly every action of the school business administrator. He is obligated to know many of them with a high degree of specificity, e.g., what size of purchase requires a competitive bid. Others he must be generally aware of in order to know he must obtain legal assistance, e.g., what kind of investments can I make with the proceeds of a bond issue?

SUGGESTED ACTIVITIES

1. Obtain a copy of your state's school code (codification of state law pertaining to schools), and determine the specific legal requirements in matters of board of education minutes, contractual authority, competitive bidding, accounting, investment of funds, budgeting, and related business functions.

2. Review the policy handbook of a school system and determine the legal bases of the school business administration-related policies which have been established.

3. Interview a school superintendent or school business official in order to identify and discuss examples of
   a. legislation (both state and federal),
   b. case law (both state and federal), and
   c. judicial opinion (opinions of the state's attorney general or state's attorney) which have influenced school business administration in your state.

SUGGESTED READINGS

Bolmeier, Edward Claude. *The School in the Legal Structure.* Cincinnati: The W. H. Anderson Company, 1968.

Drury, Robert L., ed. *Law and the School Superintendent.* Cincinnati: The W. H. Anderson Company, 1958.

Drury, Robert L., and Ray, Kenneth C. *Essentials of School Law*, New York: Appleton-Century-Crofts, 1967.

Edwards, Newton. *The Courts and the Public Schools.* Chicago: University of Chicago Press, 1955.

Garber, Lee O. *Current Legal Concepts in Education.* Philadelphia: University of Pennsylvania Press, 1966.

Garber, Lee O. *Law and the School Business Manager.* Danville, Ill.: The Interstate Printers & Publishers, Inc., 1957.

Garber, Lee O., *Tort and Contractual Liability of School Districts and School Boards*, Danville, Ill.: The Interstate Printers & Publishers, Inc., 1963.

Garber, Lee O., and Edwards, Newton. *The Law Governing the Financing of Public Education.* Danville, Ill.: The Interstate Printers & Publishers, Inc., 1964.

Gauerke, Warren E. *School Law.* New York: The Center for Applied Research in Education, 1965.

McDaniel, Jesse L. *Law Governing Acquisition of School Property.* Cincinnati: The W. H. Anderson Company, 1966.

Remmlein, Madeline K. *School Law.* 2d ed. Danville, Ill.: The Interstate Printers & Publishers, Inc., 1962.

Seitz, Reynold, ed. *Law and the School Principal.* Cincinnati: The W. H. Anderson Company, 1961.

Simpson, Robert J. *Education and the Law in Ohio.* Cincinnati: The W. H. Anderson Company, 1968.

MANAGEMENT TOOLS USED IN THE PLANNING PROCESS

THEORIES OF MANAGEMENT — APPLICABILITY TO SCHOOL BUSINESS ADMINISTRATION

With the increasing complexity of educational administration, the student of administration, as well as the practicing administrator, must avail himself of many planning tools which are available. Management tools are only a portion of the total array of tools available to enhance the human skills of the administrator. In the utilization of management tools for planning one must be constantly aware of the values and philosophy underlying the utilization of these tools.

Most current theories of management have as their core an explanation of the relationships existing between managerial actions and various organizational goals. The traditional school of management relies on lists of principles; the empiricists on historically successful patterns of action; the human relations school on the interactions between persons and groups; the rationalists on information flows and authority concepts; the mathematical school on formulae; and the decision-making school on the decision process itself. Though each theory has a particular emphasis, certain lines of reasoning are distinguishable in almost every theoretical formulation dealing with organizations. One similarity is the stress placed upon individual motivation and initiative. Other theorists emphasize the monetary aspects of motivation, the rational balancing of needs and desires, the universal importance of individual action, and the critical role of productivity. Maximum output is not always advocated, but almost every theory of management assumes that the organization must be enjoying satisfactory levels of output. The principles of short-run efficiency and long-range effectiveness permeate the literature concerning management.

The final point in similarity in theories of management is the attempt to relate the "whys" of organizational activities to the "whats" needed to reach specific goals. These "whys" and "whats" reflect the bias of the auspices: social scientists rarely advocate mathematical models to direct human activity, and mathematical-model builders seldom press for subjective judgment in a manufacturing run. Seen as a whole, the spectrum of activities recommended in various theories covers the broad categorization of using personal skills and talents to manage resources and equipment. To put it more succinctly, management theory, as it relates to school business administration, attempts to explain how organizations seek to meet their goals by integrating personal skills and learning resources. School business management behavior is concerned with functional skills, with the factors of learning, with individual and group behavior patterns, and with the role of institutions' operating environment vis-à-vis society as a whole.

KEY PLANNING – MANAGEMENT TOOLS

The basic goal of planning is to influence the future by taking logical, predetermined action in the present. Planning is the essence of effective operation, and plans carefully integrated with organizational goals are economical.

Planning involves the preparation of alternative methods, strategies, and approaches designed to assist organizations in accomplishing desired objectives or goals. More specifically, the aims of educational planning are to formulate a system-wide philosophy, general goals, and instructional objectives; organize relevant data; determine personnel, space, and material requirements; examine alternative procedures and establish priorities;

provide for communication and information retrieval for the system; analyze financial resources; evaluate the attainment of objectives; view the future; and appraise the system continually to ensure that objectives are being reformulated.

Although educational institutions do not have the profit motive of business, this is rather inconsequential. Educational institutions must produce learning increments efficiently and economically.

Planning does not always lead to Utopia. In a given situation, the effect of time, cost, and flexibility considerations could negate all the advantages that can be derived from systematic planning activities. In actuality, the success of planning efforts depends largely on the skills and abilities of the planners themselves. Many within the educational hierarchy lack training in portraying school activities as a system; they fail to integrate curriculum planning with financial administration, thereby negating the concomitant effects of all the component variables of an educational program. If they fail to state their plans clearly, if they base their suggestions on incomplete information or dubious forecasts, if they suggest alternatives that fail to meet organizational goals effectively, or if they finalize plans that are too highly structured or too inflexible to meet changing conditions, then planning can be a sterile activity. The school business administrator must, because of his exposure to management tools, assume leadership in planning. When planning is done well, the organization can gain the advantage of logical, systematic, and purposeful action. Most well-structured educational plans yield a set of returns far in excess of their costs. With the ever increasing struggle for the tax dollar and the constant shortage of exceptional educational personnel, the school business administrator must spearhead the planning for effective, efficient, economical use of educational resources, and must exhibit leadership in planning for new structures and processes.

Organization

How best to organize the efforts of individuals to achieve desired objectives has long been one of the world's most important, difficult, and controversial problems. Important forces and resources are complicating the problem. Competition from other countries with differing educational philosophies is complicating the problem of educational organization. The trend in America, generally, in our schools, in our homes, and in our communities, is toward giving the individual greater freedom and initiative. This has a compounding effect when one considers that our school systems are growing increasingly larger and more complex. Fundamental changes in American society create expectations among employees as to how they should be treated. The increasing level of professional preparation of the staff increases its expectations of participation in organizational decision making. Coupled with the cultural trend in American homes, schools, and communities is an increasing concern about mental health and the growth of individuals into healthy, emotionally mature adults. These are complicating personnel relations, another factor likely to accelerate the formulation of new organizational practices prevalent today. Finally, as school systems increase in complexity the staffs must exhibit training in diverse, complex technologies and highly specialized skills and professions. It is not at all uncommon for subordinates or staff to know far more about an important matter than does the chief school officer or board member. The superintendent and board can no longer make the best decision on the best technical information procurable. The decisions are so complex that no one subordinate has all the technical information required. To marshall all the information bearing on a decision, it is usually necessary to involve experts from all phases of the educational complex. As a consequence, there is much greater need for cooperation and participation in administering the enterprise. To meet the demands created by our more complex learning institutions, more appropriate management tools or systems of organizing human behavior are being created. Because of his expertise in personnel relations, management tools, and organizational strategies, the school business administrator must exhibit a bold approach to planning.

Congruent with the evolution of the organization has been the development of models for explaining organization concepts. Initially, we struggled with aspects of organization such as structure, hierarchy, authority, specialization, span of control, line and staff. The traditional theory was supplanted by the bureaucratic model, neoclassical model, professional model, and finally the decision-making model. None of these approaches provided a basis for an integrated, systematic organizational model. In compatibility with the rest of this text we would like to explore organization as a system of mutually dependent parts and variables. The educational organization is thought of as a social system within the totality of society. Under the systems concept, the organization is viewed as a series of parts which include the individual, the informal work groups, the formal structure, and environmental systems. Under the systems concept, consideration must be given to the means for interrelating and coordinating these various subsystems. These parts are integrated through various processes such as the information and communications network, the decision system, and built in equilibrium mechanisms which exist in every organization.

Delegation

Since delegation is the attempt to accomplish tasks by reallocating the authority required to perform those tasks, it calls for well-formulated plans and policies developed in the context of a given administrative philosophy. Work loads must be assigned to those best able to do the tasks needed to carry out the component parts of the total plan.

Once authority is delegated within a given goal framework, controls must be set up to find out how well the goals are being met. Systems of reporting are needed to measure actual achievement against expected results. Adjustments must then be made when discrepancies occur. These adjustments may be made in terms of personnel, authority granted, or task assignments. They may take the form of transfers, reassignments, removal, incentive compensation, or recentralization of decision making. Since the delegation process is dynamic, methods, results, and rewards must be reviewed continually. If individuals are given new responsibilities, they should be rewarded in some manner.

A certain amount of progress can be made toward clarifying authority relationships by developing effective ways and means of specifying exactly which matters are to be delegated and which ones are not to be delegated. The degree of specificity required in delegation, the nature of the matter being delegated, the degree of repetitiveness of the assigned duties, and other concerns such as the level of performance demanded are the critical points encountered in laying out authority relationships. In general, written delegation is good when relatively long periods of time or the written word is needed to legitimize individual action. In some cases, a document or a job description must be prepared to assure certain individuals that expressed authority has been granted to allow a particular person to perform specified deeds or to make particular decisions. For example, specific limits on capital expenditures almost always appear in written form. Oral directives are most expeditious when the time duration of delegation is short, when an extremely complex matter is being delegated, when delegation is related to the performance of minor or infrequently performed tasks, or when other factors make the preparation of written instructions either unnecessary or cumbersome.

In summary, delegation of authority is a keystone of sound operational management. If done well, proper delegation can improve the execution of the planning, organizing, and evaluating functions by developing more effective relationships between superiors and subordinates. If done poorly, the results can be chaotic and costly. The skill of delegating authority is one of the key determinants of the degree of success a leader can hope to achieve. It is also, without doubt, one of the more difficult skills to develop effectively. How the leader chooses to develop superior-subordinate relationships depend on the supervisor, his subordinates, and the situation. Since the chain of a leadership pattern can exert positive or negative influences on organizational efficiency, it is important to weigh and evaluate such a choice as carefully as possible. For a school system the team approach to planning is a viable alternative.

Control

The function of control includes the measurement of output, the comparison of output with some predetermined standard, and the adjustment of input to restore the system to its planned norm. Educators generally perceive control as negative as an end in itself, as punitive rather than as a way to add flexibility and effectiveness. The design of control in subsystems should be consistent with the objectives of the larger network, preventive rather than punitive, and no more elaborate than necessary to accomplish the established goals. Elements vital to any control system are:

1. Something to be controlled
2. Sensory device or method for measuring the characteristic or condition

3. Appraisal unit for evaluating data with prescribed goals
4. Corrective unit or mechanism

The system may be open or closed depending upon whether the appraisal unit is an integral part of the system it regulates. An illustration appears in figure 4.1.

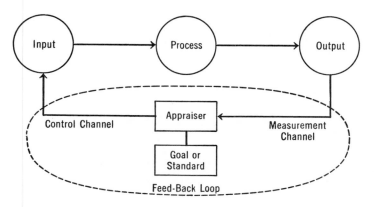

FIGURE 4.1   Control system.

Controls that are appropriate for educational systems are: cost control, educational process control, pupil personnel control, staff personnel control, and transportation system control. The objective of the systems concept is to perform a specified function within tolerance while the objective of control is to maintain the output which will satisfy the system objectives.

Information is the medium of control; it is the flow of measurement information and later the flow of corrective information which allows an item to be controlled. The information must be in a language common to the plan, accurately measured and transmitted to the appraiser for comparison, and processed rapidly. Basic to the process is the definition of information which states that it consists only of that which is communicated. The growth of organizations and increased specialization and functionalization have developed barriers to communication. Technical break-throughs in data processing equipment have provided an opportunity for development of integrated systems of information flow. In spite of this opportunity, few educational institutions have really capitalized on it. Educational systems that have established data processing centers at best utilize only the clerical aspects of the systems. Only a few "lighthouse systems" are using data processing as a decision-making instrument. Information-decision systems can be developed which provide the proper flow of information among decision points in the organization. (See figure 4.2). Both formal and informal communication must be recognized. Administrations might well analyze informal communication patterns in some detail because the information-decision system may follow "natural" patterns although they may not be recognized in the formal system.

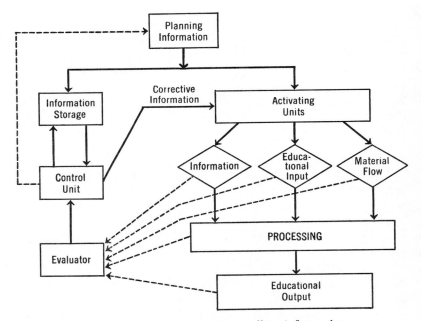

FIGURE 4.2   Flow of planning and controlling information.

Maximization — Planning

The systems concept provides a framework for integrated decision making. Within the framework a number of tools of analysis have been developed over the years which include the latest, most sophisticated techniques used in operations research. One of the objectives of this section will be to place these tools in perspective as they relate to the science and art of management. In surveying the field of management science, no attempt will be made to cover the techniques exhaustively; each warrants book-length treatment to ensure some degree of expertise or even understanding. Rather, we shall describe the technique from a school administrator's point of view, emphasizing those aspects which are important in assessing applicability. In particular, we are interested in their usefulness in implementing the systems concept — either in analysis and decision making or in systems design. Mathematics will be kept to a minimum.

Network Analysis

Network analysis is a managerial technique which is useful in systems design, planning, and control. It is as old as scientific management and as new as the latest space exploration. Although many variations of the new generation of network analysis have been developed, the two basic types are critical-path method (CPM) and program evaluation and review technique (PERT). (See figure 4.3.)

CPM was used by Du Pont in 1959 to schedule plant-maintenance shutdowns during changeover. Subsequently, it was used to plan building construction and other large projects. In CPM the primary analytical emphasis is to determine the programming strategy which will satisfy schedule requirements at minimum cost. Once again, the analyst will trace through the paths of the diagram. In this instance the shortest time in which each job can be accomplished is estimated (minimum time) and what it would cost under this condition (maximum cost). With ranges of time and cost established, the critical path and the cost of reducing the time can be determined. CPM has been very effective in areas relating to planning, scheduling, and coordinating of total developmental projects.

PERT is based on critical-path scheduling. However, there is a fundamental difference between the two. The PERT technique is applicable where there is no established system for doing the task and therefore no exact basis for estimating the required time to complete each task. Critical-path scheduling, on the other hand, usually is applied to jobs which are established or have been

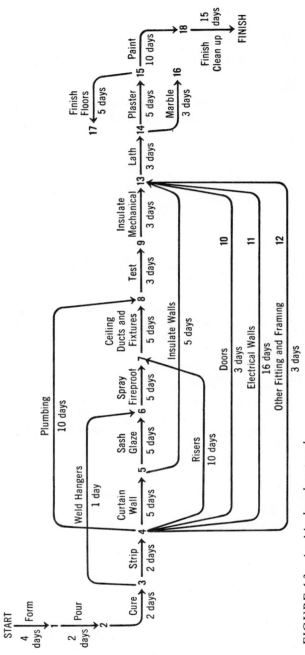

FIGURE 4.3 A critical-path network.

done before and where it is possible to predict performance accurately. Consequently, more sophisticated mathematical models must be used in the PERT technique.

During the past few years, the techniques of CPM and PERT have been refined and other variations have been added. The first developments were concerned principally with a description of a total task, the relationship among various elements, and the cost of performing various segments of the operation. More recent variations of CPM and PERT have added features of minimax theory in determining the optimum way to complete the job.

Another variation of CPM and PERT is LESS (Least Cost Estimating and Scheduling), which resolves the problem at what time and hour each and every job should be done so as to complete the project at a minimum cost or in a specified time. This technique could be very useful for larger school systems with extensive maintenance crews. Some that are equipped to do minor construction might utilize this technique.

Resource Allocation and Multi-Project Scheduling (RAMPS) considers restrictions such as quantity of resources available, priorities, "resource team" composition, additional staff, subcontracting to another educational agency, and inefficient staff utilization rates. Other related factors may be incorporated in the procedure. Considering these restrictions and requirements, RAMPS seeks the schedule which satisfies various criteria including minimum costs.

There are many other variations, many of which at the present time do not have applications in education. It is safe to say that most examples are basically the same and only the acronyms differ. Inasmuch as PERT was one of the first, and also the most widely accepted, we will use it to illustrate networking and give illustrated usages in school business management.

The PERT technique can be used in planning and developing internal and external audits; moving from a line- to program-type budget; switching from a manual to machine record system; planning and controlling the budgetary process; planning mergers or consolidations of school systems; organizing and determining priorities for school construction and acquisition of capital equipment; timing and selling of bond issues; scheduling unusual school operations; closing out a school plant and opening another; installing and integrating a new organizational structure; planning student, staff and educational resource flow; planning and implementing maintenance programs; studying the educational process; planning acquisition programs; and planning and scheduling transportation programs, especially when alternatives are available but of a complex nature.

The PERT network is the working model of the technique. It illustrates, by diagram, the sequential relationships among the tasks which must be completed to accomplish the project. PERT treats planning and scheduling separately. First the plan is developed, and then the limitations are added to the problem. The first step in developing the PERT network is to gather a list of all the activities needed to complete the project. The people associated with the project activities have the best knowledge about detailed tasks. Next, the network is constructed to show the sequential relationship among the activities.

Figure 4.4 is an example of a simplified PERT network. Each

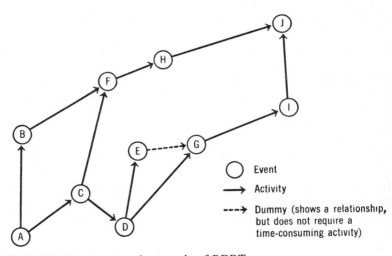

FIGURE 4.4   A network example of PERT.

event is lettered for the purpose of identification. Thus, activity A/H is the activity which takes place between events lettered A and H. It is possible to start the diagram from the completion of the project and work backward, or from the beginning and work toward completion. Length of arrows do not denote time span but logical sequence. Activities B/F and C/F must be completed before activity F/H or F/J can begin. Event F signifies the completion of activities H/F and C/F and the starting point for the following related activities.

Once the flow network has been determined for the system, the next step is to obtain an estimate of the elapsed time (in time module) required to accomplish each activity by the individual responsible for accomplishment of that element of work. This time forecast consists of three individual estimates:

> The most likely estimate (x)
> The optimistic estimate (a)
> The pessimistic estimate (y)

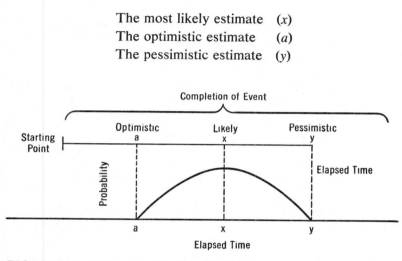

FIGURE 4.5   *Estimating the time distribution.*

The flow network, with its coded events, can be programmed for a computer. The elapsed-time estimates can likewise be used as input to the computer processing. The computer solves the mathematical problems (calculation of each estimate) and, by adding the calculated expected times for each activity, computes the expected time for each event.

When we have three estimates of elapsed time and need to find t_e,

> a–optimistic estimate of interval   Obtained
> x–most likely estimate of interval   for each
> y–pessimistic estimate of interval   interval

the expected value (mean) and t_e^2 (variance) we can use the following equations:

$$t_e = \left[\frac{\alpha + 4x + y}{6}\right]$$

Apply to each interval

$$\sigma t_e^2 = \left(\frac{y - a}{6}\right)^2$$

In summary, network analysis is a useful managerial technique for planning, organizing, and evaluation. The advantages of PERT may be summarized as follows:

—the sequence and relationship network of all significant events in planning how the end objective will be achieved is identified;

—the relative uncertainty in meeting or accomplishing all activities in the plan is measured and evaluated;

—the relatively critical condition in areas of effort required is shown to the adm·nistrator;

—slack areas are shown where some delay will not preclude the meeting of end objectives on time;

—the current probability of meeting scheduled events is provided for the administrator. Network analysis is useful; however, when the system to be described is complex, the use of computers is almost a necessity.

Queuing Theory

Another name for *queuing theory* is waiting-line theory, which applies to those decisions which arise when service must be provided to meet group needs. There are costs connected with the length of the waiting line and the time lost to waiting. There are also costs associated with increasing the capacity of the servicing unit, both capital costs and labor costs. Since arrivals may be random, there may be times when there are waiting lines and other times when there is idle servicing capacity. The appropriate number of lunchroom servicing lines, ticket booths, water fountains, and other situations around a school that might cause lines of waiting are excellent applications of this technique. Even in the simpler cases, the computations tend to get quite lengthy. Many tables are available which give general solutions to various waiting-line situations. In some instances, the Monte Carlo techniques are the appropriate management tools (see figure 4.6).

---

n = number of units in waiting line at time t

$Pn(t)$ = probability of n units in queue at time t

$\lambda \Delta t$ = probability of a new unit entering the line in the time interval t to $t + \Delta t$, which implies that λ = mean arrival rate $u\Delta t$ = probability that a unit being serviced is completed in the time interval t to $t + \Delta t$, which implies that u = mean service rate.

$\bar{n}$ = mean length of waiting line

$$\frac{dPn(t)}{dt} = Pn - 1^{(t)} + uPn + 1^{(t)} - (\lambda + u)\,Pn(t),\,(r > 0)$$

$$\frac{dPo(t)}{dt} = -\,Po(t) + uP_1\,(t),\,(n = 0)$$

FIGURE 4.6 *Single-station queuing problem showing the relationship between waiting time and service time as solution to many waitingline problems. (For a more detailed explanation, see Churchman, Ackoff, and Arnoff,* Introduction to Operations Research *[New York: John Wiley & Sons, Inc., 1957], pp. 389–416.)*

Game Theory

Game theory involves analysis of the choice of strategies. It is primarily a new way of thinking about competition decisions. Applications have been few in number and limited in scope because of the unmanageable complexities that arise once the number of contestants exceeds two and freedom of action is increased. Therefore, it would appear that game theory should have a great practical impact. Unfortunately, this has not been the case. It has received modest application in military problems, but there have been very few industrial or educational applications. The reason seems to be that game theory has only been capable of analyzing very simple situations. Thus, there has been a great gap between what the theory can handle and most competitive situations in education and industry. Thus, the primary contribution of game theory has been its concepts rather than its formal application to solving real problems. This technique, through modification, should be very useful in the future.

Linear Programming

Linear programming is one of the most useful of the operations-research techniques. This is a technique for specifying how to use limited resources or capacities to obtain a particular objective. Linear programming has been applied with good results in purchasing and inventory control determining best alternative transportation routes in urban areas at peak traffic periods, location and number of warehouse and maintenance facilities, and the best location of schools. The name implies the limitation in that it can only handle linear relationships.

Linear programming uses a mathematical model to describe the problem of concern. The adjective "linear" means that all the mathematical functions in this model are required to be linear functions. The word "programming" is essentially a synonym for planning. Thus, linear programming involves the planning of activities in order to obtain an "optimal" result, i.e., a result which reaches the specified goal best (according to the mathematical model) among all feasible alternatives.

One of the classic problems of linear programming is the diet problem. The objective is to ascertain the quantities of certain foods that should be eaten to meet certain nutritional requirements at a minimum cost. Assume that consideration is limited to milk, beef, and eggs, and to vitamins A, C, and D. Suppose that the number of milligrams of each of these vitamins contained within a unit of each food is as in table 4.1.

TABLE 4.1

Vitamin	Gal. of Milk	Lb. of Beef	Doz. of Eggs	Min. Daily Req.
A	1	1	10	1 mg.
C	100	10	10	50 mg.
D	10	100	10	10 mg.
Cost	$1.00	$1.00	$.50	

Let Xm, Xb, and Xe be the number of gallons of milk, pounds of beef, and dozens of eggs, respectively, in the daily diet. The objective is to minimize costs, and the resource restrictions are in the form of lower bounds rather than upper bounds. Therefore, the linear programming model for this problem is the following:

Minimize:

$Z = 1.0Xm + 1.1Xb + 0.5Xe$, subject to the restrictions,
$Xm + Xb + 10Xe \geqslant 1$
$100Xm + 10Xb + 10Xe \geqslant 50$
$10Xm + 100Xb + 10Xe \geqslant 10$ and
$Xm \geqslant 0, Xb \geqslant 0, Xe \geqslant 0.$[1]

Having had a glimpse at the possibilities of linear programming, it is well to survey the underlying assumptions of linear programming that limit its applicability. A primary requirement of linear programming is that the objective function and every constraint function must be linear. This requires, in turn, that the measure of effectiveness and resource usage must be proportional to the level of activity conducted individually. Activities must be "additive" with respect to the measure of effectiveness and each resource usage. In other words, the total measure of effectiveness and each total resource usage resulting from the joint performance of the activities must equal the respective sums of these quantities resulting from each activity being conducted individually. It is frequently the case that the decision variables would have significance only if they have integer values. Therefore, another limitation of linear programming in obtaining an optional solution is that fractional levels of the decision variable must be permissible. In addition, all the coefficients in the linear programming are assumed to be known constants. In summary, the user should be fully aware of the assumptions and approximations involved, and should satisfy himself that they are justified before proceeding with a linear programming approach.

Quadratic and Dynamic Programming

Quadratic programming, like linear programming, is an algebraic technique for maximizing (or minimizing) a qualitative objective function subject to linear constraints, but can also handle nonlinear relationships. Applications are similar to those of linear programming.

[1] Frederick S. Hillier and Gerald J. Lieberman, *Introduction to Operations Research* (San Francisco: Holden-Day, Inc., 1968), pp. 130–131. Used with permission of the publisher.

Dynamic programming is still in a state of development. The objective is to facilitate solution of sequential problems. It is a method of solving multistage problems in which the decisions at one stage become input into later stages. Application has been primarily theoretical to date. This will be treated more extensively in Chapter 10.

Sequential Planning

Under queuing we studied the determination of facilities to minimize human and machine waiting time. Sequencing models treat the converse problem. The problem is to schedule arrival or to sequence the operations to be accomplished so that the sum of pertinent times or costs is minimized. Mathematical analysis of the sequencing problem has just begun. The characteristic of operations research problems which involve conflicting objectives has not been brought into the formulation of sequencing problems. At the present time, the most fruitful approach to the complex sequencing problems which occur in a school system may be appropriate for operational experimentation and gaming (simulation), which may involve use of Monte Carle procedures.

In conclusion, it should be re-emphasized that the objective of this section was only to suggest the direction of current research on sequential planning. All the procedures are relatively sophisticated algorithms that require the use of a digital computer.

Input-Output Analysis

The *input-output analysis* technique was originally developed for studying an overall economy. Given the input-output matrix, detailed analysis can be made of consequences of alternative governmental expenditures. Tracing the impact of such changes throughout the economy by hand would be impossible. The input-output matrix and the computer make such analysis feasible. As educators accept school financing as a segment of the total economy this can be helpful in determining amount and level of educational expenditure for greatest overall effectiveness.

Simulation

Simulation is used to obtain the essence of a situation, without reality. The stochastic model is the feature that distinguishes a simulation from a mere sampling experiment in the classical sense. Two basic types of large-scale system simulation have been developed. In one case, the decision-making process is programmed into the simulation in order that the entire system may be run automatically without involvement of human decision makers. A second type requires recurrent decisions on the part of outside decision makers, the result of those decisions being generated by a simulated system which ordinarily is programmed for an electronic computer.

The University Council for Educational Administration has developed many simulation projects for the school administrators. Others, such as ASBO, have made contributions to the business management area and other groups to each respective area. Simulation has great potentialities for study of race relations when mistakes in real situations might cause irreversible damage. This could be used for study of new teaching and learning processes. The business segment of the school system has innumerable opportunities for simulating developments before the hard decision is reached.

Management Information System

In essence, the *management information system* approach consists of (1) defining the operating and planning decisions that are required to manage the organization, (2) exploring the types of policies available for making each decision, (3) determining the data requirements implied by each decision policy, and (4) developing preferred processsing techniques for the desired data set. The objection is not optimization of data processing systems; rather, the objective is development of better information systems for administrators.

The desirability of using a model of the proposed system cannot be overstated. The new approach may be tested by simulation in order to assess the impact of the new system. Such an approach would allow the evaluation of a systems design without running the risk of undue disruption of the present system.

The steps involved in setting up an information system are as follows:

1. Establish criteria for management information needs.
   Lay out the current information, decision, display, and report practices in graphical flow forms.

2. Make preliminary design.
   Specify reporting frequencies, types, and routing of reports, types of equipment, etc.
   Determine what can be automated and what should remain in its present form.
3. Evaluate preliminary design.
   Determine hardware and software cost.
   Determine personnel training costs.
   Assess improvements to be gained.
4. Develop revised model of the proposed system.
   Test via simulation thereby obtaining participation of ultimate users.

This provides an inclusive framework. It will work for a total system or a subsystem. A picture of the present and projected systems can be shown by graphic flow charts. An outline of principal systems and subsystems follows.

Principal Systems and Priorities

The principal systems and subsystems in an educational information system of the type described might be:

1. Student Information System
   a. Census/Elementary Information Subsystem
   b. Attendance Subsystem
   c. Scheduling Subsystem
   d. Mark Reporting Subsystem
   e. Guidance Subsystem
   f. Health Subsystem
2. Materials Information System
   a. Library Subsystem
   b. Audio-Visual Subsystem
3. Administrative/Financial Information System
   a. Employee Information Subsystem
   b. Accounts Payable Subsystem
   c. Appropriation and Budgetary Subsystem
   d. Property Subsystem
   e. Purchasing/Inventory Subsystem
   f. Transportation Subsystem
   g. Maintenance Subsystem
   h. Food Service Subsystem

4. Instructional Use System
    a. Test Scoring Subsystem
    b. Mathematics Subsystem
    c. Business Education Subsystem
    d. Science Subsystem
    e. Social Studies Subsystem

In-Service Education

Reference should be made to the need for in-service education programs. Certain of these in-service programs should be designed for persons unexposed to management information systems; others should be designed for the moderately exposed. Still other programs of a refresher nature should also be established. Individual programs should be developed for specific groups of school personnel as follows:

1. Superintendents and Assistants or Directors
2. Secondary Principals and Assistants
3. Elementary Principals and Assistants
4. Directors of Business Affairs
5. Subject Consultants
6. Teachers
7. Directors of Health Services
8. Directors of Transportation
9. Directors of Food Service
10. Librarians
11. Directors of Audio-Visual
12. Selected Secretarial/Office Personnel
13. Coordinators of Education Information System

Emphasis must be given in such in-service programs involving new data processing services to:

1. Adequate explanation of new procedures and why they should be followed.
2. How to interpret information and action that should be taken. Few persons will make significant use of information if they are not trained to interpret it and know how to take the appropriate action. In some instances more time will have to be spent on action techniques than interpretation.

    In connection with in-service education programs and the continued successful operation of any data processing services, written procedural manuals must be available and in a language and illustration easily understood by those who must originate or interpret information. Selected elements of these procedure manuals should be placed in a form that lend themselves to visual display in an in-service education program.

Considerations in Selection of a Manufacturer and Supplier

At least the following matters should be taken into account with respect to manufacturer's services:

1. Availability of back-up hardware for program testing and provision of operating services
2. Extent of educational programs available for various personnel
3. Quality and understanding of educational problems exhibited by manufacturers' personnel
4. Quality of maintenance services
5. Amount of systems design and programming assistance that the manufacturer will provide
6. Contract terms, including availability of educational discounts.

Summary on Personnel Requirements and List of Staff

The following personnel are needed to make such a system operational. Some can be used on a consultative basis rather than as full-time employers.

Administration
1. Director of Administration Services
2. Assistant Director of Administration Services

Staff Consultants
1. Educational Research Consultant
2. Mathematics Consultant
3. Business Education Consultant
4. Social Studies Consultant
5. Service Consultant
6. Advance Computer-related Consultant
7. Materials Information Consultant

Systems/Programming
1. Systems Programming Manager
2. Systems Analyst
3. Programmers

Operations
1. Operations Manager
2. Miscellaneous Supporting Personnel

Services/Conversion Personnel
1. Services Coordinator
2. Conversion Coordinator
3. Assistants

Benefits

Benefits that accrue from a management information system are many and varied. How many of these benefits will be realized by a particular school district will depend on the district itself. This implies that unless a district examines its procedures and plans properly, the following benefits may not be fully realized.

Some gross benefits that may be realized are:

1. Savings in manual effort by clerical, teachers, and administrative staff. (For example, the clerical staff would not have to complete census totals or subdivision for state reports; teachers would not have to mark cards or total absences for individual or groups of students; and administrators would not have to total class registrations or construct conflict sheets, and so forth, in building the master schedule.
2. Timely and accurate preparation of information: Staff/student ratio, test result reporting and distribution, state and/or federal reports.
3. Improved dissemination of information to all staff members. (For example, any information necessary may be printed in as many copies as desired for general distribution.)
4. Timely preparation of reports for state, other educational agencies, and school boards (for example, financial reports for school boards, superintendents and state agencies).
5. Ability to prepare reports not previously possible because of constraints of time and staff on the information-gathering process. (An example of such a report might be a summary of those students at the end of a grading period whose marks had declined seriously or whose absence pattern indicates problems at school or at home.)
6. Improvement of educational research through the utilization of electronic data processing techniques.

Benefits of cooperative action are:

1. A data processing staff can be developed for work on educational problems with skills in programming, analysis, etc.

2. Greater capability of equipment can be realized at smaller expense to the district.
3. Technological obsolescence can be more effectively handled.
4. Skilled systems analysis and programming staff members can be retained and a high degree of data processing skills can be brought to bear on common and individual district problems.
5. Desirable specialization of functions within a data processing staff may be achieved.
6. A broad base of information will be made available for the analysis of common district problems.
7. Comparable data can be developed through standardization processes. (Comparisons in the past have been very tenuous in nature because not all schools interpret or develop data in the same way.)
8. Instruction of employees in new techniques and means of operation may be accomplished more economically. (Training program costs are included in membership dues.)
9. Consultants of the highest competence can be retained and utilized in the development and realization of long-range systems planning.
10. In-service programs for teaching and administrative staff may be implemented more easily. (Data processing staff members with this responsibility would plan and initiate their activities in cooperation with participating districts.)
11. Parts of the instructional program may be more fully developed and new means of instruction developed through data processing (modular scheduling, individual construction via computer, etc.).

The benefits listed above are only a partial statement.

Cooperative System

Representative tasks which may be accomplished through a cooperative educational management information system are as follows:

Business Office
1. Reduction in time required to perform a function.
2. Improved or more timely information for decision making.
3. Improved access to information.
4. Immediate updating of information.
5. Automatic entry to expense distribution accounting.

6. Total encumbrances for each account.
7. Year-to-date expenditures for each account.
8. Complete updating of payroll information on each employee at the end of each payroll period.
9. Preparation of necessary state and federal reports.
10. Accounting of all records.
11. Payroll distribution.
12. Preventive maintenance scheduling.
13. Inventory control of all kinds.
14. Purchasing, including bid requests and analysis.
15. Food Service.

Census

Specific benefits which may accrue in the area of census are accuracy, time saved, and ease of preparation. The principal advantages would be:

1. A small reduction in the time required by the enumerator to verify or collect new information.
2. *Substantial* reduction in the time required to tabulate census data.
3. Accurate census data can be used as a basis for study of student personnel, projected district needs, and studies of particular school needs.

Student Personnel: Both elementary and secondary.

While there are innumerable applications in this area the specific benefits which are available consist of:

1. A reduction in time required to perform many clerical functions.
2. Improved or more timely information for teachers, counselors, and administrators.
3. Improved access to information.

Specific operations which can be performed through data processing for student personnel are:

1. Boundary line determination.
2. Bus routing.
3. Mailing for various purposes including kindergarten roundup.
4. Bus passes or lists, ID cards, etc.

5. Scheduling including tallying, conflict matrix preparation, teacher-pupil assignment, course selection analysis and projected need, class lists, student/class profiles, directory for students, report card marking and mailing, reading inventory, teacher-department mark distributions, cumulative record labels including attendance, test scores, behavior trait posting and grades, scheduling of conferences between teachers and parents, surveys and machine scoring of tests whether teacher-made or standardized.

ILLUSTRATIONS

Business Office

1. Accounts Payable
   a. Payroll Processing (see figure 4.7)

   b. School Activities Accounting Processing (see figure 4.8)

   c. Checks and Remittance Advices

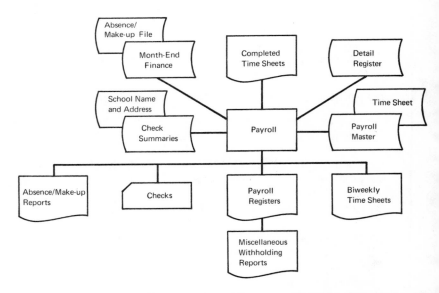

FIGURE 4.7 Payroll processing. (Courtesy Memphis City School System.)

The primary benefits of this service appear to be:

Potential savings in manual effort.

Timely and accurate preparation of information.

Ability to prepare reports not previously possible because of constraints imposed by a manual or machine bookkeeping system. Automatic entry to expense distribution accounting. Potential for handling an enlarged chart of accounts that could refine the present expense distribution system.

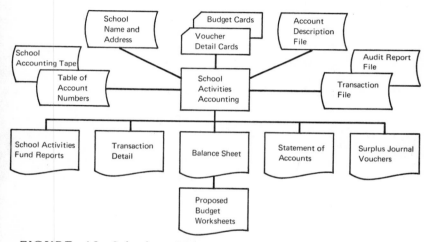

FIGURE 4.8 School activities accounting processing. (Courtesy Memphis City School System.)

2. Appropriations and Budgetary Control
    This potential data processing service would require certain information from accounts payable. This data would be in the form of expense distributions to the various accounts.
3. Payroll
4. Property Records
5. Activity Fund Accounting
6. Preventive Maintenance Scheduling
7. Maintenance Cost Accounting
8. Inventory Control
9. Purchasing
10. Textbook Inventory
11. Food Service

ELEMENTARY STUDENT PERSONNEL

ELECTRONIC STUDENT RECORD

1. Cumulative record
2. Health record
3. Personal background and interests
4. Attendance records

UTILIZATION OF ELECTRONIC CENSUS DATA FOR:

1. Boundary line determination
2. Bus routing
3. Kindergarten roundup mailing (see figure 4.9)

```
345678921

Mr. Bill Smith
125 Main
Pulaski, VA
```

```
123456789

Mr. John Doe
121 Main
Chicago, IL
```

FIGURE 4.9   Mailing labels. (Courtesy Memphis City School System.)

4. Bus passes or lists
5. Class lists (see figure 4.10)
6. Student/class profile
7. Family/student directory/locator file
8. Student family information and background
9. Reading pattern inventory
10. Mark (grade) reports
11. Teacher mark distribution
12. Mark label for cumulative record
13. Behavior trait posting

GENERAL SHOP 1   SEM 1 PER 6 DAYS ALL RM 112 SUB 9024 SEC 02 CRAIG

BLACKWELL

STUDENT NAME	NUMBER	SEX	GRADE	CONFLICT 19 -
BACK PAUL E	2251841	M	09	
BEARD JOHNNY H	1069245	M	09	
BLEDSOE BENNIE M	1068670	M	09	
BOATWRIGHT JAMES R	1080733	M	09	
BOWKER CHARLES D	2553229	M	09	
CARTER ROY L	1152718	M	09	
COLE DANNY E	1184265	M	09	
COOK JOHN E	1179855	M	09	
COOPER DAVID L	1175394	M	09	
CRUMBY MICHAEL E	1205307	M	09	
DORROUGH STEVEN T	1234859	M	09	
FEUERSTACKE JOSEPH C	1275852	M	09	
FINGER MICHAEL C	2108795	M	09	
FOSTER RICHARD	2983050	M	09	
FRYE KENNETH W	1293753	M	09	
GREEN CHARLES P	1338947	M	09	
GRIMSTEAD DANIEL R	1342027	M	09	
INMAN RANDALL L	1438743	M	09	
MCCOY JAMES C	1576549	M	09	
PADGETT GLENN M	1672731	M	09	
PEARSON JAMES O	1694001	M	09	
PRYOR DAVID L	1718894	M	09	
SANDERS LOUIS F	1729141	M	09	
SCONYERS JOHN R	2445662	M	09	
SCRUGGS JERRY G	1791117	M	09	
STOKES JOHNNY R	1640959	M	09	
THOMASON GEORGE E	2741849	M	09	
WHEELER THOMAS E	1958550	M	09	

FIGURE 4.10 Class list. (Courtesy Memphis City School System.)

14. Envelope addressing
15. Periodic attendance accumulation
16. Annual attendance report
17. Scheduling of teacher-parent conferences
18. Parent-teacher opinion surveys
19. Machine scoring of standardized tests
20. Machine scoring of teacher-prepared tests

SECONDARY STUDENT PERSONNEL

ELECTRONIC STUDENT RECORD

1. Cumulative record
2. Health record
3. Personal background and interests
4. Attendance records

STUDENT REGISTRATION

1. Course tally (see figure 4.11)

COURSE TALLY				
Course Name	Course No.	Requests	Sections	Overflow
Agric. 3	301	15	1	0
Agric. 4	401	10	1	0
English 1	101	103	3	4

FIGURE 4.11   Course tally. (Courtesy Memphis City School System.)

2. Historical course selection analysis
3. Conflict matrix
4. Student sectioning/schedules (see figure 4.12)
5. Class lists (see figure 4.13)
6. Student/class profile
7. Student directory
8. Locker room assignment
9. Student ID cards
10. Mark (grade) reports (see figure 4.14)

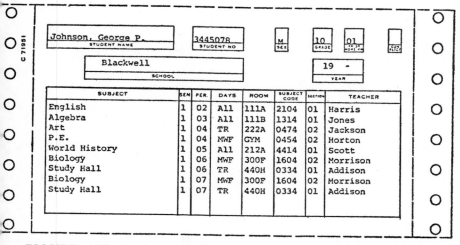

Johnson, George P.   STUDENT NAME   3445078 STUDENT NO   M SEX   10 GRADE   01 ROOM

Blackwell   SCHOOL   19 -   YEAR

SUBJECT	SEM	PER.	DAYS	ROOM	SUBJECT CODE	SECTION	TEACHER
English	1	02	All	111A	2104	01	Harris
Algebra	1	03	All	111B	1314	01	Jones
Art	1	04	TR	222A	0474	02	Jackson
P.E.	1	04	MWF	GYM	0454	02	Horton
World History	1	05	All	212A	4414	01	Scott
Biology	1	06	MWF	300F	1604	02	Morrison
Study Hall	1	06	TR	440H	0334	01	Addison
Biology	1	07	MWF	300F	1604	02	Morrison
Study Hall	1	07	TR	440H	0334	01	Addison

FIGURE 4.12 Student schedule. (Courtesy Memphis City School System.)

11. Teacher and departmental mark distribution
12. Honor point computation and honor roll list

   Failure and incomplete list
   Class rankings
   Mark label for cumulative record
   Behavior trait posting
   Student activity posting
   Envelope addressing
   Daily absentee lists

PERIODIC ATTENDANCE ACCUMULATION (see figure 4.15)

ANNUAL ATTENDANCE REPORT

TEACHER/PARENT OPINION SURVEYS

READING PATTERN INVENTORY

MACHINE SCORING OF TEACHER-PREPARED TESTS AND STANDARDIZED TESTS

MASTER SCHEDULE BY PERIOD   DATE 05/14/

BLACKWELL

PERIOD = 04

COURSE	SECTION	DESCRIPTION	SEMESTER	PERIOD- STARTS	ENDS	DAYS	ROOM	TEACHER	CTL	SEATS ORIGINAL	ASSIGNED
0182	01	LUNCH GRADE 8	1	04		ALL	400	CAFE	0	25	12
0134	01	LUNCH GRADE 9				ALL	400	CAFE	0	500	495
1282	02	ARITHMETIC (GR. 8)	1	04		ALL	204	GREEN	3	34	34
1294	08	ARITHMETIC (GR. 8)	1	04		ALL	303	ARITH B	3	34	33

MASTER SCHEDULE BY SUBJECT   DATE 5/31/   PAGE

- PERIOD -

SECTION	DESCRIPTION	SEMESTER	STARTS	ENDS	DAYS	ROOM	TEACHER	CTL	SEATS ORIGINAL	ASSIGNED	REMAINING
01	LIBRARY ASSISTANT	1	01		ALL	207	CAMPBELL	3	3	3	0
AVERAGE NUMBER OF STUDENTS PER SECTION IS 3.							TOTALS		3	3	
01	LIBRARY ASSISTANT	1	02		ALL	207	CAMPBELL	3	4	3	1
AVERAGE NUMBER OF STUDENTS PER SECTION IS 3.							TOTALS		4	3	1
01	LIBRARY ASSISTANT	1	03		ALL	207	CAMPBELL	3	3	2	1
AVERAGE NUMBER OF STUDENTS PER SECTION IS 2.							TOTALS		3	2	1
01	LUNCH GRADE 8	1	04		ALL	400	CAFE	0	25	20	5
AVERAGE NUMBER OF STUDENTS PER SECTION IS 20.							TOTALS		25	20	5
01	LUNCH GRADE 8	1	05		ALL	400	CAFE	0	560	531	29
AVERAGE NUMBER OF STUDENTS PER SECTION IS 531.							TOTALS		560	531	29

FIGURE 4.13   Master schedule. (Courtesy Memphis City School System.)

SEE REVERSE SIDE

REPORT CARD
MEMPHIS CITY SCHOOLS

JUNIOR AND SENIOR HIGH SCHOOLS

JOHNSON HIGH — SCHOOL
136 — SCHOOL NO.
11 — GRADE
03 — SECTION

Mr. Greenlee — PRINCIPAL

TO THE PARENT OR GUARDIAN OF
John Q Doe
2899 Broad Avenue
Memphis, Tennessee

123-4567 — STUDENT NUMBER

PERIOD ENDING: 05 MO — 28 DAY — YR.

REPORT: 6 PERIOD

S U B J.	S E C T.	SUBJECT DESCRIPTION	1 G/DAY R/AS	2 G/DAY R/AS	3 G/DAY R/AS	EXAM	SEM AV	SEM DAYS AB	4 G/DAY R/AS	5 DAY AS	6 DAY AS	EXAM	SEM AV	SEM DAYS AB	YR GR	YEAR DAYS ABSENT	UNITS	1	2	3	SEM AV	4	5	6	SCY AV	YR GR
009	07	ENGLISH	A02	B01	C03	B	B	06	C11	D12	D10	D		33	C	39	1	S	S	S	S	S	U	S	E	S
078	02	ALGEBRA 2ND YEAR	C02	C01	C03	C	C	06	B10	C10	C10	C		30	C	36	1	S	S	S	S	S	E	S	S	S
110	03	AMERICAN HISTORY	C02	B02	A02	B	B	06	C	8C12	C10	C		30	C	36	1	S	S	S	S	S	E	S	S	S
132	05	CHEMISTRY	B03	B02	B02	B	B	07	C	8A10	B10	C		28	B	35	1	S	E	E	E	E	E	E	E	E
264	12	INSTRUMENTAL MUSIC	A02	A02	A02	A	A	06	A	B810	A11	A		29	A	35	1	S	S	S	S	S	S	S	S	S

ACADEMIC GRADES

CONDUCT

ATTENDANCE	1	2	3	SEM.	4	5	6	SEM.	YEAR
DAYS PRESENT	28	28	28	84	22	20	20	60	146
DAYS ABSENT	02	02	02	06	08	10	10	28	34
TIMES TARDY	00	03	01	04	00	00	02	02	06

PROMOTED TO GRADE _____ 12

RETAINED IN GRADE _____

AT JOHNSON HIGH — SCHOOL

MISS ROBINSON

PROMOTION TO:
10th. REQUIRES 3 UNITS
11th. REQUIRES 7 UNITS
12th. REQUIRES 11 UNITS

UNITS	
PRIOR YEARS	08
CURRENT YEARS	05
TOTAL	13

HOME ROOM TEACHER

FIGURE 4.14 Grade report. (Courtesy Memphis City School System.)

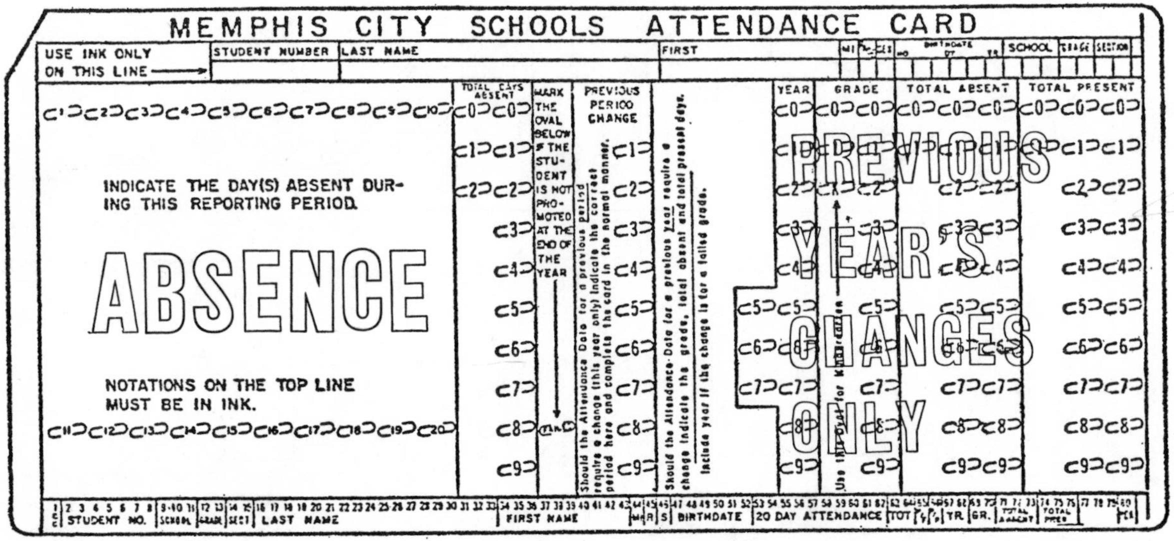

FIGURE 4.15 Attendance card. (Courtesy Memphis City School System.)

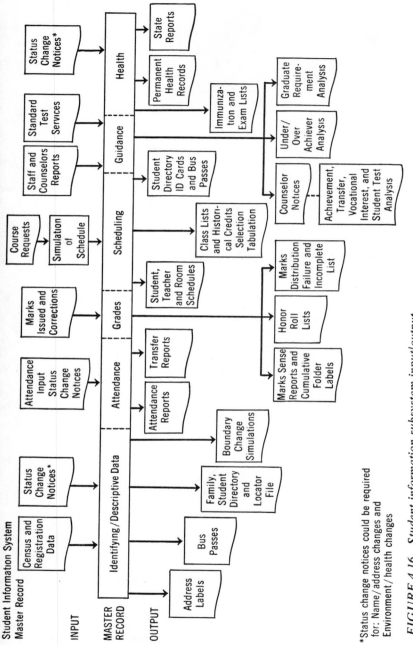

FIGURE 4.16 Student information subsystem input/output.

*Status change notices could be required
for: Name/address changes and
Environment/health changes

EMPLOYEE INFORMATION SUBSYSTEM

Employee Information Subsystem

A master record of 500 to 2,000 characters could be created in connection with this subsystem. Data contained in the record could include at least the following:

Name
Spouse's name
Address
Telephone number
Birthdate
Sex
Date of employment
Building
College of undergraduate degree
Year of graduation
Majors
Minors
History of courses beyond most recent degree
College of graduate degree
Year of graduate degree
Major filed of graduate degree
Certificate number
Certificate expiration date
Extracurricular activities
Salary history
Current salary
History of subjects taught
Subjects currently taught
Social security number
Marital status
Number of dependents
Medical report status
Position code
Salary distribution codes
Termination date and reason code
Placement on salary schedule
Sick leave data
Personal leave data
Leave of absence data
Retirement number and plan

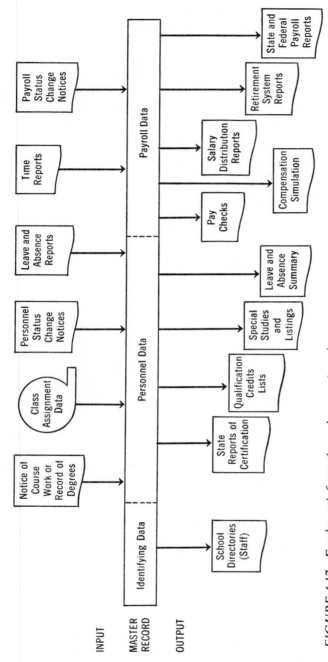

FIGURE 4.17 Employee information subsystem input/output.

Tax-sheltered annuity
Nonteacher experience
Voluntary payroll deductions

Flow Models

For learning resources and material, equipment, staff, pupils, and so forth, scale models of the layout of facilities may be utilized to model the system and point up any problems. Visualizing such physical aspects is obviously important for developing optimum learning conditions and efficient flow of materials and persons. This approach allows consideration without description of the present system. If the system can be modeled in terms of flow charts tracing material, equipment, personnel, or information flow, then alternative approaches can be tested in the abstract. While models will not guarantee success in practice, it certainly improves upon trial and error.

A modification of flow models that can be very useful to the school administrator is the use of overlays. The formal structure of an organization represents as closely as possible the deliberate intentions of its framers for the processes of interaction that will take place among its members. It must be recognized, however, that the actual processes of interaction among the individuals represented in the formal plan cannot adequately be described solely in terms of its planned lines of interaction. Coexisting with the formal structure are myriads of other ways of interacting for persons in the organization; these can be analyzed according to various theories of group behavior, but it must not be forgotten that in reality they never function so distinctly, and all are inter-mixed in an organization which also follows to a large extent its formal structure.

The interacting processes must be studied one at a time; this can be done with overlays so as not to destroy formal line relationships. The totality of these overlays might be so complex as to be nearly opaque; nevertheless, it will be a closer approach to reality than the sterile organization chart so typically used to diagram a large group structure (see figure 4.18).

The total number of such overlays is infinitesimal in quantity. Five such overlay patterns will be considered here; many others could have been utilized. The overlay approach aims to be realistic in recognizing that organization also consists of a wide variety of

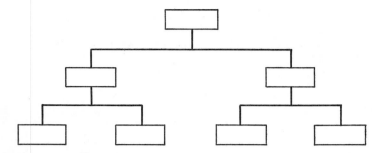

FIGURE 4.18   The typical organizational chart.

contacts that involve communication, sociometry, goal-centered functionalism, decision making, and personal power. We will present these overlays individually.

The Sociometric Overlays

The *sociometric overlay* (see figure 4.19) describes the relationships that are purely social and may be of a positive or negative nature. Some attitudes that lend themselves to sociometric measurement are as follows:

1. The *prescribed relations,* which are identical with the official or formal organization.
2. The *perceived relations,* which consist of individual interpretation of the official network.

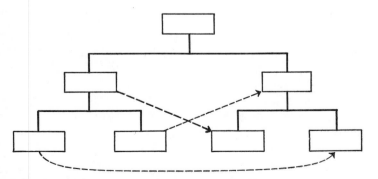

FIGURE 4.19   The sociometric overlay—"Joe understands me and will help me."

3. The *actual relations* are those interactions which in reality take place among persons.
4. The *desired relations* are personal preferences as to interrelations.
5. The *rejected relations* are interrelations not wanted by the individuals involved.

The last two categories are more sociological in nature.

The Functional Overlay

Functional contacts occur most typically where specialized information is needed. Through them the staff or other specialist, the intellectual "leader," exerts his influence upon operations without direct responsibility for the work itself (see figure 4.20).

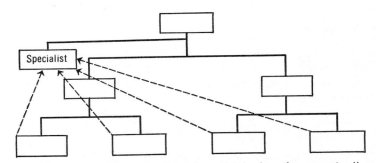

FIGURE 4.20   The functional overlay—"John has the expertise."

The Decision Overlay

Of major importance to an organization is finding out where the decisions are made and by whom. It is usually assumed that the decision pattern follows the structure of the formal hierarchy. In practice this may not be true, particularly if we study the decision process rather than the decision point. It might be more correct to say that there is a network of influence, not a network of decision.

The Power Overlay

The important consideration from the standpoint of organization theory is that there is a network or a grid of personal power centers, though sometimes latent and not expressed. They

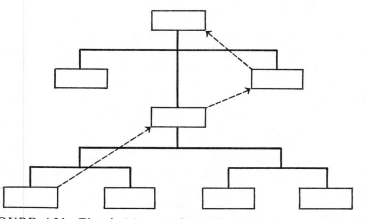

FIGURE 4.21   The decision overlay—"Pete isn't interested in this, and, besides, Roger has had the experience with this problem."

may or may not coincide with the official structure of authority. Power is not institutionalized in the sense that one can look in the organizational manual and find out where it resides. The person of comparatively low organizational status may be a power center because he knows all the informal "do's and don'ts" (see figure 4.22).

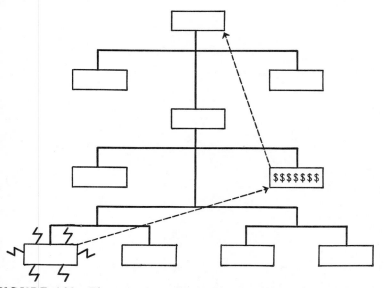

FIGURE 4.22   The power overlay—"Check with Joe because he is a 'nit-picker,' and with Barney because he 'handles the purse strings.'"

The Communication Overlay

The information process is central to the organizational system. It affects control and decision making, influence and power, interpersonal relationships and leadership, to mention only a few of the facets. A communications overlay may tell a great deal more about reality within an organization than the formal picture. Thus, an important and useful means of taking a look at an organization is to ask the question, "Who talks to whom about what?"

Answers to the question will often reveal that patterns of communication are at variance with official prescriptions. There is a possibility that the mere existence of a hierarchy sets up restraints against communication between levels. Such blockages and distortions are certainly frequent enough to force us to recognize that the communications overlay represents an important dimension of organization analysis (see figure 4.23).

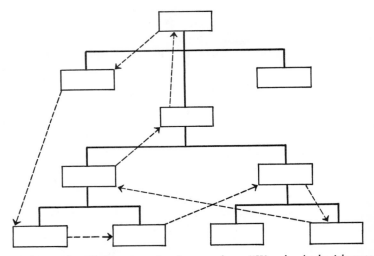

FIGURE 4.23   The communication overlay—"We checked with every-one in making the decision."

SUMMARY

This chapter attempts to review management tools that would be of particular use to the school business manager. Some techniques are more useful to varying-size school systems. Some techniques will require the utilization of computers and appropriate software. Other tools will require a familiarity with symbolic language and mathematical concepts. Many tools are in the developmental stage, and utilization will increase as ingenious school business managers work with the techniques.

The above review of the use of management tools for planning is only illustrative, not exhaustive. For a more detailed and basic approach to the utilization of management tools see one of the basic texts listed in the Suggested Readings.

SUGGESTED ACTIVITIES

1. Consider the PERT system flow plan in figure 4.24. Assume that the time required (in weeks) for each activity is a predictable constant, and that it is given by the number along the corresponding branch. Find the earliest possible time, the latest possible time, and slack for each event. Also identify the critical path (CPM).

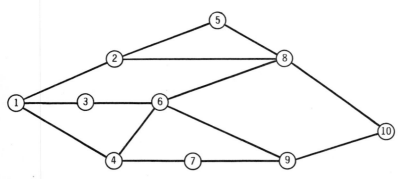

FIGURE 4.24   A PERT system flow plan.

2. A superintendent is making plans for a bond issue referendum. He has received the services of six volunteer workers for precinct work, and he wishes to assign them to precincts in such a way as to maximize their effectiveness. He feels that it would be inefficient to assign a worker to more than one precinct, but he is willing to assign no workers to some of the precincts if they can accomplish more in other precincts.

Table 4.2 gives the estimated increase in the plurality (positive or negative) of the bond referendum in each precinct if it were allocated various numbers of workers.

TABLE 4.2

Number of Workers	Precinct			
	1	*2*	*3*	*4*
0	0	0	0	0
1	25	21	32	15
2	42	38	41	25
3	58	55	48	33
4	62	64	52	40
5	68	72	54	46
6	73	81	55	51

3. A single crew is provided for unloading and/or loading each truck that arrives at the loading dock of the school system's warehouse. These trucks arrive at a mean rate of one per hour. The time required by the school warehouse crew to unload and/or load a truck has an exponential distribution (regardless of the warehouse crew size). The expected time required by a one-man crew would be two hours.

The cost of providing each additional member of the crew is $6 per hour. The cost that is attributable to having a truck not in use (i.e., a truck standing at the dock) is estimated to be $25 per hour.

a. Assume that the mean service rate of the crew is proportional to its size. What should the size be in order to minimize the expected total cost per hour?

b. Assume that the mean service rate of the warehouse crew is proportional to the square root of its size. What should the size be in order to minimize expected total cost per hour?

4. Suppose that the demand for a product from the school's carpenter shop is 50 units per month, and the items are withdrawn uniformly. The setup cost each time a production run is made is $30. The production cost is $5 per item, and the inventory holding cost is $1 per item per month.

a. Assuming shortages are not allowed, determine how often to make a production run, and what size it should be.

b. If shortages cost $5 per item per month, determine how often to make a production run, and what size it should be.

SUGGESTED READINGS

Banghart, Frank W. *Educational Systems Analysis*. Toronto: The Macmillan Company, 1969.

Catanese, Anthony J., and Steiss, Alan W. *Systemic Planning: Theory and Application*. Lexington, Mass.: D. C. Heath & Company, 1970.

Churchman, C. West. *The Systems Approach*. New York: The Delacorte Press, 1968.

Cleveland, David I., and King, William R. *Systems, Organizations, Analysis, Management: A Book of Readings*. New York: McGraw-Hill Book Company, 1969.

Correa, Hector. *Quantitative Methods of Educational Planning*. Scranton: International Textbook Company, 1969.

Hartley, Harry J. *Educational Planning-Programming-Budgeting: A Systems Approach*. Englewood Cliffs, N.J.: Prentice-Hall, Inc., 1968.

Hillier, Frederick S., and Lieberman, Gerald J. *Introduction to Operation Research*. San Francisco: Holden-Day, Inc., 1967.

Knezevich, Stephen J., and Eye, Glen G., eds. *Instructional Technology and the School Administrators*. Washington, D.C.: American Association of School Administrators, 1970.

Laughery, John W. *Man-Machine Systems in Education*. New York: Harper & Row, Publishers, 1966.

Martin, Francis F. *Computer Modeling and Simulation*. New York: John Wiley & Sons, Inc., 1968.

Tanner, C. Kenneth. *Designs for Educational Planning—A Systemic Approach*. Lexington, Mass.: Heath Lexington Books, 1971.

Van Dusseldorp, Ralph A., Richardson, Duane E., and Foley, Walter J. *Educational Decision-Making Through Operations Research*. Boston: Allyn and Bacon, Inc., 1971.

HUMAN RELATIONS AND COMMUNICATIONS TOOLS USED IN THE PLANNING PROCESS

One of the most often heard criticisms leveled at the educational system and more particularly at the business division of the school system is the accusation that decisions are depersonalized, that administrators make decisions affecting the lives of human beings based on data gathered and interpreted with little or no attention to the human element. Business administrators are often charged with being rigid automatons, of reacting only with statistics, of ignoring basic human needs, of being concerned only with balanced budgets, of not understanding unique and diverse clients — in short, of not being capable of "good" human relations.

While these criticisms are, all too often, valid charges, the school business administrator finds himself trapped in mounting pressures converging on him. On the one hand, he must guarantee the solvency of the educational system by exercising firm control over the resource pool, while on the other hand he must develop the ability to adjust to diverse pressures exerted from a variety of sources all impinging upon the already severely extended fiscal capacity of the educational system. The automatic reaction of most business administrators is the natural one: to withdraw into the protective custody of the balance sheet and to adjudicate on the basis of cold, hard facts and figures.

Actually, these mounting pressures are symptomatic of a societal change that has proceeded over time and has suddenly burst upon the conscience of most communities. This is the general dehumanization of the individual in contemporary society. In the transition from a basically agrarian society to a much more formal and structured urban society, basic values and concerns have been rationalized and sometimes lost. As the density of population grew along with the multitude of concerns that accompany density, the capacity of educational systems to react to those concerns became more and more mechanized and rigid. Concern for the individual has been replaced with concern for the smooth operation of the system. The capacity to react to individual needs has been co-opted by the doctrine of "statistical fairness" in the allocation of resources. Thus, one finds that all first-grade pupils of a typical school system have identical materials, books, and supplies and that all elementary schools are allocated resources on a formula based on enrollment with little or no attention given to the needs of particular children. Business administrators, typically, point with pride at the fact that resource allocations are thus equitable. Yet the fact remains that individuals and not groups learn and that no two people are alike in terms of needs, wants, and aspirations.

School business administrators must come to grips with the question of humanism as it relates to the educational system. Just as curriculum planners are increasingly concerned with the individualization and humanization of programs so must the business planner address the humanistic needs of clients in the development of educational plans.

As society has become fragmented and as human needs have multiplied, the ability of existing agencies to react to human needs has become severely taxed. Communications skills once confined to close interpersonal, face-to-face relationships have become very diffused and increasingly difficult. The warm, friendly, personal dialogue between two close friends has become the Madison Avenue, formal, hard-sell, impersonal message.

It is the contention of the authors that the emerging model for successful educational business administration must utilize human relations and communications tools as vital ingredients of the total planning process. It is therefore appropriate that consideration be given these tools.

PRINCIPLES OF HUMAN RELATIONS

Definitions of the term "human relations" abound in the literature. Daniel E. Griffiths presents a number of definitions in the following comment:

> We say that good human relations in administration are built upon a firm foundation of mutual respect, good will, and faith in the dignity and worth of human beings as individual personalities. It is further necessary for the administrator to develop skills in relating himself and others to the social situation in which they are placed.[1]

The fields of business and industry supply definitions that are somewhat more narrow than those found in education. Keith Davis defines human relations as "the integration of people into a work situation that motivates them to work together productively, cooperatively, and with economic, psychological, and social satisfactions."[2]

Gardner and Moore, writing in the field of industry, declared that the human relations approach as they had known it "is nothing more than another name for the application of the behavioral sciences to the study and understanding of management and organization within the business setting."[3]

William W. Savage uses the phrase *interpersonal and group relations* when writing about human relations and says that it:

> includes an understanding of the behavior of people as individuals and in groups. It also includes skills in working effectively with individuals and groups. . . . The school administrator must understand his own behavior and the behavior of pupils, teachers, other staff members, parents, and all citizens of the community who influence educational policy in any way. He must understand the group dynamics not only of school boards, school-related groups such as the Parent-Teacher Association, and groups of school personnel but also

[1] Daniel E. Griffiths, *Human Relations in School Administration* (New York: Appleton-Century-Crofts, 1956), p. 17.

[2] Keith Davis, *Human Relations at Work* (New York: McGraw-Hill Book Company, 1962), p. 4.

[3] Burleigh B. Gardner and David G. Moore, *Human Relations in Industry* (Homewood, Ill.: Richard D. Irwin, Inc., 1964), p. 20.

of the many other groups in the community which can or do affect the operation, strength, and quality of the schools.[4]

There is considerable evidence which points to still broader definitions of the term "human relations." Robert Chin identifies several usages of the term including: "Human relations is defined as the study and practice of planned social change. . . . It coordinates available resources, intellectual, technological, and ethical, so as to formulate and test strategies of change."[5]

The role and influence of human relations as they apply to educational administration are identified by Savage and include:

1. The very nature of the administrator's tasks demands knowledge and skills in interpersonal and group relations.
2. The administrator's effectiveness and success are related closely to his knowledge and skills in interpersonal and group relations.
3. The administrator who has knowledge and skills in interpersonal and group relations behaves or acts in a manner that distinguishes him from persons who lack such knowledge and skills.
4. The study of interpersonal and group relations results in changes in the behavior of many administrators and persons preparing for administrative positions.
5. The acquisition of an understanding of interpersonal and group relations and the development and actual use of skills in this field demand ability, personality characteristics that all people do not possess, and an environment in which effective relationships are possible.[6]

The importance of human relations tools to the success of the school business administrator suggests that some effort be expended in drawing knowledge of human behavior from the fields of psychology, anthropology, and sociology. More important, perhaps, is the task of gaining an understanding of oneself in order to relate to others better. This can be very threatening, for it implies a change in one's own behavior. As Carl Rogers writes:

I have found it of enormous value when I can permit myself to understand another person. The way in which I have

[4] William W. Savage. *Interpersonal and Group Relations in Educational Administration* (Glenview, Ill.: Scott, Foresman and Company, 1968), p. 7. Copyright © 1968 by Scott, Foresman and Company. Reprinted by permission of the publisher.

[5] Warren G. Bennis, Kenneth D. Benne, and Robert Chin, eds., *The Planning of Change* (New York: Holt, Rinehart and Winston, 1966), p. 70.

[6] Savage, *Interpersonal and Group Relations*, pp. 7–14.

worded this statement may seem strange to you. Is it necessary to permit oneself to understand another? I think that it is. Our first reaction to most of the statements which we hear from other people is an immediate evaluation, or judgement, rather than an understanding of it. When someone expresses some feeling or attitude or belief, our tendency is, almost immediately, to feel "that's right," or "that's stupid," "that's abnormal," "that's unreasonable," "that's incorrect," "that's not nice." Very rarely do we permit ourselves to *understand* precisely what the meaning of his statement is to him. I believe this is because understanding is risky. If I let myself really understand another person, I might be changed by that understanding. And we all fear change. So as I say, it is not an easy thing to permit oneself to understand an individual, to enter thoroughly and completely and emphatically into his frame of reference. It is also a rare thing.[7]

It is therefore important for the administrator to understand that behavior is caused and that his own and others' behavior in a given situation is the result of a myriad of influences ranging from one's culture to values to basic human needs. While many conflicting theories have been proposed as to the causes of human behavior, the authors feel that the school administrator must have some concepts that will be useful to him in attempting to work effectively with other people. Basic to this effectiveness is some understanding of human needs and the cultural milieu in which they operate.

Human Needs

Human needs have been broadly categorized into physical and psychological needs. Maslow classified "basic" needs into five categories and arranged them in a hierarchy:

1. Physiological (or physical needs).
2. The safety needs (avoiding physical danger, pain, extreme temperature, the discord and uncertainty that affect security, etc.).
3. The belongingness or love needs.
4. The esteem needs (self-respect, self-esteem, and the esteem of others).
5. The need for self-actualization.[8]

[7]Carl R. Rogers, *On Becoming a Person* (Boston: Houghton Mifflin Company, 1961), p. 18.
[8]A. H. Maslow, *Motivation and Personality* (New York: Harper and Brothers, 1954).

Savage has interpreted the work of Maslow and others into a set of characteristics that have implications for the school administrator. These include:

1. Every person, including the school administrator, has the same basic needs.
2. The manner in which a person fulfills his needs and the behavior which he exhibits when his needs are not fulfilled are influenced by his values and the culture or society of which he is a part.
3. Needs do not have the same potency or strength in influencing the actions of individuals.
4. The potency of a need varies from time to time.
5. The same need does not have the same potency in all people.
6. All of a person is involved when a need affects his behavior.
7. A person may not be aware of the impact of his needs on his actions.
8. The fulfillment of more than one need is involved in a person's actions at any given point of time.
9. Much of a person's activity is directed toward acquisition of the means to fulfill needs.
10. All of a person's needs are never fully met. Some needs are recurring, and the fulfillment of others may never be met.[9]

As one strives to fulfill his needs, there are certain barriers both within the person and outside the person that tend to block fulfillment. Such frustrations lead to tension within the individual and produce attempts to alleviate the tension in such a way that the individual can continue to function in his world. Sometimes such attempts include aggression either direct or indirect, but more often the individual utilizes a variety of adjustment mechanisms available to him. This includes: withdrawal, identification, dependence, rationalization, sublimation, repression, projection, and compensation. In other cases the individual uses what Gates and others termed "direct methods of tension reduction" and which are classified as (1) "renewed attempts to reach the original goal," (2) "substitution of other goals," (3) "analysis and decision."[10]

[9] Savage. *Interpersonal and Group Relations*. pp. 35–37.
[10] Arthur I. Gates. Arthur T. Jersild. T. R. McConnell. and Robert C. Challman, *Educational Psychology*. 3rd ed. (New York: The Macmillan Company. 1948), p. 647.

In the ongoing school system dynamic, the business administrator is frequently called upon to utilize the direct methods of tension reduction and equally often turns to the adjustment mechanisms in relieving the tensions that surface as a result of barriers to the fulfillment of basic needs.

Cultural Influences

A. L. Kroeber and C. Kluckhohn have analyzed over 160 definitions of the term culture and have categorized them into six major groups labelled as follows: "(1) enumeratively descriptive, (2) historical, (3) normative, (4) psychological, (5) structural, and (6) genetic."

Definitions representative of the six major groups are:

1. Culture embraces all the manifestations of social habits of a community, the reactions of the individual as affected by the habits of the group in which he lives, and the products of human activities as determined by those habits.
2. As a general term, culture means the total social heredity of mankind, while as a specific term, a culture means a particular strain of social heredity.
3. Culture is that whole "way of life" which is determined by the social environment.
4. Culture consists of traditional ways of solving problems. Culture is composed of responses which have been accepted because they have met with success; in brief, culture consists of learned problem-solutions.
5. A culture is an historically derived system of explicit and implicit designs for living which tends to be shared by all or specifically designated members of a group.
6. Culture is the accumulated transmissable results of past behavior in association.[11]

While most authors imply the existence of a dominant American culture, the explicit definition of such a culture is impossible. Rather it is possible to suggest that there exist a multitude of subcultures that are different from one another and that accommodate certain values that could be considered part of the dominant culture. These subcultures are the result of many variables, including race, national origin, religious beliefs, geo-

[11] Julius Gould and William Kolb, eds., *A Dictionary of the Social Sciences* (New York: The Free Press, 1965), p. 166.

graphic location, population density, historical events, and even age. Each subculture legitimizes certain behavior patterns and recognizes certain values, attitudes, customs, and artifacts that are different from those of other cultures. Behavior which is acceptable in one subculture may be unacceptable in another. The school administrator must understand the taboos if he is to work effectively with the constituency of a particular subculture.

Cultural influences on the individual's behavior must consider not only the incremental effects of environment over time but also the existing values and structure of unique subcultural milieus operating in a particular situation. Thus, the school business administrator cannot haphazardly behave according to an instinct strengthened by his own environment and experience, but he must examine and synthesize the variety of subcultures with which he interacts for appropriate behavior patterns. Therefore the planning role of the school business administrator assumes even greater importance as he gathers human relations "tools" for use in the performance of his duties.

PROCESSES OF HUMAN RELATIONS

Human relations cover a spectrum ranging from very bad to very good and can be viewed as the result of the administrator's role behavior or expectations. J. W. Getzels defines role expectations as:

> Roles are defined in terms of role expectations. A role has certain normative obligations and responsibilities, which may be termed "role expectations," and when the role incumbent puts these obligations and responsibility into effect, he is said to be performing his role. The expectations define for the actor, whoever he may be, what he should or should not do as long as he is the incumbent of the particular role.[12]

However, it is entirely possible that the role expectations of a particular position can produce bad as well as "good" human relations. This is especially so in the school business administration arena where the role has traditionally had a rather negative expectation.

[12] Andrew W. Halpin, ed., *Administrative Theory in Education* (Chicago: Midwest Administration Center, University of Chicago, 1958), p. 153.

The task of the business administrator is to change the expectations of the office by modifying his role behavior in such a way that it will produce more positive relationships with the many publics with whom he must deal. The manner in which behavior is changed can be considered a process of human relations.

In his planning role, the school business administrator assists in the development of the organizational goals of the school system. Equally important to the success of the administrator are his own personal goals, for unless and until organizational goals provide consistency and compatibility with personal goals, the conflict and frustration of trying to meet diverse sets of goals render him ineffective. Just as the goals of the organization must reflect the concerns and commitments the school system has for the individual learner, so must the personal goals of the school business administrator reflect his own concern and commitment to the individual learner. The internalization and synthesis of both personal and organizational goals will provide the basis for the establishment of goals and objectives of the school business office. If genuine commitment to the individual becomes the cornerstone, then the concomitant strengths of honesty, integrity, dedication, and technical skills will operate to reinforce the concept of "good" human relations. It is when the organization and individual members of the organization lose sight of the individual learner as the base that human relations aspects turn negative. In his book *The Human Organization,* Likert identifies four systems of management and relates their productivity to their character. He places management systems along an authoritative-participative continuum as follows:

1. Exploitive authoritative
2. Benevolent authoritative
3. Consultative
4. Participative[13]

Likert develops his research to show that organizational success is most probable as the management system becomes more participative with expanded opportunity for all members of the organization to become involved in the decision-making process. He also writes: "A science-based management, such as

[13] Rensis Likert, *The Human Organization* (New York: McGraw-Hill Book Company, 1967), pp. 14–25. Copyright © 1967 by McGraw-Hill. Inc. Used with permission of the publisher.

System 4 (Participative), is appreciably more complex than other systems. It requires greater learning and appreciably greater skill to use it well, but it yields impressively better results, which are evident whenever accurate performance measurements are obtained."[14]

Likert goes on to state:

> The leadership and other processes of the organization must be such as to ensure a maximum probability that in all interactions and in all relationships within the organization, each member, in the light of his background, values, desires, and expectations, will view the experience as supportive and one which builds and maintains his sense of personal worth and importance.[15]

Thus the superior-subordinate relationship must be one that is supportive and ego building rather than ego deflating. It is the perception of the subordinate rather than the superior that determines how supportive a situation is. To test if the superior's behavior is seen as supportive, Likert uses a series of questions to subordinates including the following:

1. How much confidence and trust do you feel your superior has in you? How much do you have in him? . . .
4. To what extent does your superior try to understand your problems and do something about them?
5. How much is your superior really interested in helping you with your personal and family problems? . . .
7. To what extent is he interested in helping you get the training which will assist you in being promoted?
8. To what extent does your superior try to keep you informed about matters related to your job? . . .
10. Does your superior ask your opinion when a problem comes up which involves your work? Does he value your ideas and seek them and endeavor to use them?
11. Is he friendly and easily approached?
12. To what extent is your superior generous in the credit and recognition given to others for the accomplishments and contributions rather than seeking to claim all the credit himself?[16]

---

[14] Likert, *The Human Organization*, p. 46.
[15] Likert, *The Human Organization*, p. 47.
[16] Likert, *The Human Organization*, pp. 48–49.

In other words, if members of the organization perceive themselves as active participants in the organization, the probability of a higher level of success is much greater than if the authoritative model is adhered to.

Processes of human relations, then, include not only the development of personal goals and objectives that are consistent with and mutually supportive of the goals and objectives of the organization but also the development of a management system that encourages maximum participation on the part of members of the organization. As the school business administrator strives toward the participatory management model, one of his prime concerns is the optimum use of communications as the vehicle for improved human relations. Communications, while not the totality of "good" human relations, are necessary to the operation of any organization and must be utilized by all administrators.

PRINCIPLES OF COMMUNICATIONS

Perhaps the oldest meaning of the word communications can be summarized as the passing of ideas, information, and attitudes from person to person. As technology invented new and different means of relaying the language, definitions began to include such things as film, television, telegraph, books, printed copy, and even the various modes of transport and travel. Raymond Williams, in his book *Communications,* defines communications as ". . . the institutions and forms in which ideas, information, and attitudes are transmitted and received . . . the process of transmission and reception."[17]

Using his definition as a base, Williams goes on to describe four kinds of communications systems that are in operation today. These are:

1. Authoritarian
2. Paternal
3. Commercial
4. Democratic

The authoritarian system is characterized by its devotion to the governance of the majority by a minority. Communications

[17] Raymond Williams, *Communications* (New York: Barnes & Noble, Inc., 1967), p. 17.

are used to perpetuate the attitudes of the minority and transmit its orders to the majority.

The paternal system does much the same as the authoritarian, but it claims the rationale of doing so in the best interests of the minority.

The commercial communication system advocates and provides a free information marketplace for those who can afford and profit from such dissemination.

The democratic communication system uses the free information marketplace but does not restrict it to those who can afford and/or profit from it.[18]

It becomes important to the school business administrator that the system of communications developed as the appropriate model be well toward the democratic side of the continuum. For if we truly believe that schools and school systems are democratic institutions, then we must strive to ensure that all components of the school and school system are founded on sound democratic principles. The democratic model presented above insists that all persons involved in an enterprise be both transmitters and receivers of ideas, information, and attitudes. Through this process of being both transmitter and receiver, the school administrator can develop capacity to encourage change in others as well as to change himself to manage this area of responsibility better.

PROCESSES OF COMMUNICATIONS

Communications tools or processes are used to accomplish specific purposes. Some popular statements of the purpose of communications suggest that it has a three-dimensional definition, that is: to inform, to persuade, and to entertain. This definition, while accepted in certain quarters, causes some concern when attempts are made to consider the three purposes as independent and unique entities. Also, the very vagueness of the terms *inform, persuade,* and *entertain* poses a degree of difficulty. Aristotle defined the study of rhetoric (communications) as the search for "all the available means of persuasion."[19] In keeping with this

---

[18] Williams, *Communications,* pp. 124–132.

[19] W. Rhys Roberts, "Rhetorica," in *The Works of Aristotle,* ed. W. D. Ross (Oxford University Press, 1946), vol. 11, p. 6.

definition of purpose, a rationale can be established that suggests that the basic purpose of communication is to enable the communicator to become an affecting agent, to increase the probability that he can become a force in determining an action.

David K. Berlo takes the position that the function of communication is that of influencing the behavior of others.

"In short, we communicate to influence—to affect with intent."[20]

Very often we ourselves are not aware of this purpose and as a result lose our effectiveness as communicators. Our communication behavior becomes habitual and often inefficient. Effective communication must not only be concerned with the general purpose of influencing, but also must take into account the specific persons to whom we wish to communicate and the appropriate methods to be used in order to communicate with them most effectively.

Berlo developed a model for the process of communication that includes six components. These are:

1. The communication source
2. The encoder
3. The message
4. The channel
5. The decoder
6. The communication receiver.[21]

As an attempt to oversimplify the use of the six ingredients, let us take the communication situation in which you are now engaged: reading this book. In this communication situation, the authors served as the source. They had a purpose in producing this message. Their writing mechanisms (with typewriters, typists, printing presses) served as encoders. The message is the way the words in this book are arranged. The channel is how the message is transmitted to you—by means of light waves. Your eye is the decoder. It receives the message, decodes it, retranslates it, and sends it to your central nervous system. Your central nervous system is the receiver. As you read, you will respond to the book.

Since the purpose of any communication is to influence or

---

[20] David K. Berlo, *The Process of Communication* (New York: Holt, Rinehart and Winston, Inc., 1960.) p. 12.

[21] Berlo, *Process of Communication*, p. 32.

to affect with intent, it follows that the channel chosen for the message depends upon the intent for which it is produced. Channels vary from one-to-one verbal and/or nonverbal situations to the use of a variety of media including the printed word, radio, television, and other sophisticated technological devices. The success of the communication depends upon how well the communicator defines the questions of whom and how.

APPLICATION TO SCHOOL BUSINESS ADMINISTRATION

The foregoing materials have presented a general overview of the fields of human relations and communications. Some of the tools have been identified and a case for the importance of communications to the broader arena of human relations has been presented. Indeed, the tools of communications are very important to the human relations effort of the school business administrator. But more important and of a higher order are those personal qualities that enable the individual to understand himself and to reconcile his own goals with those of the educational system. Unless and until the business administrator can integrate his personal needs and aspirations with those of the system, he cannot function as a top administrator of a school system.

Another level of human relations skill which the school business administration should possess is the ability to relate his role and responsibility in the organization to the roles and responsibilities of his coordinates (administrators on the same level or in the same echelon) and his subordinates (those personnel under his immediate supervision). The business administrator must see himself in the school business subsystem, and as such it is part of a larger system—the whole administrative organization of the school district. In order to develop the most creative and complementary relationships in the larger system, the school business administrator must see that his subsystem is responsive and open.

There is good evidence that the most successful managers are those who embrace the participative models of administration which involve all members of an organization in decision making. This means that the school business administrator must develop a high degree of tolerance and an ability to allow others of his staff to assume varying levels of responsibility. It also means that the business administrator must provide opportunity for cooperative planning and, additionally, assume the role of the coordinator of planning efforts for this arm of the school system. As the business division of a school system plans for the various tasks assigned it, the administrator must provide the influence that allows for smooth, orderly integration of efforts. The cooperative development of goals and objectives for the school business division that complements and supports the goals of the total school system is the logical first step of the planning cycle. Understanding of the service and support role of the business division and an appreciation of the individual client are important for all staff members. The development of positive internal relations and commitment will greatly assist the development of positive external human relations.

As a support system for the educational process, the business division must devote considerable energy in maintaining an "open" division, for if all members of the educational enterprise do not feel free to call for assistance from the business division, its effectiveness is reduced. Such "openness" begins with the internal operation of the business office through the planning process. Always uppermost must be the common thrust of the division: how can we best serve the individual child through our efforts? As goals and objectives are cooperatively developed, the process of communications assumes greater importance to the business administrator and his staff. During the initial planning phase, communications are largely of the one-to-one or group dialogue type. However, as the need for external communications grows, other channels must be utilized. These include verbal communications but also must incorporate a variety of strategies all developed to carry the message of the school system to its desired audience. For the business division, the message must also go to other arms of the school system as well as to the greater audience.

It therefore becomes important for the school business administrator to understand the process of communications and to develop means to choose appropriate channels to transmit messages. For example, when a message is intended for a single person or small group of people, an appropriate channel is the one-to-one dialogue. This is so because such transmission not only provides opportunity for a close interpersonal experience, but also the nonverbal interchange gives far more opportunity for mutual understanding. Therefore, the school business administrator must devote considerable time and energy to personal dialogue and communication. But this is not always possible or desirable. There are many instances where other channels of communications must be utilized. Then the decision must be based upon the following:

1. To whom is the message intended, and
2. How is it best transmitted?

In the typical school setting all diverse segments of the school system must be reached. It would be foolish to transmit the particular message in the same way to all clients. In communicating the school budget, as an example, the business community can probably digest the standard format with a minimum of explanation. However, if the school system has a Spanish-speaking clientele, the budget message must be encoded in a different manner. Use of interpreters, translation into Spanish, visual presentations, and so forth, are appropriate. For blue-collar clientele, another approach must be developed using the experience of the receiver as the common denominator. The school business administrator must understand the particular receiver or group of receivers and use the appropriate channel for transmission.

The business of education is a highly personal and emotional business. To succeed in the educational enterprise, the administrator must not only know and utilize the highly specialized management tools but must also develop a parallel set of tools that deal with human beings and their unique characteristics. It is often these "human related" tools and strategies that enable the administrator to accomplish objectives and goals.

SUMMARY

The human relations arena and the processes of communications have often been overlooked as important components of the skills needed for successful school business administration. This chapter presents basic considerations and concepts for the improvement of human relations and communications skills. Definitions and explanations derived from the disciplines of psychology, sociology, anthropology, and business are used to clarify concepts and to present important points.

The processes of human relations are presented and related to the role of the school business administrator. Research efforts by scholars in the field of human relations are utilized to describe certain processes. The superior-subordinate relationship is examined and suggested relationships presented.

Various styles of communications are analyzed and defined. Processes and tools of communications are presented in order that the reader can better understand its importance and applicability to the school business administrator. The goal of this chapter is to provide the reader with a basic grasp of the human relations-communications arena and the relationship of those fundamentals to the task(s) of the school business administrator.

SUGGESTED ACTIVITIES

1. Obtain and examine a table of organization of a large school system. Analyze the structure of the school business administration function and contemplate the kinds of communications that probably flow between the school business administrator and the other major administrative offices.

2. Obtain and examine the job description of a school business administrator. Try to ascertain the kinds of human relations skills which are implied in the description of this position.

3. From your knowledge of the job expectations of a particular school system's superintendency team (or the "central office"), what if any unique human relations skills are required by the school business administrator?

4. Given the emphasis or the planning approach as described by the writers, do you think this changes the human relations and communications skills required by the school business administrator as described in a more conventional role and organization? If so, why?

SUGGESTED READINGS

Bennis, Warren G., Benne, Kenneth D., and Chin, Robert, eds. *The Planning of Change.* New York: Holt, Rinehart and Winston, Inc., 1966.

Berlo, David K. *The Process of Communication.* New York: Holt, Rinehart and Winston, Inc., 1960.

Davis, Keith. *Human Relations at Work.* New York: McGraw-Hill Book Company. 1962.

Griffiths, Daniel E. *Human Relations in School Administration.* New York: Appleton-Century-Crofts, 1956.

Likert, Rensis. *The Human Organization.* New York: McGraw-Hill Book Company, 1967.

McLaughlin, Ted J., Blum, Lawrence P., and Robinson, David M. *Communication.* Columbus, O.: Charles E. Merrill Books, Inc., 1964.

Maslow, A. H. *Motivation and Personality.* New York: Harper and Brothers, 1954.

Rogers, Carl R. *On Becoming a Person.* Boston: Houghton Mifflin Company, 1961.

Savage, William W. *Interpersonal and Group Relations in Educational Administration.* Glenview, Ill.: Scott, Foresman and Company, 1968.

Williams, Raymond. *Communications.* New York: Barnes & Noble, Inc., 1967.

DATA PROCESSING TOOLS USED IN THE PLANNING PROCESS

The identification of the planning function as a paramount consideration for the school business administrator has been established in earlier chapters. This function was expanded in the chapter dealing with specific management tools used in the planning process. To utilize many of these tools effectively and efficiently, a scheme for the implementation of a data processing system will often be an integral part of planning conducted by the administrative team. These efforts will depend, at least in part, on the competence of the school business administrator.

Within the very near future, even the smallest school district will have access to some type of data processing equipment — either electronic or punched card. Several manufacturers have introduced electronic equipment with monthly rental prices compatible with the budgets of most school districts in the country. Additionally, manufacturers, data processing or leasing companies, and software organizations have developed remote data processing capabilities to such a degree that they are available for a relatively small monthly expenditure. Developmental activities are continuing at a rapid rate in all areas of computing and software and the emergence of extensive competition is having a marked effect on total cost for all aspects of the computer industry.

This chapter will give an overview of data processing (DP) activities and opportunities in school systems and the relationship each has to the school business administration function. These relationships will be both practical and theoretical and will have applicability in many areas for most school districts.

GENERAL CONSIDERATIONS

Effect on Staff

It is a foregone conclusion that the installation of data processing equipment in a school district will require the moving, retraining, or replacing of certain currently employed personnel. Additional personnel will be needed for specific positions generated by the installation of new equipment.

There are several situations to consider when data processing equipment is to be brought into a school district. Among the key considerations is the one associated with staff morale. A new level of personnel is likely to be needed—the technical employee. These persons will not fit the current structure of administrator, teacher, or clerk and will present a series of unique personnel problems. Pay scales are likely to be altered drastically and usual lines of authority may need to be changed. The type of employee associated with general machine operations will be a new breed for most school districts. His requirements for space, clerical and technical assistance, and working conditions will be significantly different from the usual needs of a school district. Physical facilities will have to be altered, and equipment and materials used by these persons will be expensive, new, and perhaps threatening to many persons within the current administrative structure.

It is possible that certain staff members may be retrained for work with the new equipment, but to expect that all positions can be filled by reshuffling current personnel is beyond reason.

A key reason for introducing these areas at this time is that activities under the direction of the school business administrator will be among the earliest applications for the machine. As such, applications of payroll, purchasing, and inventory control, among others, will be closely observed by all administrative and instructional units within the school district.

Effect on Administrators

There is a possibility that an area of conflict will be created within the central office when a data processing facility is set up in a school district. Decisions as to placement of the data processing center are often poorly thought through and can lead to future problems. The truism that a data processing facility is for service to the entire school system is often overlooked at installation time. The school business administrator should resist the approach of having the data processing operation placed under him and push for a placement within the district where the computer can serve all areas of the program. Two possible top-level organizational schemes are shown in figures 6.1 and 6.2.

Either of the organizational patterns shown in figures 6.1 and 6.2 allows the flexibility necessary to provide service to all areas of a school district with a minimum of conflict among various departments concerning control and allocation of funds.

Either of these types of organization will provide a structure for the distribution of data to the proper location within the organization without some of the problems of clearing data sources with various groups throughout the central staff.

The need to get necessary information and data into proper hands within the district cannot be overemphasized. The flow of information and data to various areas of the district is the only

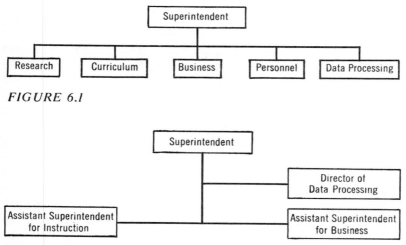

FIGURE 6.1

FIGURE 6.2

logical base for decision makers to use in working through key problem areas. As will be discussed later, the computer can serve as a key provider of planning information when correctly applied within any school district.

The capability for using the computer to augment the instructional and research programs of most school systems has hardly been tapped. Demographic information on students and the total community as well as school system material provides most areas of potential utilization for the school's computer system.

Problems associated with the placement of a computing or data processing facility often revolve around fiscal control. Many school business administrators have come up through the ranks of business applications using adding machines, checkwriting machines, and/or desk calculators. It is natural to associate the control of the physical hardware with this area of fiscal responsibility.

However, it is imperative that the tremendous resource represented by the addition of an electronic computing system be properly placed within the district so that all areas of the program will have proper access to the use of the hardware. It is to be expected that the school business manager will have responsibility for the implementation of many of the general applications for the machine once it is available.

In many districts the school business administrator would be a logical person to head the advance planning group for the district, and he should be on the committee in all cases. This committee, or one similarly constituted, must be in operation well before installation time and should continue as an integral part of the system's organization.

DETERMINING FACTORS

Need

There is no question but that a need must be established before a data processing facility should be introduced into a public school system. There are numerous instances where computer facilities have been opened in a district long before the proper cost-utilization studies had been made. The result of such

premature installation was no different than could have been expected—disaster. The center could not function in an efficient
manner and the hardware was removed. The real loser in this
instance was the school district. Once hardware has been removed,
whatever the cause, the replacement or reinstallation of computers is a difficult process. In fact, it is often much more difficult
than was the initial effort to secure equipment.

This reinforces the point of verifying the need for data processing facilities in the particular school district. The needs for
each district will vary, and unique application should be expected
for most situations.

Need for data processing equipment should be established
on a day-to-day basis, for several years in advance, and in close
cooperation with representatives of all phases of the school program. The services will be offered across several, if not all,
aspects of the school program—business, instruction, research,
personnel—and should involve representatives from these areas
in the planning of the operation. As stated before, it is necessary
to start planning early, and it is not unusual to plan in detail for
at least three years and in one or two five-year blocks after that.
The utilization of these plans then provides the director of data
processing with current and long-range, system-wide goals for
his use.

A hierarchical arrangement of needed services should be
established by representatives of each of the groups. It is to be
expected that those functions associated with school business
administration—payroll, inventory, and so forth—are sure to be
among the first identified and the first selected for implementation.
Cost figures should be computed as should time commitments
and security of data for each identified need. Needs cannot always
be computed in cost because it is not always possible to know
the value of rapid turnaround of information if none has been
available in the past. Detailed cost figures for machine utilization,
software development, personnel expenditures, and supplies
should be maintained for the various facets of the school program.
Security of data should receive high priority consideration in
terms of maintaining the privacy of the individual student and
staff member as well as providing for the maintenance of correct
and accurate data.

Visits to school districts similar to the local one and to those
somewhat larger are generally profitable. Those within the same

state are best, if this is possible, because of the similar type of state reports required and the state rules and regulations governing items from transportation to cafeterias. Care should be taken to discuss problems of implementation, user education, staff acceptance, and machine selection with all affected levels of personnel within the organization. Systems persons and supervisors are often more valuable to persons seeking technical information than are central office level personnel.

Selection of Equipment

It is impossible to give a formula for machine selection. The variables involved in this decision are many and complex. As has been previously noted, visits to other school districts, regional facilities, and university centers have merit. Discussion of need with data processing consultants is another valuable source of information. Vendors' information can be used profitably when solutions for the same problems are offered by the several companies. These solutions should be based on hardware configurations like the system proposed for the local district. Yet another source of information is the varied technical reports researched by reputable firms or national data processing organizations.

An alternative arrangement to sole ownership or rental and one which is gaining increasing national support is the concept of time-sharing. Terminals (typewriters, card reader-printers, visual display systems) are used by the local system and are tied to a large central processor at some remote location. This may be the most economical manner for some districts to secure data processing services.

A third arrangement is the use of the service center concept for data processing. The use of a service center generally involves the packaging of material at the local district and the physical movement of that material to a remote location for processing. The cost of processing is then set as per the function performed and the number of students served. For example, school scheduling is often performed for a fixed amount plus a charge for each student scheduled, assuming a standard computer scheduling program can be used. If special processing must be done, additional costs are involved.

The actual selection of a computer system, time-sharing service, or service center is a laborious, time-consuming, and generally unrewarding task. The discussions of core size, computer speed, cycle time, compiler languages, satellite devices, new personnel, expensive physical facilities, and the thousands of other details which must be examined to produce the best possible recommendation for board action are not without trauma. Decisions as to what features can be cut without hampering proposed operations are difficult to make. The aspects of service and software (program) support are especially difficult to evaluate. These latter two areas may provide an even larger consideration for a district not in proximity to a metropolitan area where large numbers of computers may be installed. Some maintenance plans include a certain number of service calls, others provide for unlimited calls, and some require a fee for each call.

Shift rental costs are another area for consideration. Some manufacturers charge additional fees for other than prime shift (normal work day) usage. Other manufacturers instead charge on a metered-hour basis after a predetermined number of hours has elapsed. Figure 6.3 gives a possible machine configuration.

UTILIZATION

Development of Suitable Software

The previous section indicates that there are problems with machine selection but that there are solutions which will allow these to be attacked by the district with likelihood of success. The larger problem for study in the area of school business administration is the development of suitable software for management problem solution in the particular school district. After the rather routine functions have been programmed, the real value of a complex computer facility will be found in the area of management decision making. These functions of management decision making where alternatives are explored, based on sufficient data, are generally lacking in the public schools. No programs for securing necessary data or projections have been available to the general school administrators, and these absences have contributed to errors in selection of building sites, program planning, personnel selection, and long-range growth projections.

The simple data processing system is a transaction-oriented system designed for the express purpose of producing reports

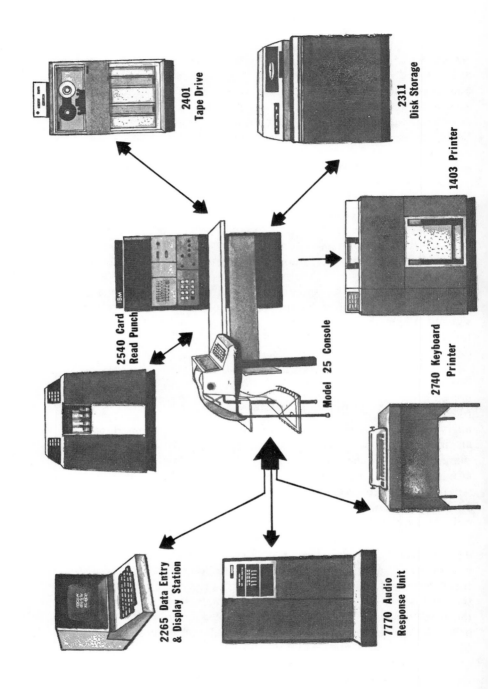

2401
Tape Drive

2311
Disk Storage

2540 Card
Read Punch

IBM

Model 25 Console

1403 Printer

2740 Keyboard
Printer

2265 Data Entry
& Display Station

7770 Audio
Response Unit

from a set of data. These reports include the general set of attendance, grade reporting, and general bookkeeping functions associated with the area of school business management and student personnel work. The value of an integrated data processing system is to go beyond these transactions, use the collected data on many facets of the school program, pose questions of a sophisticated data base, and utilize this data to discover alternative courses of action.

The Administrative Role

There is little doubt that the availability of the computer is an asset to a school business administrator. However, as noted above, the true value of the computer will come in the combined use of the machine by several key staff members, including the school business administrator, and the creation of imaginative software to make proper use of the hardware. As was stated previously, the personnel to do these jobs are difficult to hire but invaluable in assisting in conceptualizing systems and their applications in a public school district.

The school business administrator is in reality one key member of the school administrative team charged with properly charting the growth of the local district. This is a relatively new role for the school business manager. It requires that he serve an analysis and planning role as well as manage the day-to-day operation of his office. This new role gives the proper emphasis as a planner and initiator of change to the position of school business administrator.

STANDARDIZATION AND MAINTENANCE

The determination of computer program needs as a part of the overall program of systems analysis for a school district is but the initial step in a series of steps. The programs necessary for the total operation must be a part of an integrated system meeting the total requirements of a district. Without some general standardization of programming efforts, replacement of personnel is difficult, and the maintenance of the system through hardware changes is virtually impossible.

Figure 6.4 gives a picture of a scheme for converting a prob-

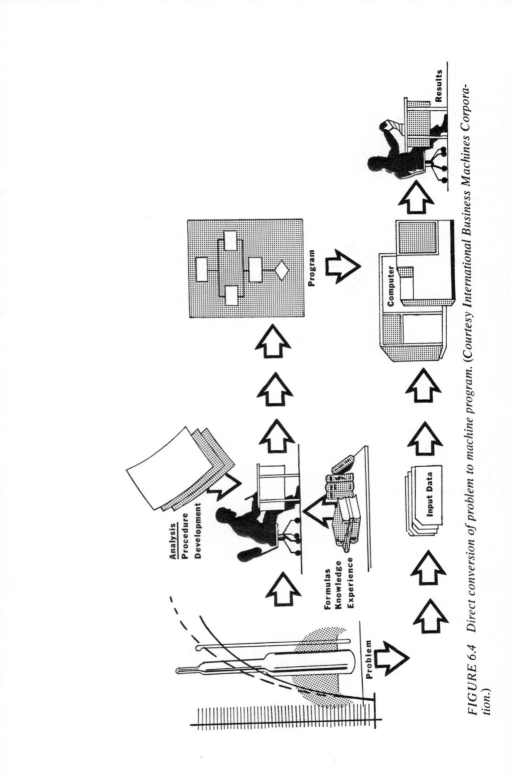

FIGURE 6.4 Direct conversion of problem to machine program. (Courtesy International Business Machines Corporation.)

lem into results. Each step is detailed, but each is a part of the overall plan.

An illustration of the cooperative use of data by members of the management team could be within the areas of personnel, business, and administration. The data collected on personnel forms will serve administrators of local schools and the business manager. Figures 6.5 and 6.6 show an example of two personnel cards containing information of use to all three groups. For example, administrators will be concerned with the type of certificate each teacher has (see card columns 55–56, card number 1), and

Explanation of Selected Card Columns

Columns 1–9	Teacher's permanent number
Columns 10–35	Teacher's name
	Cols. 10–23: Last
	Cols. 24–33: First
	Cols. 34–35: Middle
Column 36	Race and sex (combined)
− − − − −	
Columns 66–67	Years of experience
− − − − −	
Columns 72–74	School number (assigned by state)
Columns 75–78	School grades

FIGURE 6.5   Teaching personnel card number 1, State of Tennessee Department of Education. (Reprinted with permission.)

teaching assignment (see card columns 53–54, card number 1). The business manager will be interested in Allowed State Salary Schedule (see card columns 49–55, card number 2) and State Increment (see card columns 56–61, card number 2).

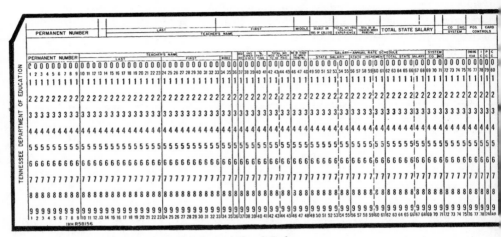

Explanation of Selected Card Columns

Columns 1–35	Same as card number 1
Column 37	Degree or years of college
Columns 38–39	Total number of years of teaching experience
Columns 49–68	Salary—annual rate schedule Cols. 49–55: State salary Cols. 56–61: State increment Cols. 62–68: Total state salary

Figure 6.6 Teaching personnel card number 2, State of Tennessee Department of Education. (Reprinted with permission.)

Single-shot, special-purpose programs should be avoided if at all possible. This approach tends to be wasteful of scarce resources and produces a type of unstructured working environment not conducive to efficient operation. The areas where this general approach may not hold are in the activities of research and instruction sections. The needs for processing in these two areas are variable and will, on occasion, require special applications.

Another argument favoring strict standardization and maintenance procedures is the control process. Without strict control of programming and machine usage records, it is difficult for the business manager to get an accurate picture of costs. These costs are, of course, invaluable to the business manager when projecting areas of growth and the attendant costs associated with that growth.

There are many ways to illustrate the need for strict practices relative to standardization and maintenance. The illustration of "financial applications" shown in figure 6.7 and the illustration of a "pupil record file" shown in figure 6.8 will indicate some of the complexities and detail characteristics of these and other computerized applications. The minute details required for each subset of the operation to contribute successfully to the total scheme are evident as is the need for proper documentation of each subset and for the total system. Figure 6.9 shows a flow chart for a typical inventory-control application.

TYPES OF EQUIPMENT

Unit Record Systems

Many school districts have had access to unit record data processing systems for several years. These systems include accounting machines, reproducing punches, collaters, and so forth, to provide basic accounting procedures and produce large amounts of company data on punched cards. For example, these card systems allow simultaneous production of payroll checks and an updated employee payroll record card. Mechanical card sorters are a necessary part of these operations since they allow for the rapid division of card files into subsets. These subsets can be alphabetic, numeric, or alphanumeric. Figure 6.10 shows available letters, numbers, and special characters punched into a standard eighty-column card. Figure 6.11 shows the mock-up of a typical data card.

Card systems are still very much in use in many small business installations and can play a valuable role in the management of business functions. A number of considerations are associated

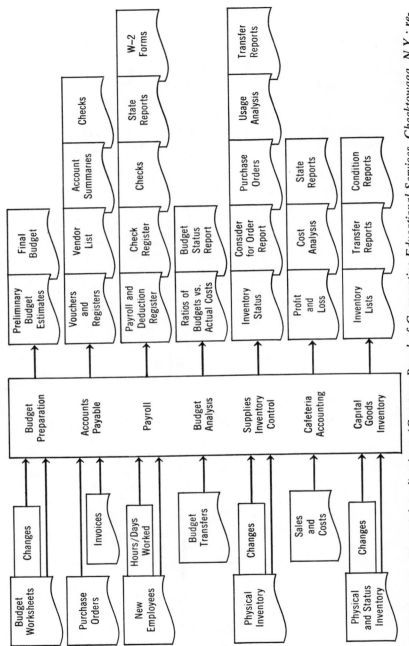

FIGURE 6.7 Financial applications. (Courtesy Board of Cooperative Educational Services, Cheektowaga, N.Y.; reprinted with permission.)

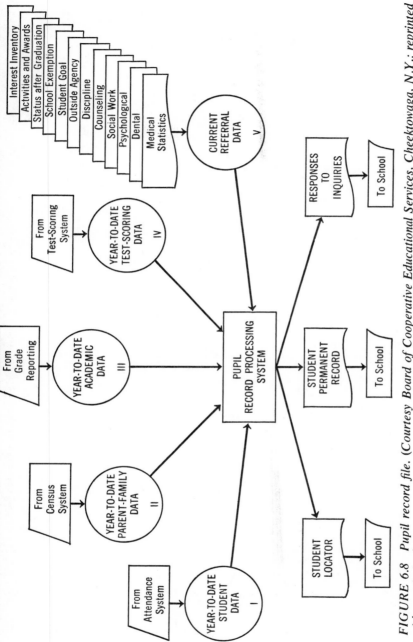

FIGURE 6.8 Pupil record file. (Courtesy Board of Cooperative Educational Services, Cheektowaga, N.Y.; reprinted with permission.)

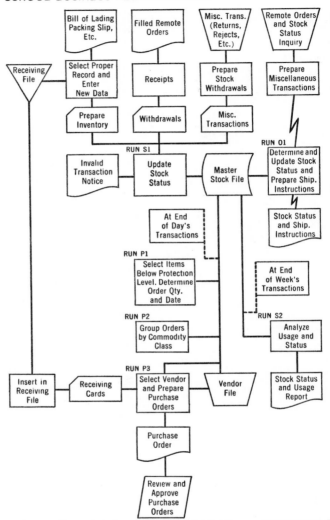

This chart uses specific symbols for certain processing functions and input/output. The application involves a multiple-warehouse system: items are stocked in a central warehouse for distribution to remote warehouses; all customer orders are received by remotely located warehouses and transmitted by teletype (lightning-type communication-link symbol) to the central data processing installation. The system provides four major groups of operations: (1) updating stock status (RUN S1), based on actual transactions; (2) response to inquiries (RUN O1) from auxiliary warehouses and central warehouse; (3) reorder analysis (RUNS P1, P2, P3), including purchase order preparation; (4) weekly analysis reports (RUN S2) to show slow-moving items, major changes in usage rates, behind-schedule deliveries, economic lot sizes, etc.

FIGURE 6.9   Flow chart for a typical inventory-control application. (Courtesy International Business Machines Corporation.)

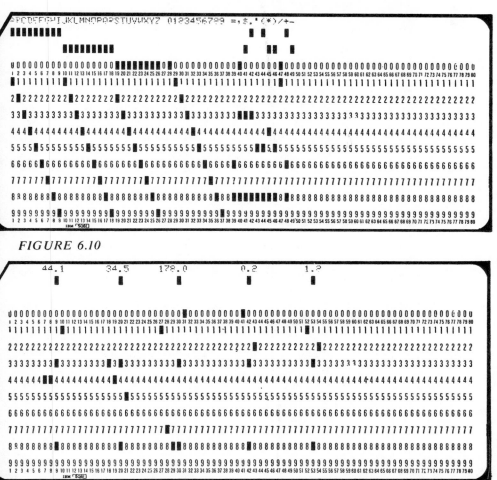

FIGURE 6.10

FIGURE 6.11

with the punched card system when its utility for a school district is questioned. A major consideration is that the punched card system does not operate under program control but by a control panel into which wires have been plugged to connect one control point with another. As an outgrowth of this, a single panel can be wired (plugged) to do a single task or a very limited number of tasks. A second consideration is that the accounting machine has no memory unit. Additionally, satellite storage devices with the capability of tapes, disks, drums, etc., are not available for accounting machines. Cost is also a consideration. Several small-scale computer systems can be leased for a cost figure approximating that of a large unit record installation.

The final consideration is the most important. Unit record equipment is not capable of providing the inputs for management decision making that are vital for solving today's educational problems. The speed, capability, and versatility of the computer cannot be replaced with unit record equipment.

While unit record equipment such as sorters, interpreters, and key punches will continue to be used with computers, the total system unit record installation is a thing of the past.

Digital Computing Systems

It would be impossible to provide a detailed explanation of a digital computer system in a brief discussion, but certain key explanations are important. The business administrator will not be required to operate or repair a computer, but some knowledge of the physical construction and operating principles of the hardware will be helpful.

Generally, a computer may be defined as an electronic device having the capability to manipulate data under the control of a program or programs stored within the device. There are few exact terms in computing work, and discussion of hardware components is no exception. There is really no typical computer system, but most systems will contain these components:

1. Central processor
2. Input/output devices
3. Storage unit
4. Control devices

The central processor is that component of the computer system which actually performs operations on data. This component performs various mathematical operations, shifts data elements from one place to another, and produces information which may be written on storage facilities, such as tapes or disks, or may be printed onto paper or punched into cards. Input devices are peripheral components which enable information to be read into the memory component of the central processing unit. These devices include card readers, tape drives, teleproc-

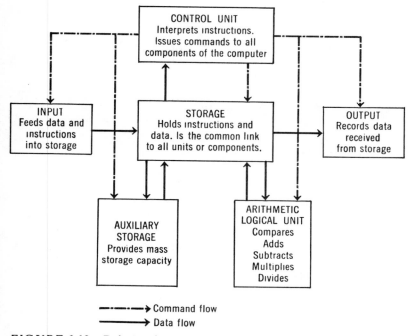

FIGURE 6.12   *Relationship of functions of a computer system.*

essing remote input stations, etc., available to computer users. Conversely, output devices are such machines as tape drives, disk drives, printers, card punches, etc., which allow for material which has been produced to be returned to the user in whatever form he wishes. Control devices are those components of the computer system which supervise the entire operation and are responsible for the interface of one machine with another. These are the least well-known types of hardware devices in any computer system but are necessary for the operation of the entire system.

Figure 6.12 shows the relationship of the functions of a computer system.

Other Equipment Needs

The installation of an electronic computer system in a school district has implications for the selection of peripheral equipment and the disposition of equipment which may currently be in use in the school district. As is evident from previous discussion, there are supporting devices which will be necessary for any computing system. These include such devices as key punches, card verifiers, sorters, interpreters, and other unit record devices directly supporting the operation of the computing facility.

An additional problem created by the installation of a computing system in a school district is the disposition of current bookkeeping equipment or decision making relative to its continued use. It is evident that the school business administrator will be involved in decisions of this nature because there are problems of amortization, rental credits, and lease agreements. The school business administrator will be a key person in a complete study of the district's noncomputing hardware to determine whether it needs to be augmented, whether certain types of equipment such as checkwriting machines need to be removed, or whether certain types of equipment need to be transferred to other divisions or units within the district.

Such a complete review of equipment needs within a district provides an opportunity to look critically at how monies are spent on equipment of this type. This will ensure that persons are given proper equipment with which to work and that equipment is utilized in a proper manner in the overall scheme of district operations. Checkwriting procedures within the district illustrate this point. The school business manager will be involved with the writing of checks within any district, and these can certainly be written on any electronic computing system as one of the initial computer applications. This means that any checkwriting equipment might be sold or turned back to the company, depending on any existing lease/purchase arrangement in effect.

MATERIALS SELECTION

Materials selection for a computing facility is not a simple or easily accomplished task. Those items of material necessary for a computing facility to operate efficiently seem to be without number. These fall into categories of consumable and nonconsumable, including paper products, cards, ribbons, etc., in the consumable section, and desks, cabinets, tape racks, tapes, disk packs, etc., in the nonconsumable section.

Consumable Supplies

The consumable supplies that will be needed in any computing facility certainly will include the necessary paper products, such as daily attendance records, checks, transfer vouchers, invoices, other billing materials, and necessary personnel reports, charts, and graphs, as well as other administrative information. Standard computer printer paper is intended for general purpose reports, for testing, and for production of rather limited amounts of material. There is wide use for preprinted forms on which material may be printed in special blanks. General applications of these special forms are payroll checks, W–2 forms, monthly reports, class registers, invoices, transfer vouchers, and other material on which heading information can be given routinely, lines can be drawn, and certain columns can be preprinted to save both time and money. Any computing facility will use tremendous amounts of paper due to the very nature of the materials which programmers, analysts, and administrators need for their day-to-day work. This will include single-part or multipart paper (with or without liner). Other types of paper products which might be used by a computing facility include punched cards and multilith master forms for producing multiple copies of reports.

Expenses for paper are just a part of those associated with computing facilities. Additional supplies which are not always considered in relation to computer facilities include rubber bands, marking pencils, batch tickets, separator cards, and any other products generally associated with the operation of a large-scale data processing center. Figure 6.13 shows a sample inventory record for a large computing facility. Obviously, all centers will not use all types of materials; but as any school business administrator will know, many kinds of supplies must be available in order to make the operation run smoothly enough so that the cost can be justified.

Nonconsumable Supplies

Consumable supplies make up a rather large expenditure for a computing center, but expenditures for nonconsumable supplies must also be considered. When one includes such items as magnetic tapes at approximately $20 per reel or disk packs leasing for $15 to $25 per month or purchased for $200 to $500, the cost

INVENTORY RECORD

DATE _____

PAPER

g r e e n b a r					
size & pts.	stk#	on hand	order	vendor	
14-7/8 x 11"	1	059I			
	2	059J			
	3	059K			UT t.v.
	4	059L			
	5	059M			

b l a n k					
size & pts.	stk#	on hand	order	vendor
14-7/8 x 11"	1			
	2			
	3			
	4			
9-7/8 x 11"	1			
	2			UT t.v.
	3			
	4			

CARDS

type (all are #5081)	on hand ordered	C O L O R						pvd
		RED	YEL	GRN	BLU	PURP	ORNG	
solid	on hand							☒
	ordered							
stripe	on hand							☒
	ordered							

type	plain	for	map	
IBM#	5081	888	820	
on hand				
ordr				
rcvd				

RIBBONS

type	part number	on hand	order	received
1403 multipurpose	IBM 414489			
1403 black red	IBM 457937, Col. 1510124			
407 black record	UT 333, IBM 426033			
1443 line printer	IBM 428032			
557 black, interp	UT 332, IBM 425018			
key punch	UT 335, IBM 424810			
selectric carriage	IBM 1136138			

MISC. ITEMS (order detail on back and/or separate sheet)

item	on hand		item	on hand	
magnetic tape			multilith long		
lib tape save card			multilith short		
lib tape release card			multilith heavy duty		
7040 batch tickets			3M type cleaner		
360 batch tickets			rubber bands		
card paks			transfer vouchers		
carriage tapes (poly)			carriage tape adhesive		
reflective spots					

FIGURE 6.13   Sample inventory record for computing facility.

of nonconsumable supplies can rise sharply. For example, tapes must be stored in racks and must be provided with either tape seals or canisters for storage to prevent a dust accumulation problem which would relegate them to uselessness in the computing center. It is not uncommon to have a tape library of hundreds or thousands of reels. The disks must be stored in a relatively secure place so that there will be no damage to the actual disk pack. Special cabinets are provided and these are generally used by most computing installations.

Other nonconsumable supplies needed by the computing center include breakdown and setup desks, chairs, programming desks, key punch chairs, and other storage devices. These must include facilities for the storing of cards and card boxes. This is generally done in card cabinets or in large bulk-type storage facilities which allow for the storage of cards in their user-supplied boxes.

It is not unusual to involve thousands of dollars in inventory for supplies to support a facility. However, it would be false economy not to provide a computing facility with the necessary consumable supplies with which to operate. As an illustration, it is not unusual that the rental of equipment for a computing facility is several thousands of dollars a month. Not to provide proper consumable supplies for the effective utilization of the center would doom the center's operation to inefficiency.

OFFICE PROCEDURES ALTERATIONS

By the time the school business administrator has participated in the decision-making process mentioned in the previous sections of this chapter, it is doubtful that he would wish to take on more reorganization or alteration projects. However, the opportunity to examine the totality of his office procedures will never be better. Staff reorganization, filing processes, and record management would be logically examined at this point.

With the introduction of computer processing, many of the procedures for filing and record keeping will be automatically altered. Current records, permanent files, transfer vouchers, purchase orders, etc., can all be generated by the computer system. This causes a restructuring for filing and may call for the removal of certain files, as in the case of the on-line inventory control system. Files of computer output will differ from current files and may produce more detailed records requiring more space. But they will be organized in such a manner as to facilitate data retrieval.

Security of data, including personnel and financial records, is a current concern and will remain so with any computerized system. If data is maintained on-line, this is especially crucial. Centralization of responsibilities for these data and the identification of persons to assume these responsibilities will be vital parts of any look at the current organizational scheme.

Computer-generated output, including paper and punched cards, will grow as the school system grows in ability to use the data processing system. Remote inquiry stations may become an integral part of financial and personnel records. Storage locations for printed material will be needed and an access scheme or system for this material must be generated. Most computer systems costs must be prorated to many areas within the system, and a machine program and accounting scheme must be developed for this.

Output will build up rapidly and a procedure for retention and disposition of all levels of records—nonessential, useful, important, and vital—must be established. Microfilming is a useful technique for producing more easily retrieved material. Some records will automatically be replaced with periodic updates from the system. Others will be special purpose, and all will present problems of retrieval.

The installation period gives an opportunity for the business administrator to examine his total set of office procedures and practices. The machine will impart these procedures, and care must be taken to prevent a complete deluge of paper. Personnel must be taught to interact with the machine and to get production as needed without becoming subjugated to the system.

SUMMARY

The school business administrator's role in planning within the local district involves many applications of management tools and processes. However, no tool at his disposal is of more potential assistance in decision making and management operations than the computer.

Computers allow for the storage, manipulation, and retrieval of vast amounts of data on a multitude of subjects. Data may be of a routine nature or may feed to a total management information system where interaction responses between the school business administrator and the machine take place. Demographic, financial, personnel, and pupil data are but a few illustrations of what can be utilized in a computer system.

Considerations as to personnel, administrative control, hardware and software selections, and space allocations are but a few of the problems to be dealt with in the operation of a computer facility. Results of machine activities must be monitored and evaluated on an ongoing basis throughout the system and across the various types of activities within the district. No single development can have as much impact on the district as the electronic computer.

SUGGESTED ACTIVITIES

1. How would you plan for the introduction of an educational data processing capability in your school system?

2. Discuss the role of the computer in administration, research, and teaching for public schools.

3. How would you determine uses of a computer in your role as school business administrator?

4. Rank in terms of priority of need the major uses of the computer in your school system. In your administrative area.

5. Design a PERT chart for the selection and installation of a computer in your school system.

6. What will be the role of the computer in decision making in your school system? In your administrative area?

SELECTED READINGS

Computer Education Directory. South Pasadena, Calif.: Data Processing Horizons, Inc., 1968.

Computers: New Era for Education? Washington, D.C.: National School Public Relations Association, 1968.

Feingold, Carl. *Introduction to Data Processing.* Dubuque, Ia.: William C. Brown Company, Publishers, 1971.

Gentle, Edgar C., Jr., ed. *Data Communications in Business.* New York: American Telephone and Telegraph Company, 1965.

Gerard, R. W. *Computers and Education.* New York: McGraw-Hill Book Company, 1967.

Grossman, Alvin, and Howe, Robert L. *Data Processing for Educators.* Chicago: Educational Methods, Inc., 1965.

Gruenberger, Fred. *Computing: An Introduction.* New York: Harcourt, Brace & World, Inc., 1969.

Introduction to IBM Data Processing Systems. White Plains, N.Y · International Business Machines Corporation, 1967.

Marker, Robert W., McGraw, Peter P., and Stone, Franklin D. *Computer Concepts and Educational Administration.* Iowa City, Ia.: The . Iowa Educational Information Center, College of Education, University of Iowa, 1966.

Myers, Charles A., ed. *The Impact of Computers on Management.* Cambridge, Mass.: The M.I.T. Press, 1967.

Sackman, Harold. *Computers, Systems Science and Evolving Society.* New York: John Wiley & Sons, Inc., 1967.

Whitlock, James W. *Automatic Data Processing in Education.* New York: The Macmillan Company, 1964.

SCHOOL BUSINESS
ADMINISTRATION TASKS

Educational administrators, regardless of their specific areas of responsibility, are thought to be action oriented. They are expected to get things done. The things that the school business administrator gets done — or the "what" of his job — are seen as his tasks, or his area's substantive accomplishment.

Thus far we have spoken to the role of the school business administrator and the setting for it, and have described some major conceptual tools which imply useful ways of thinking about and approaching the school business administrator's tasks. In Part III we will build on these notions of role and conceptual tools and describe the tasks or more substantive aspects of the responsibility.

The authors' approach to tasks involves more than a classification and description of problems, work expectations, and the like. We also find the "cookbook" or "how-to-do-it" approach inadequate, since a specific solution to a given problem is often dysfunctional to an individual and a particular school system because of the variation of circumstances. The single recipe is, of course, inappropriate when considered in the planning context, which is a basic premise of this book. Instead, the several chapters in Part III include discussions on the nature and relevancy of the task—both within the school system structure and within the responsibility of the school business administrator. These task chapters also describe the relationships of the task with other aspects of this field: the task may be seen as a subsystem in interaction with the greater system. Each chapter describes some of the problems indigenous to the task, and suggests how the problem nature of a specific task is manifested in the unique environment of individual school systems.

Most of the task chapters include the application of several of the conceptual tools in the context of the specific administrative task, e.g., an identification of the legal constraints in accomplishing the task, the application of appropriate management tools, the need for and utilization of communication and human relations capabilities, and the design and operation of appropriate information systems and data processing facilities.

The several task chapters also include the application of other factors, principles, guidelines, theoretical constructs, and techniques which must be considered and which might be useful in successfully completing the given task.

A last major component of several of the task chapters is approaches to the evaluation of the school business administrator's performance in accomplishing the task. Naturally the unique nature of each task dictates the mode of evaluation, and so each task chapter has a unique evaluation format.

The tasks of the school business administrator as described in the text vary somewhat from the treatment afforded them in conventional texts. The authors take the position that the nature of the task is markedly influenced by the approach taken and the methodology used by the school business administrator as he works toward task accomplishment. The planning approach which underlies our concept of school business administration therefore influences the definition of the task as well as the processes used in order to accomplish it.

PLANNING AND BUDGETING

Educational planning, i.e., the weighing of priorities of alternative offerings and the weighing of alternative means to accomplish the stated objectives, is the essential feature of effective budgeting in the schools. The significant role of planning in the budgetary process was not always clearly recognized. The division of powers between executive and legislative branches in our governmental structure, the superfluity of public revenues in the last quarter of the nineteenth century, and public acceptance of graft, corruption, and boss rule were factors which tended to retard the development of systematic budgetary practices in the United States.

The important role of planning in the budgetary process was not always fully comprehended. Several developments have caused attention to be focused upon the importance of planning. Administrators are becoming more astute in budgeting. The growth in pupil population, the demands of the public for new and expanded programs, the need to employ the services of more highly trained instructional personnel and support personnel, the new instructional media and equipment with leasing or purchasing possibilities, and growing sophistication of the public concerning an understanding of school financing have all added to the need for more complex budget planning. In short, the rate of change in the educational environment calls for periodic and intense examination of alternative ways to allocate school funds. Traditional methods of budgeting have not given the school administrator proper insight into weighing alternative plans of education. Past definitions of the term "budget" reflect the traditional methodology of budget development. For example, the educational budget is the translation of educational needs into a financial plan which is interpreted to the public in such a way that, when formally adopted, expresses the kind of educational program the community is willing to support, financially and morally, for the budget period.

The school budget is the numerical translation of the educational program of a school district. It expresses to the citizens of a community the dollar value of the program of education provided them.

The school budget is basically an instrument of educational planning and, incidentally, also an instrument of control. It reflects the organizational pattern by breaking down the elements of a total plan into their sectional and departmental components, allowing costs to be more easily estimated. It then forces a coordination of these elements by reassembling costs in a whole so that a comparison may be made with total revenues. This very process requires a kind of orderly planning that otherwise might never take place. Budgeting, then, forces the administrator and his staff to plan together on what needs to be done, how it will be done, and by whom.

Among the benefits of budgeting can be included:

1. It establishes a plan of action for the future.
2. It requires an appraisal of past activities in relation to planned activities.
3. It necessitates the establishment of work plans.
4. It necessitates foreseeing expenditures and estimating revenues.
5. It requires orderly planning and coordination throughout the organization.
6. It establishes a system of management controls.
7. It serves as a public information system.

CONCEPTS OF BUDGETING

Concepts of budgeting can generally be plotted on a continuum ranging from very poor to outstanding. At the lower end of the scale are those methods presently used that are rooted in the historical development of educational budgeting as a closed, authoritarian, unresponsive, negative system with little planning evident. The upper end of the continuum expresses the emerging concepts of budgeting with their emphasis on educational planning and evaluation as the basis for budget development. For purposes of this discussion, the concepts included below contrast those judged to be obsolete for modern systems of education with those being utilized by the more innovative, dynamic school systems of the country.

Concepts of Budgeting Not Viable for Today's Needs

Mechanical Budget

The mechanical type of budget can be set forth on two sheets of paper, one presenting the estimated yearly receipts of an institution and the other showing how the money can be divided in order to run the school. Under this concept, budgeting is strictly a revenue-and-expenditure operation—a bookkeeping chore, required by law, which is feverishly pored over near the end of the year and then is quickly forgotten until the end of the next year. This type of budgeting forces expenditures to fit income expectations and pays no attention to needs. Any planning is negative, calculating what can be eliminated or what can be padded so that the budget will come out right. The main task of this type of budgeting is to keep costs at a minimum without regard for needs or educational improvements.

Yearly Budget

The yearly or periodic type of budget approach attempts to construct a school budget in a short (three- to four-week) period for presentation to the board of education and to the community. It is almost a refinement of the mechanical type in that it forces quick decisions on expenditures and revenues with little effort made to evaluate its impact. Decisions on staffing, salaries, programs, supplies, and services are often made without any consideration of educational needs or evolving educational opportunities. The object of the challenge is to get the budget document completed and approved before the deadline date. Mostly this concept attempts to adjust the previous year's document to include such items as pay increases, enlarged staff, and increased numbers of students and does not consider change in program, availability of new materials, differing needs, and emerging concepts. Once completed, this type of budget becomes a strait jacket with little opportunity provided for shifts in priority.

Administration-Dominated Budget

This concept views the development of the budget as strictly a responsibility of management. No help is asked or desired in making up the budget. The staff must take what they get as far as the budget is concerned. The central office gives the impression that budgeting is a very complex process with only the "chosen few" sufficiently sophisticated to participate. The prevailing philosophy seems to be that the fewer who know about the budget, the less will be the static, and the fewer the questions. Often value judgments are made without proper evaluation and with no options to affected persons. This "tight ship" approach has been symptomatic of authoritarian systems and has hastened the coming of our present era of negotiations, citizen involvement, and student awareness. While still in existence, it is dying and will not be an effective concept in the future.

Centralized Budget

This concept of budgeting treats all schools in a system as if they were only one. While it is a very efficient way of developing a budget, little consideration is permitted for differing needs among the various communities served. Allocations are made on a per-pupil basis with no attention given to existing resources or to any backlog of requests. Decisions concerning teacher-pupil ratio, supplies, materials, texts, curriculum, etc., are made at the central office and all schools must conform. This concept tends to treat the entire system as a homogeneous unit rather than recognize that even the smallest systems are most heterogeneous, made up of very diverse persons with unique needs, abilities, and capacities. The trend today is toward decentralization in order to permit schools to be relevant and responsive to the needs of a local area.

Concepts of Budgeting More Suited to Present and Future Educational Systems

Functional Budget

This concept of budget development requires that the planners attempt to determine the educational objectives of a school district as the first step in the budget process. Out of the objectives, the planners must then develop an educational plan suited to the school system. The educational plan is then translated into a budget for presentation to the community for reaction and adoption. Out of this usually comes a compromise between what people are willing to pay for and what the planners think is needed. It actually represents the best program of education the people of a community will buy at a particular time.

Under the functional approach, the budget committee considers the educational plan before it considers money. It translates the qualitative and quantitative aspects of the educational program into expenditures and then attempts to show the people what their needs are so they will provide the resources.

Continuous Budget

The concept of continuous budget development considers budgeting an integral part of daily operation. Immediately upon adoption of a budget, work starts the development of the next budget document. Strengths and weaknesses in the operation of the present budget are appraised and proposed budget plans are made. Educational plans are conceived on a long-range basis and hastily formulated educational programs are not considered. All program plans are developed in the context of proposed financing for implementation. With year-round budget development, various areas of the school can be better coordinated, and the board of education can be given time to consider an addition or deletion on the basis of educational merit as well as of cost. The continuous consideration of the budget is not an automatic operation; certain administrative devices must be used including: (a) scheduling discussions of the budget throughout the year at staff, teachers', and board meetings; (b) setting up "tickler" files around the system which prod people to think about and make suggestions concerning the budget; (c) establishing a calendar which distributes the various phases of budget making over a twelve-month basis; (d) requiring reports which force consideration of items that should be included in the budget.

Participatory Budget

This concept recognizes two basic principles. First, schools, being tax-supported institutions, must consult citizens in the planning process if they expect to obtain continued and expanding support. Second, persons who teach in a school and use its equipment and facilities should be given an opportunity to suggest procedures and materials that they believe would be most effective in carrying out the job.

Education is big business. It is the most important and largest undertaking of the United States. This is true if one is thinking of education as an investment to develop our human resources. It is not true if one has in mind school costs as compared with some other expenditures. As an example, public education expenditures for grades kindergarten through twelve are running about 3 percent of the gross national product and considerably less than the amount spent on autos, alcohol, and defense each year. However, public education is the largest governmental unit controlled and administered at the local-community level. People must be convinced of the desirability of a particular educational program before they will support it. By the same token, teachers must believe in and understand a plan before they will actively contribute to its success.

The participatory concept of budget development involves and provides for the interplay of the school staff and public representatives on the various levels of budget making. This process uses a combination of formal and informal methods to get involvement in budget development.

Teachers and other staff are asked to submit individual requests for needed supplies and equipment. In addition, staff participation on formal committees dealing with budget development is encouraged. Many schools also conduct staff hearings and in-service meetings on the budget.

Citizens are involved as members of advisory committees and study groups. The budget hearing is one of the best ways of keeping all citizens informed and of reporting committee findings.

Public sentiment in the long run will favor a clear unbiased presentation of the problem and an honest seeking for advice and suggestions.

Attempts to involve teachers, staff, and citizens often fail because of inadequate preplanning and a lack of role definition. Clear delineation of the advisory nature of the participants is important before any work is completed. However, all participants deserve to know the disposition of their proposals and the results of their efforts. Staff and citizen participation helps create a better understanding of education for the future and assists in giving direction and scope to budget development.

Decentralized Budget

This concept applies especially to large multiunit school systems. It is an effort to enable the large system to react to particular and unique needs as they are identified at a particular school. Each school in a system establishes individual budgets and establishes its own educational priorities within the parameters of the total system.

The decentralized budget, by its very nature, forces wider participation in budget development. Principals and teachers, working together, create a custom-made program. It stresses the individuality of each particular building and staff and breaks down the large district into units which are small enough to permit face-to-face planning and follow through.

The central office acts as the coordinating and guiding agency, establishing general guidelines, i.e., salary allocations, staff allocations, and so forth. Educational priorities and specific needs are established in the subunits, and resources are allocated according to these priorities. In well organized, decentralized systems, flexibility to react to needs as they are identified by local staff is a major strength. At the same time, overarching educational policy is established at the district level and educational goals are consistent throughout the system.

Perhaps the biggest advantage of a decentralized system is its ability to react quickly to unusual situations and needs. Budget flexibility in terms of supplies, equipment, and personnel allocation allows for a more viable system of education.

However, decentralization is not without danger. It tends to compartmentalize education in the community. Each school becomes a small kingdom within itself and cooperative efforts among and between schools can become difficult. Pressure groups may take over particular schools, and quality of education may vary significantly from school to school.

Therefore, the decision becomes one of planning decentralization so that certain functions are continued centrally. These include the setting of goals, the evaluation function, and the long-range planning function. In this way, a check and balance is provided as a framework for effective decentralization.

Evolution of the Planning, Programming, Budgeting Evaluation System (PPBES)

Some of the principles of the Planning, Programming, Budgeting, Evaluating System — PPBES — have been recognized in much of the writing by professional educators over a long period of time. Many times the principles were fragmented, and little attempt was made to make the total concept operational.

The essential aspects of PPBES are as follows:

1. A careful specification and a systematic analysis of objectives;
2. A search for the relevant alternatives, the different ways of achieving the objectives;
3. An estimate of the total costs of each alternative — both direct and indirect costs, both initial costs and those to which the alternatives commit us for future years, both dollar costs and those costs that cannot be measured in dollar terms;
4. An estimate of the effectiveness of each alternative, of how close it comes to satisfying the objective;
5. A comparison and analysis of the alternatives, seeking that combination of alternatives that promises the greatest effectiveness, for given resources, in achieving the objectives.

PPBES is not a panacea. It is not a substitute for the experience, the intuition, and the judgment of the educational planners. Its aim is to sharpen that intuition and judgment by stating problems more precisely, by discovering new alternatives, and by making explicit the comparison among alternatives.

Although computers may expedite PPBES, they are not the decision makers. Decisions will continue to come, as they should, from the educational planners and from the political process, influenced by value judgments; from the pressures coming from the various interested parties as well as from the process of systematic analysis. PPBES through systematic analysis seeks to aid the educational planner by being clearer and more explicit about objectives, assumptions, and facts; by trying to distinguish relevant issues from irrelevant ones; and by tracing out the costs and consequences of the alternatives, to the extent that these are knowable.

Computers and machinelike analysts cannot by highly abstract mathematical or economic techniques solve the value-laden problems of educational financing. However, these persons, machines, and techniques may make important contributions to the budgeting process.

PPBES and systematic analysis are not limited to cost accounting, or to economic consideration in the narrow sense. PPBES should not neglect a wide range of human factors and it should not attempt, naively, to measure those factors that are really unmeasurable. Wherever relevant, quantitative estimates are to be encouraged. Good systematic analysis does not try to assign numbers to every element of a problem, does not ignore the intangible, does not rule out subjective evaluation and the appropriate use of judgment. On the contrary, the very name PPBES reminds us that the question of who benefits and whom it costs is a question involving values as well as analysis.

The term "program budgeting" is not equivalent, in this context, to PPBES. Program accounting and program budgeting are basic conceptual elements of a PPBES but are limited to accounting and budgeting systems emphasizing categorization schemes by programs. The primary distinctive characteristics of PPBES as defined by Hatry and Cotton are:

1. It focuses on identifying the fundamental objectives of the government [education] system and then relating all activities, regardless of organizational placement, to these.
2. Future year implications are explicitly considered.
3. All pertinent costs are considered — including capital costs as noncapital costs, and associated support costs (such as employee benefits, associated vehicle and building maintenance costs) as well as direct costs.
4. Systematic analysis of alternatives is undertaken. This characteristic is the crux of PPBES. It involves: (a) identification of the governmental [educational] objectives; (b) explicit, systematic identification of alternative ways

of carrying out the objectives; (c) estimation of the total implications of each alternative; (d) estimation of the expected results of each alternative; and (e) presentation of resulting major costs and benefit tradeoffs among the alternatives along with the identification of major assumptions and uncertainties.[1]

Dr. Selma Mushkin, Director of the State-Local Finances Project of George Washington University, outlines the following system requirements in the preparation for implementing a PPBES:

1. Clarifying and specifying the ultimate goals or objectives of each activity for which a government (educational institution) budgets money.
2. Gathering like activities into comprehensive categories or programs designed to achieve the specified objectives.
3. Examining as a continuous process how well each activity or program has done — its effectiveness.
4. Analyzing proposed improvements or new program proposals to see how effective they may be in achieving program goals.
5. Formulating a plan, based in part on the analysis of proposed cost and effectiveness, that leads to implementation through the budget.[2]

Five major categories of data must be developed in order to estimate, evaluate, and report within the multiyear framework of a PPBES system. They pertain to (a) pupils, (b) programs, (c) personnel, (d) facilities, and (e) finances.

Pupil Data

It has been pointed out that one of the major ingredients of PPBES is program evaluation. The criteria developed in each district to evaluate programs will vary and may include not only classroom test results, but other pupil statistics such as dropout rate, college entry rate, job entry rate, or return-to-school rate. The school districts implementing PPBES will find it necessary to record in a consistent format such statistics and report these statistics in specific time frames and against specific programs.

[1] H. P. Hatry and J. F. Cotton. *Program Planning for State. County. City* (Washington. D.C.: State-Local Finances Project of the George Washington University. 1967). p. 15.
[2] George Washington University State-Local Finances Project, *Planning Programming. Budgeting for City State County Objectives,* PPB Notes-8 (1967), p. 1.

The districts should also be prepared to utilize these statistics in the preparation of new programs, as well as in the evaluation of current programs, and to maintain such statistics for long periods of time to develop behavior patterns, trend reports, and long-range pupil-need evaluations.

In the multiyear financial planning portions of PPBES, the districts will find it necessary to project pupil enrollment data, not only in numbers of students, but also in socioeconomic changes within the community.

Program Data

Goals, objectives, evaluation criteria, and program memoranda pertaining to each individual program operating in the school district must be recorded, stored, and reported for the successful operation of a school district PPBES. This is true for both the educational program (i.e., math, English, social studies), as well as the special programs (counseling, career guidance and ancillary services, transportation, maintenance, custodial).

Personnel Data

At least two major clusters of information on school district employees are required by a PPBES system: payroll information and assignment information.

Within the PPBES framework, a district may choose to distribute the first-grade teachers' pay to several different first-grade programs, while charging all of the kindergarten teachers' salary to a single preschool program. For a high school Spanish teacher who works two periods a day as a counselor, who is also assigned as an assistant football coach three months of the school year, and who teaches driver training on Saturdays, specific portions of this teacher's salary must be prorated to the Spanish program, the counseling program, the athletic program, and the driver training program. The allocation of personnel assignments and costing are a necessary part of PPBES.

Facilities Data

The expenses involved in the operation of each school district facility must be recorded by specific facility in order to accommodate the reporting requirements of a PPBES system. This will require the development of location and sublocation codes and the assignment of these codes to such items as inventory supplies, equipment, custodial and overhead costs, maintenance projects, and construction projects in the school district.

Financial Data

In addition to the program-oriented budgeting and accounting, the traditional (and often state-mandated) line item budgeting and accounting should be maintained by responsible levels (school districts, subdistricts, buildings), funds, and functional areas as long as they are required. It should be emphasized that in order to preserve data comparability for state, federal, and local analysis by existing functions—such as instruction, administration, and transportation—budgets can be cast by line item within the function format and in a program format.

A caution should be inserted here to allay the fears of educators who are unfamiliar with school fiscal affairs. Accounting, enriched by cost accounting and budgeting, is crucial for the successful operation of PPBES, but it is merely a tool of the organization, not the end. Educational decision makers must guard against forming conclusions about instructional activities solely on the basis of costs. Costs must be weighed against benefits and values held by citizens for the development of their children.

Procedure

While PPBES is not a step-by-step procedure per se, we shall, for the purpose of illustration, use a step-by-step approach in further describing PPBES (see figure 7.1).

Step 1. State measurable objectives and measurable planned accomplishments for a given school thrust, program, subject area, courses, and activities over a specified period of time—possibly five years.

Step 2. Assign priorities to the various objectives and planned accomplishments of the school.

Step 3. Determine alternative plans for achieving the objectives expressed in step 1 above. Alternative plans would be expressed in terms of inputs and processes over a specified time span.

Examples of inputs are: staff, including the number of paraprofessional and professional, and level of preparation, experience, staff mix; pupil-teacher ratio; number and types of learning facilities, learning resources, curricula, etc.

Examples of processes are: instructional methodology, length of periods and school day, research and development, in-service training, assignment of teachers, etc.

Step 4. Assign a dollar estimate to the various alternative plans based upon the inputs and processes of those plans. Remember the dollar amounts would be expressed over a possible five-year period.

Step 5. Select within dollar constraints those alternative plans that appear to foster efficient and effective accomplishment of the predetermined objectives.

Step 6. Place the system in operation, that is, the inputs and processes that have been determined and budgeted.

Step 7. Analyze and evaluate the outputs of the school, thrusts, programs, subject areas, courses, and activities. Follow-

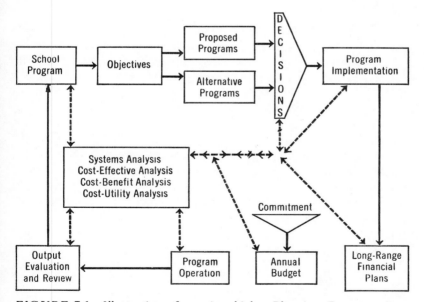

FIGURE 7.1   Illustration of way in which a Planning, Programming, Budgeting, Evaluating System (PPBES) might work. The process is continuous, cyclical, and requires feedback into all parts of the system.

ing evaluation, it may be necessary to change the inputs and processes in order that next year's budget can better achieve the objectives set forth.

Step 8. Review the stated objectives set forth in step 1. This review could result in changing the previously stated objectives, reordering the priorities assigned to previously stated objectives, or continuing to utilize the previously stated objectives and their respective priorities.

Step 9. Review and prepare continuously alternative plans (inputs and processes) in search of a more efficient and effective means for achieving the stated objectives.

Step 10. Return to step 3 and restart the cycle.

The selection of program alternatives is no less promising in its potential payoff at the school district level than at state and federal levels, but to date there is little application of PPBES among school districts throughout the nation. This is caused by (1) the lack of specific knowledge of the PPBES, its associated techniques, and its potential rewards on the part of most school administrators, and (2) the shortage of qualified analysts and selected personnel to design, implement, and operate a successful PPBES.

Categorizing proposed expenditures by object or character is probably the most uninformative way the human mind can conceive to show what government agencies really propose to do with the money they hope to get from legislators. One learns nothing of the work to be undertaken from a listing of proposed salaries, transportation, educational equipment and supplies, operation, maintenance, communication, or other objects of expenditure. The significant thing for the citizen and his school board representatives is the knowledge of what is to be served by them, what plans are a part of the permanent program of departments, what new plans are being undertaken for contractions or expansions of services involving such objects. If a government budget is regarded as a prospectus for the sale of certain services to the public, then most jurisdictions today are playing a guessing game with the citizen-financier so long as they continue merely to show objects of expenditure.

Program budgeting, which involves the activity classification of proposed expenditures, is designed to remedy this defect by showing the public what services and benefits it is purchasing. Emphasis, however, is on the doing of certain tasks rather than the buying of certain items with which to do the tasks. An administrative management concept is introduced into the direction of many activities from which it was previously absent. Budget execution in the form of follow-up to ensure that departments are actually doing what they said they would do when requesting their budget is an essential step in program budgeting procedures.

Analytical Process

This is an integral part of the PPBES. The primary objective of analytical effort is to systematically examine alternative courses of action in terms of benefit and cost with a view to clarifying the relevant choices (and their implications) open to the decision makers in a certain problem area.

In terms of the types of problems encountered in the total budgeting process, perhaps one might think of a wide spectrum ranging all the way from the most major allocation decisions on the one hand, to progress reporting and control on the other. Major allocative decisions involve such questions as should more resources be employed in different educational programs, police protection, welfare and health programs, or in preservation and development of natural resources and control of pollution? Ideally, the decision makers would like to allocate resources in the future so that for a given budget, the estimated marginal return in each major area of application would be equal. But this is more easily said than done; and at the current state of analytical art, no one really knows with any precision how the "grand optimum" might be attained. In the main, the analytical tools now available—particularly the quantitative ones—are only partially helpful in dealing directly with such problems. Intuition and judgment are still of major importance.

At the other end of the spectrum—progress reporting and control—the main problem is to keep track of programs where the major decisions have already been made, to try to detect impending difficulties as programs are being implemented, and to initiate remedial action through a feedback mechanism when programs are deemed likely to get out of control in the future. Numerous techniques are available for dealing with these types of program—management problems. Examples, explained more fully in other chapters, are as follows: financial and management accounting techniques; network-type systems for planning, scheduling, reporting, and controlling progress; critical-path methods (within the framework of a network-type system); plus many others.

The Budget Process

The educational plan is the starting point. The school budget is the educational plan translated into dollars. The school budget can be conceptualized as an equilateral triangle with the educational program as the base and expenditures and revenues as the other two legs (see figure 7.2). If any one of the three sides is shortened, the other two must also be shortened. Only when the three sides meet is there a budget document.

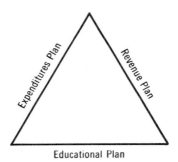

Educational Plan

FIGURE 7.2

For many, the budget may be seen as both a needs and a working budget. In the needs budget, program costs are projected as if all educational needs are to be met. The working budget is the final document drawn according to educational priorities and will serve as the financial plan throughout the year.

More specifically, the needs budget calls for cooperatively defined educational plans, both short and long range. The development should involve the staff and community and be initiated at the building level under broad guidelines established by the central office administration. The educational needs must be translated into financial terms. As the community and staff gain experience in this type of activity the level of sophistication in budget development increases. Important considerations in the development of a needs budget are:

1. Special programs
2. Innovations
3. Staff increases
4. Salary adjustments
5. Operations and maintenance
6. Fixed costs
7 Supplies, equipment requests

A further step in the development of the needs budget is the determination of resources needed to meet the budget. The total spectrum of local, state, and federal sources must be considered. Decisions should be made as to the disposition of the budget. Plans should be made for staff and community involvement in the important step of budget appraisal.

The working budget is really a further refinement of the needs budget. The needs budget is more idealistic, in that it lacks the realistic parameters that surround the working budget. The working budget calls for the establishment of program priorities. Again the staff and community are involved. Costing must be developed for each level of priority. Determination of the level of support from each source must be figured. At this stage the working budget can be established. This should include appropriate documentation throughout. Approval by the board of education is absolutely necessary, but approval by the community is also desired. Again, plans for involvement in budget appraisal would be desirable.

The Budget Calendar

July 1	Budget year begins.
October 1	Quarterly revision – to incorporate accurate revenue and enrollment figures (present budget).
November	Population (enrollment) projections.
	Staff needs projections.
	Program changes and addition projections.
	Facilities needs projection.
December	Staff requisitions – supplies.
	Capital outlay preliminary requests.

January 1	Budget revisions (present budget).
January	Central staff sessions on needs.
	Maintenance and operations requests.
February	Rough draft of needs budget.
March	Meet with staffs and principals to establish priorities.
	Citizens committees' reports and review.
	Central staff and board of education budget sessions.
April 1	Budget revision (present budget).
April	Working budget draft.
	Meet with staff and community groups to revise working budget.
May	Final draft of working budget.
June	Budget hearings and adoption of working budget.

Cost-Utility

The essential features of cost-utility analysis are to formulate numerical utility values for specific activities and also formulate specific cost factors with those same activities. Thereby one can derive cost-utility ratios and make decisions regarding selection from alternatives based on the relative size of the cost-utility ratios.

As the emphasis upon education as an investment in human resources has increased in recent years, so too has the attitude toward obtaining and allocating resources in order to optimize their utilization. During the previous decade new uses regarding the budgetary process have come into existence. The trend is to view the budget as a dynamic, flexible instrument which encourages adaptation to an evolving society. Long-range planning is encouraged because of this increased emphasis upon flexibility.

Analyzing, planning, controlling, appraising, and evaluating are processes of educational budgeting. The advantages of program budgeting over former methods of budgeting are to provide a framework for more clearly defined alternatives among which choices must be made and to create an information system that will assist in measuring cost in relation to accomplishments.

Fisher has listed the following as major characteristics of cost-utility.

1. The fundamental characteristic is a systematic examination and comparison of alternative courses of action that

might be taken to achieve specified objectives for some future time period.

2. Critical examination of alternatives typically involves numerous considerations; but the two main ones are assessment of the costs (in the sense of economic resource costs) and the utility (the benefits or gains) pertaining to each of the alternatives being compared to obtain the stipulated objectives.

3. The time contracts are in the future (off in the distant future five, ten, or more years).

4. Because of the extended time horizon, the environment is one of uncertainty (very often a great uncertainty).

5. Usually the context in which the analysis takes place is broad (often very broad) and the environment very complex with numerous interactions between the key variables and the problem.

6. While quantitative methods of analysis should be used as much as possible because of items 4 and 5 above, purely quantitative work must often be heavily supplemented by qualitative analysis.

7. Usually the focus is on research and development and/or investment-type decision problems, although operational decisions are sometimes encountered.[3]

Williams has delineated a number of valid precautions for those who base educational policy decisions on cost-utility analysis. Included among these are:

1. Although costs of educating one student one year can be described in general terms by use of averages, one could not adequately understand the activities of an institution, or administer or support an institution by the use of such average costs alone.

2. There are so many variations in the factors affecting costs that comparisons of average costs, with implied meanings for efficiency of operation without consideration of quality, become of highly questionable value.

3. Statements of average costs of instruction are simple numerical descriptions of an operation. They may stimulate study of an instructional process but they should not control the process.

4. High costs in a given instructional area are not sufficient cause alone to abandon the educational program. Any

[3]G. H. Fisher, "The Role of Cost-Utility Analysis in Program Budgeting," in *Program Budgeting: Program Analysis and Federal Budget*, D. Novick, ed. (Cambridge, Mass.: Harvard University Press, 1965), pp. 37–8.

curriculum with a small enrollment will have high unit costs. . . . These facts do not alter the necessity for training people in urgently needed specialities.[4]

A cost-utility approach involves four distinct steps:

1. Careful delineation of the objectives
2. Stipulation of various ways of achieving the objectives
3. A cost-utility analysis of the various alternatives
4. Selection of the most appropriate alternatives based upon systematic analysis.

Emphasis throughout is based upon interrelatedness of the many parts and how those parts contribute to the total operating system. Stated another way, analyses are made of the programs and activities currently underway in the school system. A coding scheme is derived for the basic elements which become the building blocks for activities and programs. In addition, determination is made by element regarding the costs and utilities of the program and activities.

The basic formula for a cost-utility analysis (see figure 7.3) is given by $U(A_1)p_1 + U(A_2)p_2 + \ldots + U(An)p_n$, where $U(A) =$ utility of A, $U(A_1) =$ utility of A_1, and $p_1 =$ probability of A_1. The additive property of utility theory is essential to the formulation of utility numbers which are to be associated with the activities and programs because the utilities are built upon elements. The utility of a program will read as follows: $U(A) = U(E_1)p_1 + U(E_2)p_2 + \cdots + U(En)p_n$. The utility numbers will be based on the basic elements and can be utilized in terms of elements, activities, or programs. This can be used in determining whether we should go to contracted or board-owned buses, board-operated custodial programs or contracted custodial services, cooperative purchasing for several districts rather than purchasing by single districts, plus many other uses.

Cost-utility analysis is a macrolevel analysis. It is most difficult to measure and is also very expensive because it calls for sophisticated measurement and longitudinal studies. Data processing is imperative to handle the management information system necessary for cost-utility analysis.

---

[4]R. L. Williams, "Cost of Educating One College Student," *Educational Record*, 29 (Oct., 1961), pp. 327–28.

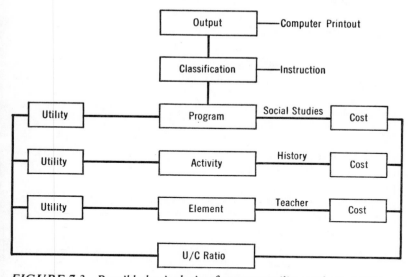

FIGURE 7.3 Possible basic design for a cost-utility analysis. (Adopted from Richard H. P. Kraft in Cost Effectiveness Analysis of Vocational-Technical Education Programs *[Tallahassee, Fla.: Florida Department of Education, 1969], p. 27; reprinted with the permission of the Florida Department of Education, Tallahassee, Florida.)*

Benefit-Cost Analysis

Benefit-cost analysis has generally been defined as an analytical approach to solving problems of choice that requires the definition of objectives and indentification of alternatives and that yields the greatest benefits for any given costs, or yields a required or determined amount of benefits for the least costs.

This form of analysis can be used in two ways: (1) to determine the worth of planned projects, and (2) to determine the benefits which have accrued to a project previously initiated. Generally the benefit-cost ratio is considered as the ratio of present value of future benefits to the present value of future costs. Because of this the decision rules are obvious (1) if the benefit-cost ratio for a program is less than one, in which case the program should not be considered (with the exception of a program in which the intangible objectives cannot be adequately weighted in monetary terms); and (2) when comparing alternative programs, in which case the higher ratio is associated with the more desirable program.

This intermediate form of analysis evaluates programs in terms of their objectives. Benefits unrelated to objectives are not considered benefits; these by-products are referred to as spill-overs. This type of analysis would seem supplementary to cost-effectiveness. However, a program may be quite effective yet not meet the necessary requirements of its objectives; thus, cost-benefit analysis is quite essential. The goal is to choose the program that allows the maximum benefits for the least cost or similar cost. At all times benefits should exceed costs: $C/B < 1$. Measurement criteria for the benefits must be specified in advance and in terms of program objectives. Cost-benefit analysis will probably be of the most use to the educational planner and the economist.

Davie suggests that benefit-cost analysis is particularly applicable in the evaluation of public education expenditure programs due to the time element involved. He feels that the application of this procedure to individual students certainly was appropriate. Individual benefits would be the present value of future additional earnings after taxes. The student would have two types of costs: direct and opportunity. The program with the highest ratio would be the logical choice, provided the student goal was oriented toward economic return.

The benefit-cost formula for the individual participants in a one-year program was:

$$B_j = \frac{\sum_{t=1}^{N} \dfrac{R_{t_j}}{(1 + i_j)t}}{O_j + C_j}$$

N = number of years over which additional income is expected.

R_{t_j} = additional income net of taxes in year t expected by individual j to accrue as a result of completing a program of vocational education.

i_j = rate of interest used by individual j to discount expected future additional income.

O_j = opportunity costs as seen by individual j.

C_j = direct costs of program to individual j.[5]

[5] Bruce F. Davie "Using Benefit-Cost Analysis in Planning and Evaluating Vocational Education," (Paper prepared for Davis S. Bushnell, Director, Division of Adult and Vocational Research, Bureau of Research, U.S. Office of Education, 1965), pp. 7–19.

Formulas can be generated for determining cost-benefit ratios from a societal point of view, alternative programs of study, and many others. General limitations of cost-benefit analysis are as follows:

1. The failure of the procedure to deal with nonmonetary returns.
2. The difficulty of establishing the comparative value of similar monetary sums for different people.
3. The failure of the analysis to necessarily identify the best possible program.
4. The lack of adjustment for where students will find employment.
5. The intangible nature of many costs and benefits which often does not permit the calculation of a ratio which is comparable to the unity rule.
6. Ratios of projects that are comparable only if the cost elements are similar in scope.
7. The tendency to inflate benefits and make ultraconservative estimates of costs.

Cost-Effectiveness Analysis

The purpose of cost-effectiveness analysis is to aid the decision maker in choosing among feasible alternatives on a basis of least cost and greatest effectiveness. While cost-benefit is a pre-programming process, cost-effectiveness analysis is primarily a postevaluation technique. Cost-effectiveness, therefore, should be considered a tool for microanalysis. It appears that the information generated by this analysis will be of the most value to the educational administrator. This technique should answer such questions as: (1) How effective has our program been? (2) How could it be better? (3) What were our failures? Some suggested ratios for educational programs are:

1. $\text{Effectiveness Ratio} = \dfrac{\text{Actual Output/Time Period}}{\text{Planned Output/Time Period}}$

This formula will show clearly whether or not targets were reached. It is commonly agreed that program effectiveness should be determined by analysis of outputs achieved compared to planned outputs.

2. Effectiveness Ratio $= \dfrac{\text{Standard Cost/Unit of Output}}{\text{Actual Cost/Unit of Output}}$

If we are to engage in reasonably intelligent planning we must consider variances. This ratio is an expression of overall variance.

Much of the educational analytic process has been concentrated upon the costs of education, especially earnings foregone and potential higher incomes due to benefits derived from additional education. An investigation of this concentration on dollar amounts reveals this as a factor that has great influence upon such analysis. It is relatively easy to obtain the input costs to education, the tax load, the bonds sold, and contributions from the public and industry. Also, there is little difficulty in determining the short- and long-term financial returns to the studies as a result of certain amounts and types of education. The difficult measure is with personal and social outcomes, with effective domain development, and with benefits to society as a whole.

In summary, program planning budget system is perhaps the first serious attempt at scientifically measuring product as an important criterion in budget development. Its refinement will force educators to more clearly define and establish measurable goals in order to justify inputs. While much research must still be completed, program planning budget system is a very intriguing and promising budgetary concept that will force greater sophistication in budget development.

SUMMARY

Long-range fiscal planning and the establishment of goals for future programs are a logical outgrowth of budgeting. The natural extension of this, in turn, is the development of better educational program plans and the synthesis of these plans into broad fiscal plans. These plans, because they are based on educational programs, will strengthen and unify the budget process. When these activities are accomplished, not only will school system operations be much more comprehensible, there will be a meaningful basis and systematic techniques for planning, reviewing, modifying, and carrying out educational programs. This, we think, will help both the superintendent and the school board to weigh the value and effectiveness of educational programs, and to balance and decide upon the essential policy alternatives available to them. It will also help interested citizens to understand and evaluate the services their school system provides.

SUGGESTED ACTIVITIES

1.   Develop a budget calendar that would allow involvement by community staff and student body but still meet proper time sequence for each of the budget steps.

2.   Develop a line item and programmatic type of budget for some phase of the school program. How would each type of these cost allocations lend itself to program-cost analysis?

3.   Develop a cost-benefit analysis for some phase of the educational program with which you are most familiar.

4.   Design a cost-effectiveness analysis for some segment of the educational program.

5.   Relate the utilization of budget building to a community information program or system.

SELECTED READINGS

Catanese, Anthony J., and Alan W. Steiss. *Systemic Planning: Theory and Application.* Lexington, Mass.: Heath Lexington Books, 1970.

Churchman, C. West. *The Systems Approach.* New York: The Delacorte Press, 1968.

Davis, James W., Jr., ed. *Politics, Programs, and Budgets: A Reader in Government Budgeting.* Englewood Cliffs, N.J.: Prentice-Hall, 1969.

Hatry, H. P., and Cotton, J. F. *Program Planning for State, County, City.* Washington, D.C.: State-Local Finances Project of the George Washington University, 1967.

Gerwin, Donald. *Budgeting Public Funds: The Decision Process in an Urban School District.* Madison: University of Wisconsin Press, 1969.

Golomiewski, Robert T., ed. *Public Budgeting and Finance: Readings in Theory and Practice.* Itasca, Ill.: F. E. Peacock Publishers, Inc., 1968.

Knezevich, Stephen J., ed. *Administrative Technology and the School Executive.* Washington, D.C.: American Association of School Administrators, 1969.

Ovsiew, Leon and Castetter, William B. *Budgeting for Better Schools.* Englewood Cliffs, N.J.: Prentice-Hall, Inc., 1960.

Piele, Philip K., Eidell, Terry L., and Smith, Stuart C., eds. *Social and Technological Change: Implications for Education.* Eugene, Ore.: The Center for the Advanced Study of Educational Administration, 1970.

Schultze, Charles L. *The Politics and Economics of Public Spending.* Washington, D.C.: Brookings Institutions, 1968.

PLANNING FOR PERSONNEL ADMINISTRATION

PHILOSOPHICAL AND THEORETICAL FOUNDATIONS

An integral part of classified personnel administration is the establishment of and adoption by the board of a philosophy undergirding its application within the school district. This philosophy must include such elements as: selection, retention, and promotion of classified staff based on ability; establishment of detailed job descriptions; implementation of the principles of human relations in dealing with staff members; provisions for an equitable salary and fringe benefit package; and the establishment of an appeals procedure for employees.

The planning function provides the key for the development of an effective and efficient plan for administering classified personnel in any school district. Proper attention is often not provided for classified personnel due to lack of understanding of their role in an organization dominated by certified employees. Classified personnel, ranging from custodians to accountants, provide a major challenge to the school business administrator who often assumes major responsibility for the administration of this phase of personnel administration in the district.

Several years ago F. W. Taylor pointed to the fact that human variability and performance could be used to discover better ways of doing work.[1] In no other place in the district office is this difference more obvious than in dealings with those personnel administered through the office of the school business administrator.

It is here that technically oriented persons who are working with clerically oriented persons and supervisors of skilled and nonskilled persons must come together to discuss and work out common problems. For example, personnel from sections reporting directly to the school business administrator, such as operations and plant maintenance, data processing, and accounting, are of such different backgrounds and varying interests that personnel administration often taxes the most ardent advocate of better human relations.

The school business administrator generally works with classified (noncertificated) personnel in the district while certificated personnel administration is carried out through the office of the assistant superintendent for personnel or by the superintendent in small systems. Office management is another key role of the school business administrator in his own area of responsibility. He may also be responsible for selection of clerical personnel in individual schools, although the building principal will supervise them.

In order to meet more properly the demands of the diverse types of staff members who are associated with the school business administrator's operation, a plan for the classification of the personnel is a logical outgrowth of the adoption of the philosophy of personnel administration by the district. The classification plan should provide for activities in the areas of recruitment, selection, orientation, in-service training, evaluation, promotion, and termination for all classified employees. The classification plan serves the system in such ways as the grouping of similar duties and responsibilities in common classes, which allows for recruitment and examination processes to be simplified through the use of common plans for performance tests; through the use of the same benefit packages, and through the use of common evaluations built around the class of descriptions.

Relationship to Subordinates and Superiors

The general line-and-staff organizational chart of any school district will show the formal subordinate-superior relationship

---

[1] Rensis Likert. *New Patterns of Management* (New York: McGraw-Hill Book Company, 1961). p. 3.

existing in the organization but will often fail to show the actual organizational operating procedures for the system or the so-called informal organizational structure. It is imperative that the proper superior-subordinate relationship be established and that these be established in terms of the district's operational goals. Ability to do the job, as well as to relate to other persons, is of importance in selecting staff applicants, but the weight of each often needs to be considered in specific instances within a district.

A major application of the use of human relations tools can be found in the area of administration of classified personnel. Concern for the individual can be exhibited while ensuring a smooth operation of the system. Mutual perceptions of the definition of a job and consensus decisions relative to job expectations can serve as a major area for integration of human relations tools into the planning role for classified personnel administration.

PERSONNEL PLANNING AND RECRUITMENT

Job Analysis

It is in this area that the school business administrator can be of greatest assistance to the total school district. Nothing needs a detailed analysis more than the general question of what transpires in a school district from the local school through to the operations at the central office. It is imperative that each district constantly reevaluate the requirements and responsibilities of each particular job within the school district. This will enable a procedure to be established for consistent revision and growth within the area of job analyses.

Job Descriptions

A detailed, explanatory job description is a must for each specific position within a school district. For example, a key punch operator's job description is no less important than the job description for the data processing manager, the school business administrator, or the superintendent. Certain job descriptions will be more routine, more easily established, and involve fewer nebulous statements than will others. However, it must be realized that all job descriptions must be as detailed as possible and must be written in such a manner that the interviewer and the interviewee are able to evaluate the requirements of the position.

Job descriptions are developed from a job analysis which details the specific activities, responsibilities, and requirements of a certain position. These guidelines include skills necessary (60 words per minute, operates IBM 300/65 computer), types of responsibility (plans and administers building department budget), and limitations imposed by the job (stands for eight-hour shift, third-shift time, lifts over fifty pounds). The more detailed the job description, the fewer are the problems generally associated with the determination of whether a prospective employee fits. Job descriptions vary for areas, but the Dictionary of Occupational Titles service is a handy general reference. Following is the DOT's job description for "Superintendent, Building."

> SUPERINTENDENT, BUILDING (any ind.) [see Janitor].
> —— (any ind.) II. 187.168. building-service supervisor; custodian; manager, building. Directs operation and maintenance of buildings, such as apartment houses or office buildings: Hires, trains, and supervises building personnel, such as maintenance men, elevator operators, and guards. Plans sequence of maintenance work. Inspects property and confers with subordinates to determine condition of property, and alterations or repairs required. Determines work that can be performed by building personnel or obtains bids from contractors. Prepares construction specifications or plans, obtaining advice from engineering consultants. Assembles and analyzes contract bids. Submits bids and recommendations to superiors. Supervises contracted projects to verify adherence to specifications. Purchases building and maintenance supplies, machinery, equipment, and furniture. Plans and administers bui ding department budget.[2]

The final make-up of a job description can be influenced by the results of union agreements or civil service contracts in effect within the district. In areas of high unionization, the slightest alteration in a job description will require union agreement or at least be a subject for negotiation at the time of the next bargaining session. Until that time, the job description will have to remain unchanged.

[2]*Dictionary of Occupational Titles.* vol. I: Definitions of Titles. 3rd ed. (Washington. D.C.: U.S. Government Printing Office. 1965).

Personnel Selection

Supply and demand often influence personnel selection. The cliché "Select the best man for the job" is certainly not wrong, nor is it to be cast aside. It may be better to leave a position unfilled than to fill it with an improperly trained person or a person with a poor or unrealistic attitude toward the job or the world of work in general. No effort should be spared to select competent personnel and to compensate these personnel adequately for each job within the school district. Personnel selection procedures should be detailed and available for review as a part of general school board policy and procedures. In several states, laws have been adopted which require that certain city school districts secure clerical personnel from approved civil service lists. These lists are constructed from test results and personnel records for use by all governmental units. This brings about uniformity of pay scale across all agencies and is generally combined with a detailed employee classification structure.

An active recruitment program in a district where civil service lists are not available is a useful procedure for securing top candidates for classified positions. Advertising, working closely with state employment agencies, and securing the best of system-trained personnel are the three ways of securing top-level classified personnel. A budget item for recruitment should be allowed, and an active plan for securing top personnel should be ongoing.

Nothing is more damaging to a school district's reputation than to have the board of education dabbling in personnel selection, recruitment, and/or retention of staff members rather than setting policies for these activities. Once again the school business administrator should exert whatever professional influence he can to be certain that proper personnel policies are established at the board of education level and that proper personnel selection is carried out within his own department.

Orientation

Job orientation is a key element in the success of any employment program. Proper instructions, job descriptions, and job analyses all give the newly hired staff member a way to orient himself to what is expected and required of him so that he may be successful in his position. An organization of any size should have a detailed orientation program. A specific plan should be implemented to introduce the new employee to the various functions of the organization. This will give the person a *feel* for who does what, why it is done, and how this fits into the overall operation of an effective school district. It is imperative that the orientation program be developed to such an extent that the person is made to feel important as a viable part of the organization, rather than "just a certain person at a certain desk in a certain row."

Material covered in an orientation session includes information on employee welfare, such as the district's fringe benefit package, insurance, sick leave and/or maternity policy, vacation schedules, and medical and hospital benefits. Additional points to be covered include job-related information on promotion policy, grievance procedures, and the manner in which jobs are classified and defined. Detailed information as to the nature of the specific position being filled and its role in the system should be offered. Since many classified positions are filled as opened, rather than in large groups, a checklist covering these would be a valuable resource for the school business administrator.

For example, on a predetermined schedule, new employees could be introduced to the directors of the various sections through which their work passes. An explanation of the flow of work through the district would be invaluable. Special attention should be given to identifying the first person in each area to be contacted in the event of a special problem. An overall look at the goals and objectives of the district through its various programs, as well as the specific responsibilities of the particular section where the employee is assigned, would be an excellent way of initiating district loyalty and a feeling of being a part of the larger picture.

Personnel Development

As important as personnel planning and recruitment are to the overall development of an effective program within a school district, the development of employees once they are members of the organization is even more significant. The expenditures which are made on staff selection, orientation, and recruitment can be wasted if an effective developmental program is not established for the total school district and for those specific areas considered a part of school business management. Within the area of school business management, many people will function in a multitude of ways. These ways can be reinforced through employee in-service training or additional structured course work, through motivational experiences, through proper use of supervision, through the effective implementation of evaluation procedures, and through proper overall personnel supervision.

In-Service Training

In-service training, while as old as the concept of the professional teacher, continually plagues the school district in the selection of meaningful and rewarding experiences for its employees. In-service programs are generally planned for the central office professional personnel and the teaching staffs of school districts but are often overlooked for nonprofessional and technical personnel. In-service training or, more properly, staff renewal (given the proper philosophical and managerial foundations) can be quite useful in upgrading skills and developing knowledges which staff members lack when they come to an organization. For example, in-service training programs for a technical person might involve participation in manufacturers' training seminars or in local technical school courses. Released time may be provided for attendance of these functions and incremental pay schedules may be based on completion of certain predetermined courses or experiences. Clerical-level personnel could participate in in-service education programs directed primarily at use of newly installed or purchased equipment, familiarization with new office procedures, or improvement of staff-public relations through proper answering of the telephone, questions or requests for information. For example, the very apex of a secretarial in-service program might be the encouragement to prepare for and take the Certified Professional Secretaries examination. Whether specific prerequisites for every step of upgrading staff can be identified as precisely as those for the CPS is questionable, but staff members can be given rewarding and meaningful experiences when some thought and preparation are involved in their selection.

It is, of course, important that the staff members be involved with the school business administrator and his subordinate personnel within the division in determining those areas for staff in-service or staff renewal activities. Current employees may have the expertise to conduct certain classes or demonstrate the use of certain types of equipment. It is not unusual to pull selected personnel from other divisions within the school system to give meaningful presentations in the staff renewal process. Cost and time considerations may also be facilitated by the use of in-house personnel.

Employee Motivation

The area of employee motivation concerns all administrative personnel. A school business administrator is concerned not only with the day-to-day operations of his division, but also with the efficient and effective operation of that division in relation to staff motivation to do the job. Motivation is directly tied to good personnel practices. For example, most employees work more efficiently if predetermined, established goals are set within each job description and when basic procedures for accomplishing these are established. More specifically, if a list of available staff renewal opportunities, insurance and other fringe benefits, educational opportunities, and policies on coffee breaks and lunch hours are written, detailed, and developed from a cooperative base for administrative and staff positions, most persons function more effectively.

Motivation is also enhanced by the existence of salary increments based on predetermined and established criteria. To have established goals and to have responsibilities where assumption of these can be rewarded in terms of positional authority or financial remuneration are important to almost all employees. Small increments, awarded frequently, are generally more effectively used with clerical- and technical-level persons than are yearly increments, which are awarded to professional level personnel.

Personnel Supervision

There is little question that supervision is necessary for all employees, whether it be specific and direct ongoing supervision or whether it be supervision reflected in the general personnel policies of the organization. The supervision of any staff position is directly related to staff evaluation and, therefore, staff retention and/or termination. Insofar as possible, supervision should be a direct, responsive part of the organization in which the lines of supervision are open for two-way communication. Supervision is more effective when both parties are informed of the boundaries of the supervision and the person responsible. While supervision is distasteful to many professional-level personnel, it is essential in establishing an effective and well-ordered program.

Staff Evaluation

All staff members are evaluated at periodic intervals. Much staff member evaluation occurs on a day-to-day basis, is informal, and is nonstructured. However, any well-structured organization will have predetermined patterns for the evaluation of staff members. Whether evaluation takes the form of interviews, rating sheets, tests, or a combination of several of these, it must be done on a periodic and established basis.

Any attempt at staff evaluation should be a cooperative venture. Under no circumstances should staff evaluations be construed to be a "witch-hunt" procedure in which a supervisor is looking for fault with a staff member's performance. As with student evaluation, the goal is to determine areas of strength to build upon and areas of weakness to try to eliminate. One of the best ways to establish an evaluation policy is to provide within the policy for some degree of self-evaluation. This will provide an opportunity for each employee to look at himself seriously and give him an opportunity to predetermine areas of less-than-acceptable performance. It is in consort with these results that the supervisor and the staff member must be very careful that the proper weight is placed upon the proper activity within the staff member's job description. To give too much weight to an area which is not defined or understood by the employee to be a prime area responsibility is quite unfair to the employee and is very damaging to total employee-employer relations.

It is imperative that the evaluation scheme mirror the activities which are detailed in the job descriptions. An employer's responsibility, whether or not covered by union agreement, is determined by what he has been told in his job description. Evaluation then becomes a direct outgrowth of that which is expected and provides both employer and employee with usable information. Vast differences may emerge in determining the degree to which responsibilities have been met and job requirements have been fulfilled.

The total evaluation effort on the part of supervisors and staff members should be viewed as a constructive effort toward the improvement of the performance of the particular staff member and the betterment of the supervisory process under which that staff member operates. In keeping with this idea, it is well to consider that other resources beyond the local division, or even the department, may be called upon to facilitate the evaluation procedure. For example, if the staff member's work has involved field work which is not directly supervised by the person primarily responsible, then it would certainly be appropriate to involve persons from the field in the overall evaluation process.

Evaluation is an overall attempt to provide staff members and supervisors with the proper determination of who is doing what and how effectively they are doing it. It can be a very constructive portion of an employee's work history with a company, or, if improperly maintained or augmented, it can be a very trying and very difficult experience for both supervisor and employee.

Promotion policies in a school district should provide for the rewarding of competence and experience on the part of employees and should be detailed in those areas associated with time in position (grade) or skill levels necessary to be upgraded. Promotion policies for professional employees within a district generally involve the school business administrator in his planning role with the entire team, while he is often directly responsible for promotion policies affecting a large number of noncertified personnel.

In many districts, union agreements will have determined most of the ground rules for promotion, both within a section and across division lines. Stipulations as to training, seniority, and pay schedules will be covered in all union agreements insofar as these affect promotion policy. In those districts where noncertified personnel are not covered by union agreements, a set of personnel policies should be established which would guarantee rewards for those deserving them and yet protect the district against exploitation by certain staff members. Some employees could be covered under civil service, with the attendant rules and regulations associated with this appointment.

The school business administrator will play a key role in negotiations with both union representatives and his board. He will be required to have cost figures, projections of need, and budget details for use in prediction of overall cost to the district.

Personnel Termination

Generally speaking, personnel terminations are not pleasant. However, some terminations are routine and should be viewed as that. Those for which there are board policies relative to their implementation, such as having to do with health, residency requirements, and so forth, are viewed as any other action based on personnel policy would be and are carried out accordingly. There should be no ill will toward either party; nor should there be any hesitance to give this policy as the reason when requested to provide justification for termination of the employee.

As with many facets of promotion, termination procedures are often covered in union agreements. If this is the case, then most of the reasons for termination and the avenues open to both parties are outlined in detail. The alteration or abandonment of these procedures then becomes a point for union-management bargaining, and all situations remain static until this can be negotiated.

In certain school districts, employment of noncertified personnel falls under civil service, with the rules and regulations associated with termination being outlined in detail. It is also possible for some noncertified personnel to have tenure status in the school district.

In any situation involving employee termination, the school business administrator and the system's legal staff must determine that due process has been granted the staff member. As was stated in Chapter 3, an employee has every right to due process, and the school system is obligated to see that he is informed of his rights and the avenues of appeal open to him.

Terminations become unpleasant when a lack of productivity, a lack of ability, or an unwillingness on the part of the supervisor or the employee to work out a difference of opinion necessitates the termination "with cause" of an employee. The key word here is, of course, "cause." To replace persons summarily in nonunion systems without justifiable cause is very damaging to the total morale of a school system. There is no formal method for this information's "getting around," but it will. Just cause should be provided by the immediate supervisor, and proper review and appeal procedures should be built into the board policies to cover any application in terms of professional or nonprofessional terminations within the system. It should be made clear to the employee at the time of employment that there are avenues for appeal and that he can pursue his grievances through the necessary legal channels. Under most instances this will be a rare occurrence, but it can occur, and parties are under obligation to each other to be apprised of the situation.

PROFESSIONAL NEGOTIATIONS

The results of professional negotiations are felt throughout an entire school district. Negotiation activities on the part of one group of employees effect changes in the day-to-day activities as well as in the thinking of all other well-defined and not so well defined groups within the district. The interaction of one group with another cannot be denied, nor can the direction the change produces be predicted. Success on the part of one group may not ensure success on the part of another group; nor does failure in one area by one group guarantee failure in that area or selected areas by other groups.

Lieberman and Moskow define professional negotiations as:

> A process whereby employees as a group and their employers make and counter offers in good faith on conditions of their employment relationship for the purpose of reaching a mutually acceptable agreement, and the execution of a written document incorporating any such agreement if requested by either party. Also, a process whereby a representative of the employees and their employer jointly determine their conditions of employment.[3]

Negotiations are relatively new to the majority of school boards, but they are becoming a fact of life at a rate to negate any belief that they can happen "elsewhere, but not here." As of 1970, twenty-three states had statutes relating directly to collective negotiations or "discussion" in the schools. School boards must be alert to the possibility of multiple kinds of negotiations, as well as the ramifications all have for the short-range and for the long-range operation of the school district. The school business administrator may be a key member of the negotiation team of the local district. The majority of all negotiation activities have

---

[3] Myron Lieberman and Michael H. Moskow. *Collective Negotiations for Teachers: An Approach to School Administration* (Chicago: Rand McNally & Company. 1966). p. 418.

fiscal results or ramifications of both short- and long-range duration. His expertise and knowledge in these activities will arm the board and/or other negotiation personnel with ample data on which to base decisions and/or make concrete offers, whatever type of negotiation pattern is established. However, negotiations are the responsibility of the total team in the planning efforts as well as in its implementation of these plans.

Individual Negotiation

In total number of persons affected, the individual negotiation is one of the least used by school districts. The vast majority of certified personnel and a similar size group of technical and supporting personnel in most systems are subject to some type of union, civil service, or local predetermined salary schedule. Whether the schedule is restrictive or flexible, a large percentage of persons in virtually all entry-level positions will be covered by a set salary schedule. If such a schedule does not exist, it implies that the school board is in the business of administering the schools rather than setting policy for its administrators to follow.

Individual negotiations have a valid place in most school districts relative to certain key personnel such as the superintendent, selected other central staff personnel, and possibly some technical employees. In its elementary form, individual negotiations boil down to a decision between "What am I offered?" versus "What will I accept?" The district will generally be operating within a predetermined salary and fringe benefit range with key elements providing override capabilities. The employee will have in his thinking a basic salary figure set by the job market, geography, and salaries of peers.

The system negotiator or negotiation team is concerned with salaries of employees with similar responsibilities, willingness of the board to agree on these terms, attitudes of the community, and the job expectations of key staff members. Key override points on both sides may include experience, training, needs of the district or of the prospective employee, and/or specialized skills.

Final terms of the agreement should be subject to board approval and should be a matter of public record. Individual contracts are few, but they often cover the key employees within a district. It should also be remembered that individual negotiations often involve expenditures of funds in excess of those allocated for salary only These additional expenditures show in selected fringe benefits paid directly to or for the employee as well as those associated with providing that employee extra or expanded auxiliary services in such areas as clerical assistance, office space, or transportation.

Group without Outside Consultation

Within certain limitations, the ability for groups of school employees, either certified or noncertified to organize and act effectively without outside consultation is severely limited. Rarely can a single uniform goal or set of goals override personnel and group differences to a degree sufficient to offset the cohesion and disengagement that outside consultation brings to personnel negotiation. It is unrealistic to assume that a board of education would enter into negotiation without readily available, expert consultation services. The group pursuing this avenue may soon find itself in the same position as the person who chooses to represent himself in a court of law – virtually without representation.

Initial points for consideration may be prepared and key points for further consideration or confrontation may be identified if not resolved through this avenue. If time permits and the atmosphere will allow, this avenue may be pursued. The group seeking negotiations, however, should not be shocked if this approach fails to materialize as expected.

Group with Outside Consultation

Outside consultant services provide expertise that is generally unavailable within most local employee groups. These professional negotiators offer a balance in background useful in discussions with board representatives. Consultants can be armed with much information and then use their abilities to reduce this material to a set of desired goals and purpose alternatives including the degree of demands a group is willing to seek.

The school business administrator is intimately involved with these negotiations, since each result impacts the funding of the school district for subsequent years. These results may be evidenced in salary figures, fringe benefits, and/or a multitude of other ways. Additionally, the business administrator will be a prime resource for the board throughout all negotiation considerations. He must have his organization functioning in such a manner that he can respond rapidly with accurate fiscal information and predictions.

Mediation

As with group activities with or without outside consultation, mediation within the school district places tremendous demands upon the school business administrator. With mediation activities, multiple combinations of fiscal results may be needed by the board as certain specific negotiation patterns begin to emerge. This fiscal information will need to be available in multiple forms and for varying periods of time. The results and predictions must be accurate to date, and the predictions must be within acceptable confidence limits to provide a reasonable degree of fiscal responsibility for the future. Mediation may be asked for or imposed on the district or its employees in certain instances. These generally result from union agreements or court orders which will generally spell out the procedure to be followed in either instance.

The mediation activities place a different, but not unexpected, demand on the school business administrator. Again, the responsibility is to be able to provide the board (or its elected representative) the fiscal information needed in a usable manner. His responsibilities to the employee group and its representative may be defined by the board.

Arbitration

Arbitration differs from mediation in many ways, but the most significant difference for the business administrator is in the providing of certain information at the request of the arbitration board rather than at the direct instruction of the school board. The demands for data will be similar to those previously identified, but the thoroughness of information provided the employee group may be well beyond that provided in any other type of negotiations. In certain situations, an arbitration board may be established to work out a specific impasse. This could result in the establishment of a deadlock procedure which is a method adopted to resolve some particular disagreement or stalemate in a part of the negotiation process.

Civil Service–Union–Association

Any or all of the forms of negotiations noted above could be used by employees working under union agreement, using their professional association as a bargaining agent, or operating within civil service salary guidelines. The school business administrator is concerned with the activities of all these groups within his district because of the previously established or potential impact on the budget. He must constantly keep the board apprised of future trends in the budget produced by contract items and/or the impact if requested items are granted.

Grievance Procedures

Grievance procedures are those mechanisms which provide for the peaceful settlement of disputes that arise over the application or interpretation of the agreement or "contract" during the time it is in effect.[4]

Any grievance procedure should be handled through normal administrative channels. The general order of a grievance should be from employee to superintendent and finally to the board with the principle of due process always observed. An employee should have the right to seek advice from any group he chooses and should always have the right of legal counsel.

PERSONNEL BUDGETING

The establishment of detailed, written salary policies for all levels of employees within the school district will greatly facilitate the solution of numerous personnel problems. A set salary policy for both certificated and noncertificated personnel is a must for effective and truly efficient operation of any school district.

Step increment salary increase policy is the type used by most school officials. Most school districts give little real thought to the more innovative and less understood salary policy of merit pay schedule. Lack of ability to establish guidelines to be applied by supervisors at all levels reduces the merit system to a single step system.

[4]T. M. Stinnet, in Report of the School Administrators' Conference on Professional Negotiations (Denver: Bureau of Educational Research of Denver, July, 1964), p. 57.

The concept of equality of treatment for secondary and elementary teachers is rarely questioned in school districts. Other differentiations, such as directing the band and coaching, have received the most attention. The number and size of supplements must also be considered in the long-range planning within any school district.

Regardless of the system used, a detailed picture of the plan is a "must." Salary projections for general budgeting purposes are little better than guesses without an established framework within which to work. Staff turnover, court action, annexation, and union agreements all have impact on salary policies within a school district. However, none of these can be allowed to set salary policy. Established policies for both certificated and noncertificated personnel have been identified as priority items. It has also been established in a previous section of this chapter that salary policy and its implementation are important elements in staff motivation. An established and published board policy relative to salary and fringe benefits is a necessary element of information for a school business manager as he attempts to do his job more efficiently and effectively.

Table 8.1 shows an example of a state salary schedule for certificated personnel and table 8.2 shows an example of a local salary schedule for noncertificated personnel.

Budget Areas

Technical areas of budgeting such as line budgeting, object and function budgeting, and organizational budgeting all play an integral part in the overall budget planning of the school business administrator. Major considerations of the role of the school business administrator relative to each of these is included in chapter 7.

Fringe Benefits

Fringe benefits and the budget impact they cause are of increasing concern to school business administrators and the total administrative team of a district. As union agreements are negotiated, as civil service contracts are set, or as general employee contracts are established, the total dollar value of fringe benefit packages continues to grow. These benefits include vacations with

TABLE 8.1. Sample state salary schedule for certificated personnel

Description of Training	Experience															
	0 Yrs.	1 Yr.	2 Yrs.	3 Yrs.	4 Yrs.	5 Yrs.	6 Yrs.	7 Yrs.	8 Yrs.	9 Yrs.	10 Yrs.	11 Yrs.	12 Yrs.	13 Yrs.	14 Yrs.	15 Yrs.
Doctor's Degree	7200	7290	7380	7470	7560	7650	7740	7830	7920	8010	8100	8190	8280	8370	8460	8550
Ed. S.	6700	6790	6880	6970	7060	7150	7240	7330	7420	7510	7600	7690	7780	7870	7960	8050
Master's Degree plus 45 Quarter hours	6600	6690	6780	6870	6960	7050	7140	7230	7320	7410	7500	7590	7680	7770	7860	7950
Master's Degree	6100	6190	6280	6370	6460	6550	6640	6730	6820	6910	7000	7090	7180	7270	7360	7450
Bachelor's Degree	5600	5680	5760	5840	5920	6000	6080	6160	6240	6320	6400	6480	6560	6640	6720	6800
Three Years College	4720	4775	4830	4885	4940	4995	5050	5105	5160	5215	5270					
Two Years College	4505	4560	4615	4670	4725	4780	4835	4890	4945	5000	5055					
One Year College	4210	4255	4300	4345	4390	4435	4480									
0 Years College	4160	4205	4250	4295	4340	4385	4430									

Note 1: Only the training acceptable for certification and shown on the certificate will be counted when applying salary rating. Teachers employed full time shall not be allowed credit for the purpose of certification on more than 6 quarter hours earned during any one quarter of the school year.

Note 2: The Doctor's Degree rating shall be given only to those teachers who earned the Doctor's Degree in a college or university approved by recognized accrediting agencies for granting graduate degrees and who by the nature of courses pursued in the doctorate program indicated that public education was their primary aim as a career.

Note 3: The Master's Degree plus 45 quarter hours rating shall be given to those who have earned 45 additional quarter hours of graduate credit after the date the requirements for the Master's Degree were completed.

Note 4: The Master's Degree rating shall be given only to those teachers who earned the graduate degree in a college or university approved by recognized accrediting agencies for granting graduate degrees and who, by nature of courses pursued in their graduate training, indicated that public education was their primary aim as a career; otherwise, rating will be based upon the Bachelor's Degree.

Note 5: To the above annual salary schedule for the school year 1972–73 shall be added the amount of one hundred fifty ($150.00) dollars per year to each training and experience category to arrive at the State salary schedule for the school year 1972–73 for full-time approved Special Education teachers who hold certificates in the area or areas of assignment.

TABLE 8.2.   Salary Schedule Example for Noncertificated Personnel

School Clerks' Salary Schedule
1972–1973

	S–2 Group II (200 days) Annually			S–1 Group I (200 days) Annually	
0	.535	$3,531.00	0	.647	$4,270.20
1	.562	3,709.20	1	.673	4,441.80
2	.589	3,887.40	2	.699	4,613.40
3	.616	4,065.60	3	.726	4,791.60
4	.643	4,243.80	4	.752	4,963.20
5	.671	4,428.60	5	.778	5,134.80
6	.698	4,606.80	6	.805	5,313.00
7	.725	4,785.00	7	.831	5,484.60
8	.752	4,963.20	8	.857	5,656.20
9	.779	5,141.40	9	.884	5,834.40

Maximum of three (3) years is allowed for previous experience.

Clerks classified in Group I are those assigned to junior high schools, senior high schools, and elementary schools with an enrollment of over 700. The minimum work hours per day shall be from 8:00 A.M. to 3:45 P.M. and such additional time and/or days as required by the principal in the performance of his duties.

Clerks classified in Group II are those assigned to elementary schools with under 700 enrollment. The minimum hours worked per day shall be from 8:00 A.M. to 3:30 P.M. and such additional time and/or days as required by the principal in the performance of his duties.

All school clerks (Group I and II) are employed for the same number of days as the principal of the school to which they are assigned.

SOURCE: Knoxville Board of Education. Used with permission.

pay, medical insurance costs for the employee and his family, group life and disability insurance, and many others. Continual attention to the direction and quantity of this change is an important job for the school business administrator.

Figure 8.1 gives one example of a list of fringe benefits for noncertificated personnel.

SUMMARY

Planning for personnel administration is a multifaceted feature of the school administrator's position. He must clearly understand his role in the organization in respect to superior-subordinate rela-

MONETARY:
  Supplementary Pay
  Guaranteed Annual Wage
  Merit Increases
  Guaranteed Pay Advantages
  Seniority Increases
  License and Dues Allowance

LEAVE:
  Vacation
  Sick Leave
  Maternity Leave
  Personal Leave
  Jury Leave
  Military Leave
  Holidays

INSURANCE:
  Health and Accident
  Life
  Retirement
  Disability

SERVICES AND MISCELLANEOUS:
  Meal Allowances
  Uniform Allowances
  Equipment Usage
  Housing
  Credit Union
  Recreational Activities
  Rest Periods
  Pay Roll Deductions
  Automobile Allowance
  In-Service Training Opportunities
  Conference Visitations

FIGURE 8.1   Types of fringe benefits for noncertificated personnel. (Frederick W. Hill and James W. Colmey, School Business Administration in the Smaller Community, Book One [*Minneapolis: T. S. Denison & Co., Inc., 1964*], p. 172. *Reprinted with permission of the publisher.*)

tionships and his position in the overall structure of the district. He must take a lead role in personnel planning and recruitment as well as working in all areas of personnel development. His role in personnel budgeting is plainly visible but not nearly so easily accomplished. The professional negotiation role is yet another dimension of his responsibilities.

SUGGESTED ACTIVITIES

1. What would be the role of the school business administrator in setting performance standards for classified positions within his district?

2. How does the school business administrator function as a part of the professional negotiations team?

3. What elements are needed in an evaluation model for clerical personnel within a school district?

4. How is due process provided in personnel terminations in your district or school?

5. How does the school business administrator plan for the institution of collective negotiations in his area of responsibility?

SELECTED READINGS

Fawcett, Claude W. *School Personnel Administration.* New York: The Macmillan Company, 1964.

Gibson, R. Oliver, and Hunt, Harold C. *The School Personnel Administrator.* Boston: Houghton Mifflin Company, 1965.

Likert, Rensis. *New Patterns of Management.* New York: McGraw-Hill Book Company, 1961.

Michigan Association of School Boards and Michigan Association of School Administration. *Labor Relations Handbook for School Boards and Superintendents.* Lansing, Mich.: The Associations, 1966.

Neagley, Ross L., Evans, N. Dean, and Lynn, Clarence A., Jr. *The School Administrator and Learning Resources.* Englewood Cliffs, N.J.: Prentice-Hall, Inc., 1969.

Stahl, O. Glenn. *Public Personnel Administration.* New York: Harper & Row Publishers, 1962.

Walter, John. *Administration and Policy Making in Education.* Baltimore: The Johns Hopkins Press, 1969.

ACCOUNTING, AUDITING, AND REPORTING

The tasks of accounting, auditing, and reporting have been associated with school business administration since its inception. In the past few years, however, the function of this set of tasks has changed considerably. In the initial period of development, accounting-related tasks were oriented to control, i.e., the public monies had to be accounted for to assure the school district's patrons that tax dollars were being spent in the proper amounts and for the proper purposes.

More recently accounting-related tasks have been expanded to incorporate the contemporary concepts of accountability. With this orientation, accounting, auditing, and reporting are used to provide necessary data and its interpretation in order to relate costs and benefits in the financial support of educational institutions. The school business administrator employs accounting techniques to describe (1) the nature, sources, and amounts of revenue inputs; (2) the appropriation of revenues to various programs (or funds and accounts); and (3) the actual expenditures in these programs. These data are then related to program outputs or educational benefits in ways that citizens can understand financial implications of program decisions and program implications of financial decisions. In this way, the schools are accountable to the public, and the public has information on which it can exercise its decision-making power in areas of financial policy.

Despite the fact that only a small minority of school systems in the nation has made significant progress in the "program budgeting" type of public accountability, the authors suggest there is another level of application of the accounting, auditing, and reporting task: an internal accountability prerequisite to integrated and comprehensive planning. As the central focus of this book is the planning approach to school business administration, it has been established that the planning process must be a team effort. Planning inputs from individual specialists responsible for discrete functions within the superintendency team are interactive. The programmatic and financial character of a staff personnel administrator's proposal will have an impact on a proposal lodged by the administrator in charge of instruction. There must be a free flow of adequate and valid information among the planning team. Each member is accountable to the team in order that individual planning and specific proposals may coalesce into an integrated educational program which in turn may be proposed to and evaluated by the public in the accountability context described earlier.

In the authors' view, the tasks of accounting, auditing, and reporting are crucial since they provide not only control in fiscal management, but also because they make possible school system accountability to the public and internal accountability for the superintendency team as a planning unit.

Although the tasks of accounting, auditing, and reporting are closely interrelated, they will be discussed separately and in the sequence mentioned.

SCHOOL ACCOUNTING

A Definition

School accounting has been defined as . . . recording and reporting activities and events affecting personnel, facilities, materials, or money of an administrative unit and its programs. Specifically, it is concerned with determining what accounting records are to be maintained, how they will be maintained, and the procedures, methods, and forms to be used; recording, classifying, and summarizing activities or events; analyzing and interpreting recorded data; and preparing and issuing reports and statements which reflect conditions as of a given date, the results of operations for a specific period, and the evaluation of status and results of operations in terms of established objectives.[1]

Several ideas in the definition deserve to be highlighted. First, accounting deals with activities and events which affect both operational inputs (money, material) as well as the school's program. Secondly, the process of accounting incorporates acts of recording, classifying, analyzing, and interpreting data. A third idea expressed in the definition is that of reporting conditions of a given date and the evaluation of the status and results of operations in terms of established objectives. From this definition, it is apparent that the accounting function is an integral part of the planning process employed as a part of the work of the superintendency team as it constitutes important financial and programmatic inputs.

Objectives of School Accounting

The definition implies that the accounting function serves several varied purposes in schools. Among the most important are:

1. Maintaining an accurate record of significant details in the business transactions of the school system.
2. Providing a basis and medium for planning and decision making by both policy-making and administrative bodies at local, state, and federal levels.
3. Providing a control system to assure the appropriate use of resources in the educational enterprise.
4. Expediting the process of setting priorities; establishing, analyzing, and selecting alternatives in the budgeting process; and establishing an operational blueprint for the school system.
5. Providing a medium for reporting the financial condition of the school system to the patrons of the school district as well as other groups and agencies at the local, state, and federal levels. This is done for purposes of planning and policy making, accountability, control, and comparative study.
6. Providing basic input information to calculate and extend school district budgets, tax levies, and state and federal subventions or transfer payments.

[1] Bert K. Adams. Quentin M. Hill. Allan R. Lichtenberger. Joseph A. Perkins. Jr.. and Philip S. Shaw. *Principles of Public School Accounting.* State Educational Records and Reports Series: Handbook II–B (Washington. D.C.: U.S. Government Printing Office. 1967). p. 260.

Emergence of School Accounting Systems

Since school accounting had its genesis in public accounting, which in turn sprang from accounting practices developed in the business world, several basic principles of the latter type of accounting should be appropriate in designing or evaluating an accounting system to be used in a public school setting. A primary difference between public school accounting and that practiced in the business world (other than the absence of a profit motive) is that of the legal restrictions or controls placed on both the sources of and procedures for obtaining revenue and the purposes and processes for expending it. The fiscal controls placed on the school district by the state typically limit revenues to taxation, gifts, tuition, fines, fees, and transfer payments from state and federal governments. In many instances very specific controls are written into some state laws. Strict control over expenditures tends to be the rule rather than the exception in most states. For example, in some states teachers' salaries may not be paid unless a valid teaching certificate is on file in the appropriate office, or monies may not be expended for paying the moving expenses of the superintendent.

States exercise their plenary legal authority over the school districts as quasi-corporations by specifying the accounting and other fiscal procedures to be used. Typically, the state requires a public school fund accounting system. Thus, all districts use a common system with common funds, accounts, definitions, and procedures. Usually a series of funds is set up including discrete sources of revenue to be used in each for specified purposes. Thus, each fund tends to be a unique entity. Within each fund, the uniform accounting laws typically provide for a group of accounts which define, as legal restrictions, those transactions which may be made within the given fund. For example, in Ohio the expenditure for replacing a typewriter used for instruction must be charged to the D-4 account — Equipment Replacements, Educational — in the general fund, whereas an additional typewriter used for instruction to be included in equipping a new school built with monies from a bond issue would be charged to the building fund — account BF-5, Equipment.

School accounting systems with their rather rigid state controls serve another major purpose as the state acts to meet its obligation of providing educational services to its youth. The designation of funds and the construction of school budgets around the funds provide the baseline decisions and information needed to determine tax rates. Thus, in many states the officials or agencies so empowered use these financial data to designate the required tax rates, and these in turn are extended by the tax department in the appropriate jurisdiction. For example, two basic property tax levies are calculated in Ohio—the current operating levy (that required by the general fund budget) and the building fund levy (that required to finance debt service).

Principles of a School Accounting System

Given the unique function and nature of fiscal accounting in the public school setting, several basic principles have been identified to describe such an accounting system:

1. A school financial record system should be adequate to provide financial and related operational information for all interested parties—the school board; the administration; the public; auditors; local, state, and federal authorities; and school employees. The adequacy of the accounting systems depends on whether both current and historical information is available for decision-making purposes.

2. The accounting system should be designed to demand accuracy and a reasonable degree of internal control. If so designed, it will automatically assist those who are performing the daily work on the records as well as those who supervise them.

3. A school accounting system should be consistent with generally accepted governmental accounting principles, and consistent as between one period of time and another. Valid comparisons of monthly or yearly operations in different time periods can be made only if the items are treated in the same way throughout. Changes and improvements in the accounting system may prove necessary, and these should be made at logical times in the accounting period.

4. A school accounting system should be flexible. Change is inevitable. New programs will develop; old programs will be dropped. Provisions should be made for taking care of changes with as little disruption as possible.

5. School financial accounting systems should be uniform; to permit maximum usefulness, they should allow for financial, operational, or performance comparisons with

other school districts on local as well as state and national levels. Uniformity will insure that the items being compared are similar items, and standard terminology and definitions should be used. This is one of the primary reasons for the cooperative development of the handbook series published by the Office of Education of the U.S. Department of Health, Education, and Welfare.

6. A financial accounting system should be as simple as possible and still fulfill the pertinent requirements. It is essential that the system not become merely frustrating "busy" work. A good accounting system will assist in improving the education processes, not hinder them.

7. A school financial accounting system should provide ready access to information about individual financial transactions as well as summaries of information about groups of financial transactions. Unless the record keeping system is organized as indicated in the criteria above, it may be exceedingly difficult to gain ready access to information about the current and projected financial operations and status of the school district.[2]

Basic Concepts in School Accounting Systems

The science of accounting is made up of an organized body of knowledge and an orderly application of procedures. Together three basic concepts are used in the accounting function in public school systems. School personnel with responsibility for general and fiscal policy decisions and those with responsibility for executing them must apply the concepts in order to utilize the information resources afforded by an accounting system. Frequently, specific terms used in an accounting context carry meanings quite different from those used (or misused) in layman's jargon.

The Accounting Equation

The first concept is related to describing financial status at a given moment. What a school system or an individual is worth is equal to what is owned minus what is owed. Thus, the basic accounting equation is stated as: Owned − Owed = Net Worth.

Accounting terminology translates the equation by substituting standardized terms.

Assets are things owned.

---

[2] Adams et al., *Principles of Public School Accounting*, pp. 3–4.

Liabilities are things owed.

Equity is the difference between things owned and things owed and thus equates with net worth. When applied to school accounting the term *fund balance* is used.

Thus, the equation becomes:

$$\text{Assets} - \text{Liabilities} = \text{Equity.}$$

If a school system has $500,000 in its bank account and owes $450,000 for teachers' salaries, its equity equals $50,000. The equation can be stated in several different forms with the above example:

1. Assets = Liabilities + Equity
   $500,000 = $450,000 + $50.000
   or $500,000 = $500,000

2. Liabilities = Assets − Equity
   $450,000 = $500,000 − $50,000
   or $450,000 = $450,000

3. Equity = Assets − Liabilities
   $50,000 = $500,000 − $450,000
   or $50,000 = $50,000

Since the accounting equation is an algebraic expression, it can be added to or subtracted from, provided the same amount is added to or subtracted from both sides of the equation.

In the following example, suppose that the school system increased its assets by $100,000. Using the equation Assets = Liabilities + Equity, assets would be increased by $100,000, and so it would be necessary to add $100,000 to the other side of the equation. The actions and reactions of adding to or subtracting from any of the elements of the equation are governed by the following concepts:

1. One asset can be increased while another can be decreased by an equal amount. Invested funds, for example, can be converted to cash. Thus, the amount of assets remain the same although investment assets decrease and cash assets increase.
2. An asset can be increased while a liability is increased by an equal amount. Material which was ordered has been received but has not yet been paid for. The assets have been increased by

the value of the material, but the liabilities have been likewise increased since the school system now owes the vendor for the material.

3. An asset can be increased while equity is increased by an equal amount. Fines, charges, and gifts received increase assets and at the same time increase the school system's equity.

4. A liability can be increased while another can be decreased by an equal amount. Money can be borrowed to pay a vendor's bill.

It must be recognized that changes in the equation may be made in combinations of the above actions and reactions since a single transaction may result in several simultaneous changes.

The Accounting Process

The financial status of a school system changes as it transacts business which effects changes in its accounting equation. It is these transactions which are recorded, classified, and summarized in the accounting process. Transactions are originally recorded in a journal and from it are posted to accounts. Accounts are established for each asset and liability, and for equity. Because of the unique nature of school district accounting specified by individual states which mandate discrete funds and accounts, public school system accounting procedures use the term *fund balance* rather than equity.

The accounts which reflect the action and reaction of the several transactions are commonly known as *T accounts*. The concept of debits and credits is built around the way data is recorded in each account. The left side of the T account is the debit side while the right side is the credit side.

The derivation of the words *debit* and *credit* in the accounting context can provide one with an important insight into this concept. Tidwell states:

> The Latin word *debeo* means "owe." The history of the use of this word as it applies to accounting began when the only transactions necessary to be recorded were those with customers or suppliers. A charge against a person who owes appears on the left side of the account with that person. The left side of the account is the "debit" side.
>
> The Latin word *credo* means "trust" or "believe." The history of this word as it applies to accounting began at the same time as the word debit. The amount shown as owed to a

person who trusts us appears on the right side of the account, which is referred to as the credit side.[3]

As transactions are posted from the journal to the appropriate account, data incorporated in the account include the date, description, journal page reference, and the amount of debit or credit. The determination of how the transaction is debited and credited is governed by the following rules:

1. In asset accounts:
   a. The value of an asset is recorded as a debit (in the left side of the account)
   b. Increases in assets are recorded as debits (in the left side of the account)
   c. Decreases in assets are recorded as credits (in the right side of the account)

2. In liability accounts:
   a. The amount of a liability is recorded as a credit (in the right side of the account)
   b. Increases in liability are recorded as credits (in the right side of the account)
   c. Decreases in liability are recorded as debits (in the left side of the account)

3. In fund balance accounts:
   a. The amount of a fund balance is recorded as a credit (in the right side of the account)
   b. Increases in a fund balance are recorded as credits (in the right side of the account)
   c. Decreases in a fund balance are recorded as debits (in the left side of the account)

In summary, the T accounts for the basic equation of school fund accounting appear as shown in figure 9.1.

ASSETS		= LIABILITIES		+ FUND BALANCE	
Debit	Credit	Debit	Credit	Debit	Credit
Increase	Decrease	Decrease	Increase	Decrease	Increase

FIGURE 9.1   T accounts for basic equation of school fund accounting.

[3] Sam B. Tidwell, *Public School Fund Accounting* (New York: Harper and Brothers, 1960), p. 30.

To keep accounts in balance, or to maintain the accounting equation, there must be an equal use of debits and credits for each transaction. As indicated earlier, a single transaction might have two or more debits and two or more credits. However, the total amount of debits must still equal the total amount of credits. In a series of transactions the total debits must be equal to the total credits. The fact that the accounts are self-balancing through equal

	ASSETS	=	LIABILITIES	+	FUND BALANCE	
	Debit	Credit	Debit	Credit	Debit	Credit
	Increase	Decrease	Decrease	Increase	Decrease	Increase
(1)	$ 500,000					$ 500,000
(2)		$ 450,000	$ 450,000			
(3)	$1,000,000			$1,000,000		
(4)	$ 100,000			$ 100,000		
(5)		$ 150,000	$ 150,000			
(6)		$ 100,000	$ 100,000			
(7)	$ 500,000					$ 500,000
(8)		$1,000,500	1,000,500			
	$2,100,000	$1,700,500	1,700,500	$1,100,000		$1,000,000

Transaction 1: The school system receives $500,000 in taxes, so Assets are increased by a debit and Fund Balance is increased by a credit.

Transaction 2: The school system pays $450,000 in teachers' salaries, so Assets are decreased by a credit and Liabilities are decreased by a debit.

Transaction 3: The school system borrows $1,000,000 from a local bank, so Assets are increased by a debit and Liabilities are increased by a credit.

Transaction 4: The school system orders and receives $100,000 in supplies from a vendor, so Assets are increased by a debit and Liabilities are increased by a credit.

Transaction 5: The school system pays $150,000 in salaries for noncertificated personnel, so Assets are decreased by a credit and Liabilities are decreased by a debit.

Transaction 6: The school system pays $100,000 to the vendor for the supplies previously received, so Assets are decreased by a credit and Liabilities are decreased by a debit.

Transaction 7: The school system receives $500,000 in state aid, so Assets are increased by a debit and Fund Balance is increased by a credit.

Transaction 8: The school system pays $1,000,500 of principal and interest on the $1,000,000 borrowed previously, so Assets are decreased by a credit and Liabilities are decreased by a debit.

FIGURE 9.2 Illustration of application of the accounting equation and double-entry bookkeeping.

entry of both debits and credits identifies such a system as *double-entry bookkeeping*.

An application of the concepts of the accounting equation and double-entry accounting with debits and credits can be illustrated in a rather simplistic example. A school district has completed a series of transactions, and they are to be recorded in the accounting system. In chronological order the transactions include:

1. $500,000 in local taxes is received
2. $450,000 is paid for teachers' salaries
3. $1,000,000 is borrowed from a local bank
4. $100,000 in supplies is ordered and received from a vendor
5. $150,000 is paid for salaries of noncertificated personnel
6. $100,000 is paid to vendor for supplies
7. $500,000 in state aid is received
8. $1,000,500 principal and interest on loan is repaid.

These transactions would be recorded as shown in figure 9.2.

The Trial Balance

In order to be certain that transactions have been properly analyzed and recorded, and that debits and credits have been equally applied, a trial balance is run. Using the above series of transactions, the trial balance should appear as in figure 9.3.

	Debits	Credits
Assets	$2,100,000	$1,700,500
Liabilities	1,700,500	1,100,000
Fund Balance	– –	1,000,000
	$3,800,500	$3,800,500

FIGURE 9.3   Trial balance.

Another type of trial balance shows the balance within each of the several accounts. Such a trial balance for our specimen set of transactions would show whether the balance is a debit balance (debits exceed credits) or a credit balance (credits exceed debits). This trial balance would be as shown in figure 9.4.

	Debits	Credits
Assets	$ 399,500	
Liabilities	600,500	
Fund Balance		$1,000,000
	$1,000,000	$1,000,000

FIGURE 9.4   Trial balance.

Application of School Fund Accounting

Thus far in the discussion, several basic concepts of accounting have been explored. These have been fundamentals necessary to understand before the whole accounting process can be understood. The remainder of the section on accounting will be devoted to an examination of the process. It will be built around the business administrator's responsibility for and in the accounting cycle.

Tidwell identifies the ten basic steps in the accounting cycle as:

1. Journalize transactions
2. Post transactions
3. Prepare a trial balance
4. Prepare a work sheet
5. Prepare financial statements
6. Journalize closing entries
7. Post closing entries
8. Balance, rule, and bring forward balances of balance sheet accounts
9. Rule temporary accounts
10. Prepare post-closing trial balance.[4]

As the school business administrator assesses his responsibility in the area of accounting, he must recognize the legal mandates and constraints in this context. States exercise their plenary authority by usually requiring an accounting for school district resources; by specifying the data, forms, and procedures to be used; and by assigning individuals fixed responsibilities in accounting and related functions. In many states these functions

[4]Tidwell, *Public School Fund Accounting*, p. 77.

involve responsibilities shared among superintendents, boards of education (or their counterparts) and/or board secretaries, treasurers, clerks, school business administrators, and other local and/or state officials or agencies. Thus, it is extremely important that job expectations and working relationships be set up carefully and clearly to avoid confusion, role conflict, and muddled role expectation.

The problem is not simply solved by a precise set of job descriptions. Ongoing working relationships must be developed and maintained if the organization so necessary for effective school fund accounting is to function. This is particularly true if part of the accounting responsibility is lodged with a layman reporting to the board while another part of the accounting responsibility is resident in the position of the superintendent or his subordinate(s).

Initiating Transactions

The accounting cycle begins with the initiation of a financial transaction. This may occur in many different sectors of the school system. It may be the certification that taxes are to be collected, the board of education might consummate a contract for construction of a building, or it might originate with a teacher's requisition for art paper. In most systems the last type of transaction is the most prevalent.

The approval procedure for requisitions is usually a local administrative decision of which the business administrator must be knowledgeable. When the approved requisition data is committed to a purchase order, the school system becomes liable for its payment. Many state-mandated accounting systems require that funds be encumbered or "ear-marked" to pay this obligation and thus subtracted from an asset account. When a school system recognizes revenues as soon as it gains a right to them and recognizes an expenditure as soon as liability occurs, it may be said to be on an "accrual basis" of accounting rather than a cash basis, which records only those financial transactions involving cash receipts and disbursements.[5]

Thus, the encumbering process finalizes the contracting or

---

[5] See Tidwell, *Public School Fund Accounting*, pp. 57–58, for a more comprehensive discussion of cash, accrual, and modified accrual systems.

purchasing act and initiates the accounting act by providing the document and data for the journal—a book of original entry in the accounting process. The contract or purchase order becomes a voucher—a business document which provides evidence of a business transaction.

Journalizing Transactions

The accounting office continuously gathers all the vouchers generated by the school system. These are analyzed in terms of debits and credits and recorded in the general journal. This book of original entry records all the transactions in a chronological order (hence the term *journal*). Specific data on each page of the general journal includes the data of the transaction, the specific accounts affected by the transaction, an explanation of the transaction, the posting reference, which indicates the specific location of the posting in the ledger(s), and debits and credits to all accounts affected by the transaction. The concept of debits and credits as discussed earlier is applicable to the general journal as well as ledgers of the several different accounts.

A general journal might reflect the following kind of transactions as the fiscal year (July 1–June 30) begins. Figure 9.5 shows an opening general journal entry.

At the beginning of the fiscal year, July 1, a school system had cash in the amount of $500,000 and was to receive goods from a vendor valued at $20,000. At the same time it owed teachers

GENERAL JOURNAL   Page 1

Date	Account and Explanation	Posting Reference	Debit	Credit
July 1	Cash		$500,000	
	Accounts receivable		20,000	
	Teachers' salaries payable			$450,000
	Accounts payable			36,000
	Fund balance			34,000
	To record current assets, current liabilities, and fund balance of July 1, 19__.			

FIGURE 9.5   General journal.

$450,000 and a vendor $36,000. Fund balance at the beginning of the year would be $34,000.

After the opening entries have been recorded in the general journal, they are posted to the appropriate account in the general ledger. The general journal entries include the date, account identification, explanation, posting reference (the account number in the general ledger where the transaction will be posted) and whether the entry is a debit or a credit.

The General Ledger

A *ledger* is a group of accounts. All asset, liability, and fund balance accounts make up the general ledger. In actual practice the simplistic examples of accounting concepts presented earlier have given way to more complex forms of recording and analyzing these data. The asset account in the accounting equation has been replaced by a whole series of asset accounts including those of cash, taxes receivable, revenue receivable from various local, state, and federal sources, and so forth. Liability accounts can run literally into the hundreds in some states. For example, there are ten separate accounts for the payment of teachers' salaries in the Ohio *Classification of Receipts and Appropriation Accounts for School Districts* (see figure 9.6). Equity, or the fund balance accounts, are used in each individual fund of the accounting system and reflect the difference between current assets and current liabilities in these individual accounts.

An additional group of accounts has been created to reflect a unique feature of governmental and school district accounting. Since revenues available to school systems are relatively fixed through local property tax levies, state aid appropriations, and rather predictable amounts of other income, and since there are rigorous state controls over expenditures, it is both possible and necessary to build in safeguards for raising and expending school system monies. As a result a fourth order of accounts has been developed. These accounts, which assist in financial planning, are known as *revenue and expenditure summary accounts*. These accounts and their functions are:

1. Estimated revenue summary: summary of all revenue estimated to accrue during the given fiscal year
2. Revenue summary: summary of all revenue actually received

Account Number	Data Processing Reference Number	Description
A–16–1 Salaries–Regular Teachers–Day School	4 010 01001	Salaries of regular teachers properly certificated to teach or instruct students, including driver training and vocational education classes.
A–16–2 Salaries–Substitute Teachers–Day School	4 010 01001	Salaries of substitute teachers properly certificated to teach or instruct students, including driver training and vocational education classes.
A–16–3 Salaries–Teachers –Tutors–Day School	4 010 01001	Salaries of teachers properly certificated by the State Department of Education for home tutoring.
A–16–4 Salaries–Teachers –Special Classes– Day School	4 010 01001	Salaries of teachers properly certificated to teach or instruct handicapped students.
A–16a–1 Salaries–Regular Teachers–Summer School	4 010 01002	Salaries of regular teachers properly certificated to teach summer school.
A–16a–2 Salaries–Substitute Teachers– Summer School	4 010 01002	Salaries of substitute teachers properly certificated to teach summer school.
A–16b–1 Salaries–Regular Teachers–Evening School	4 010 01003	Salaries of regular teachers properly certificated to teach evening school.
A–16b–2 Salaries–Substitute Teachers– Evening School	4 010 01003	Salaries of substitute teachers properly certificated to teach evening school.
A–16c–1 Salaries–Regular Teachers–Trade School	4 010 01003	Salaries of regular teachers properly certificated to teach in trade schools.
A–16c–2 Salaries–Substitute Teachers– Trade School	4 010 01003	Salaries of substitute teachers properly certificated to teach in trade schools.

3. Appropriations summary: summary of the total amount appropriated by the board including authorization of fixed amounts for specific purposes during the given fiscal year.
4. Expenditure summary: summary of all expenditures incurred including those paid and unpaid which result in benefits enjoyed during the given fiscal year
5. Encumbrances: summary of all encumbrances which are chargeable to and included in an appropriation for the given fiscal year.

The revenue and expenditure summary accounts provide the school administrator with information on what the nature and amounts of expenditures are set up in the appropriations, the nature and amounts of expenditures to date, and the nature and amounts of expenditures which are not yet encumbered. As a result these provide important planning tools for the school business administrator.

Posting the General Ledger

Transactions entered in the general journal are posted to the appropriate accounts in the general ledger. This process brings together or summarizes all similar accounts. The general ledger is made up of individual accounts. Each account incorporates data regarding its designation (cash, accounts receivable, etc.), its account number (usually the state-mandated classification system), date of the transaction, explanation, the posting reference (designation of page or location of the transaction in the general journal), and the designation as to whether the transaction was a debit or credit to the particular account (same designation given the transaction in the general journal).

Several transactions which have been posted from the general journal are illustrated in figure 9.7.

In figure 9.7 and in the illustration of the general journal in figure 9.8, note that the first entry is in the cash account. It is a beginning balance; its posting reference is J1—page 1 of the general journal—and it is a debit amount. Since we are opening

---

FIGURE 9.6 Classification of appropriation accounts, teachers' salaries. (Bureau of Inspection and Supervision of Public Offices, Classification of Receipts and Appropriation Accounts for School Districts [Columbus, O.: The Bureau, 1967], p. 5. Reprinted with permission.)

GENERAL LEDGER

Account __Cash__   Account No. __701__   Page __1__

Date	Explanation	Post Ref.	Debit Amount	Date	Explanation	Post Ref.	Credit Amount
July 1	Beginning balance	J1	500,000				

GENERAL LEDGER

Account __Accounts Receivable__ Account No. __703__   Page __1__

Date	Explanation	Post Ref.	Debit Amount	Date	Explanation	Post Ref.	Credit Amount
July 1	Beginning balance	J1	20,000				

GENERAL LEDGER

Account __Salaries Payable__ Account No. __850__   Page __1__

Date	Explanation	Post Ref.	Debit Amount	Date	Explanation	Post Ref.	Credit Amount
				July 1	Beginning balance	J1	450,000

GENERAL LEDGER

Account __Accounts Payable__ Account No. __870__   Page __1__

Date	Explanation	Post Ref.	Debit Amount	Date	Explanation	Post Ref.	Credit Amount
				July 1	Beginning balance	J1	36,000

GENERAL LEDGER

Account __Fund Balance__   Account No. __1010__   Page __1__

Date	Explanation	Post Ref.	Debit Amount	Date	Explanation	Post Ref.	Credit Amount
				July 1	Beginning balance	J1	34,000

FIGURE 9.7   *Transactions posted from the general ledger.*

the general ledger, similar dates, explanations, and posting references appear on all other entries as well. However, cash and accounts receivable are debited, while salaries payable, accounts payable, and fund balance accounts are credited.

Recording Budgets and Appropriations

At or near the beginning of the fiscal year, school systems adopt budgets and appropriations for their operations during the fiscal year. These basic financial decisions are transactions and must be recorded. The budget is used to establish estimated revenues and expenditures. These data are entered in the general journal and general ledger in a fashion similar to the entries which originally opened the books. The journal entry account title in the operating or current expense fund would be "Estimated Revenue" and would be a debit amount. The equal credit amount would carry the title "Fund Balance."

When the general journal entries for estimated revenue are posted to the general ledger, the same account titles and debit and credit assignments are entered as they were entered in the general journal. Subsidiary ledger forms for the revenue ledger include account descriptions and numbers for each of the several revenue sources. Estimated expenditures or appropriations are entered in a similar fashion.

Recording Transactions

The several sections above have discussed the principles of accounting, how the books are opened, and how budgets and appropriations are recorded. The latter two aspects are done only once each year as preparation for the entry of the normal daily transactions.

Assuming that the school system opened the school year with a bill outstanding to a vendor for $2,500 for supplies, the transaction for paying it would be reflected as shown in figure 9.8.

Processing Accounting Data

Manual, machine, and electronic data processing have all been used in accounting systems in recent years. The basic principles of school accounting apply, however, in any of these. The latter two types of processing have advantages over manual accounting in terms of speed, multiple use of a given entry, and mechanical or electronic reliability.

Accounting machines are frequently used in small- and medium-sized school systems. Through the use of carbons, mul-

GENERAL JOURNAL

Date	Account Title and Description	Post Ref.	Debit Amount	Credit Amount
July 2	Accounts Payable		2,500	
	Cash			2,500

GENERAL LEDGER

Page ___1___

Account _____ Account No. _____

Date	Explanation	Post Ref.	Debit Amount	Date	Explanation	Post Ref.	Credit Amount
July 1	Previous Bal.		2,500	July 2	Payment to Vendor		2,500

GENERAL LEDGER

Account ___Accounts Payable Vendors___ Account No. _____

Date	Explanation	Post Ref.	Debit Amount	Date	Explanation	Post Ref.	Credit Amount
	Pay off Vendor		2,500	July 1	Beg. Balance		2,500

FIGURE 9.8

tiple carriages, and the like, relatively complex accounting systems can be maintained by a few well-trained people.

Unit record systems using the punched card as input to verifiers, sorters, and printers when used with wired program boards in data processing equipment have increased the speed, accuracy, and productivity of manual and machine systems.

Computers with high-capacity memory units, vast data storage capability, and the capacity to interface with other computers with their stored data and programs are now being used in large school systems, state government agencies, and regional bureaus, etc.

The major problem emerging in this type of accounting system is not handling or processing the data but instead is related to the programming of the data in order to have the right data in the correct form at the right time to optimize the planning and decision-making processes. Thus, the problem becomes one of "software" rather than "hardware." Frequently our technical capability outruns our conceptual capability, and we do not know how to treat data in order to have it help us resolve a problem.

AUDITING

The concept of an audit is a logical part of the whole idea of the state's responsibility for public education and its accountability to the public. Auditing is the study of an accounting system in general and specific accounts in particular to verify their accuracy and completeness. Since states specify much of the accounting system used in most school districts, audits usually include checks on the legality of expenditures as well as the accuracy of the many entries and calculations.

Audits may be classified by at least two criteria. In terms of time sequences, audits may be described as:

1. Preaudits which are conducted before a transaction is completed. In this type, accounts are checked to see if expenditures are proper and/or within the appropriation. Initiating the encumbrance procedure is a type of preaudit.
2. Postaudits are conducted after a series of transactions has been completed. Usually the annual audit by a certified public accountant hired by the board at the end of a fiscal year, or a periodic audit by a state auditor is considered a postaudit.
3. Continuous audits are conducted by very large organizations to ascertain net worth or cash flow. School systems with computer capability might conduct their own continuous audit, especially if unique fiscal problems require monitoring the flow of revenues and expenditures.

The organizational affiliation of the auditor makes possible another classification of audits:

1. Internal audits are conducted by individuals within the organization. In school systems this might be done (and even mandated by the state) by a designated official reporting directly to the board of education, e.g., the secretary, clerk, treasurer, comptroller, etc. Usually someone on the superintendency team will verify the figures of the accounts in order to prepare various financial reports. Both of these constitute a form of internal audit.
2. External audits are conducted by individuals from outside the school system. These may be private auditors employed by the board, or state, regional, and federal auditors checking

on legal conformity to the particular governmental requirements.

Auditors' reports are not exclusively designed to find crooks and embezzlers. Instead they can be used by school officials to improve their practices and build bridges of confidence with the community and professional staff. Educational needs can be evaluated with more confidence if these kinds of assurance of validity are provided.

If computers are used in accounting and auditing, an "audit trail" must be established wherein actual documents are available for each major step in the processing of the transaction.

REPORTS

The accounting and auditing processes have to do with generating and verifying information pertaining to the financial status of the school system. Reporting deals with disseminating the information to persons or offices which through the use of it can upgrade their understanding and concomitant decision making in school matters. The reporting aspect of accounting is extremely important, and without adequate reporting nearly all else which goes on before would have little impact on understanding, decision making, or planning. As a result, the accounting system should be considered as a part of a total information system. Thus, accounting reports are output for the accounting subsystem but are input to other sub- and suprasystems.

In considering reporting from this posture, one can look at reporting to external agencies and internal units within the school system.

External Reporting

Federal and state law along with local policy dictate much of the data and its format which is reported to external agencies. Federally funded programs usually specify the accounting procedure to be used in describing the financial status and transactions made in connection with these grants. Probably the most important decision for the school business administrator (once involvement in the federally funded program is assured) is how the specified accounting responsibility is to be executed. The total information system perspective is helpful as the school business administrator plans for the design of a flow of school system information relevant to the data required in the federal specifications. In essence, it requires the integration of local data and data channels with the required data and procedures.

Much the same is true for the state-mandated financial reports. However, in most school districts, the information system for the local district is structured around the state mandates. Thus, the monthly financial report for the board members usually uses the same data, format, and terminology as that required in monthly or annual financial reports which the school system must file with the state education and/or finance department.

Financial reports to local agencies or groups are not usually limited to those mandated by the state. Thus, local boards and administrators have considerable freedom in providing data of their own design for these groups. Most school systems are required to publish or make available some kind of an annual financial statement or report. In addition, school boards frequently integrate this with an annual or "state of the school system" report to inform citizens of the status, problems, and accomplishments of the system. Thus, a considerable amount of interpretation of both program and finances is included.

Special reports of the fiscal status of the educational enterprise are frequently generated to illustrate the need for issuing construction bonds, passing tax levies, and enacting other public policy related to fiscal affairs. Unfortunately, the public often perceives such reports as attempts to inform only when the school feels a problem exists, when it has a predetermined solution to it, and when it needs public ratification in the form of allocating more resources. Out of this perception has grown the public demand for greater accountability on a continuous rather than a sporadic, crisis-oriented basis. The school business administrator should be aware of his responsibility and capability in providing one kind of data to meet this emerging public demand. With an understanding of school accounting, he can provide important input to the administrative team in designing and developing meaningful kinds of reports which can relate the school system to the community in the most open and honest sense possible.

Internal Reporting

The internal reports which involve school accounting can also be perceived as one aspect of an information system. It is in this form that accounting can best be described as a planning tool for the superintendency team. If administrators in the office of the superintendent think of themselves as a team and if they see their roles and behaviors in an interactive milieu, then it follows that each must have access to the data as well as the thinking of the others. Thus, the accounting system must provide data of a financial nature to each member of the team. These data are (1) indigenous to that member's responsibility and (2) relevant to all other operations of the school system and are sufficient to provide a financial context to the programmatic character of these operations.

Furthermore, it is important that information regarding the nature of all available data and the channels which may be used to obtain it be made available to the whole team. In this way accounting information is accessible to but does not inundate a whole staff which doesn't want or cannot use it at a given time.

Planning and decision making can be expedited through optimizing the quality and availability of relevant data. The school business administrator fulfills his team responsibility in not only providing appropriate information but also integrating his data production process into the larger information systems at the federal, state, and local levels. A significant move in this direction has been made by the Office of Education with its development and publication of the State Educational Records and Reports Series. In addition to *Financial Accounting for Local and State School Systems—Standard Receipt and Expenditure Accounts* (1957), other handbooks have been developed for property accounting, school activity accounting, and staff accounting. These handbooks established uniform definitions and classification systems which have provided a great deal of help to state- and local-level administrators who seek to upgrade quality and uniformity of data among the several levels of government.

SUMMARY

School accounting requirements and current practices have been drawn from the accounting arts and sciences developed in the business and public administration sectors. This chapter describes the function and objectives of school accounting. Principles of accounting are reviewed in order to afford an overview of the fundamental concepts and terminology and thus provide a school business administrator with sufficient knowledge to understand the data and reports generated by the school system accountant. The accounting equation is reviewed to provide an understanding of assets and liabilities. The process of accounting is reviewed in order to acquaint the reader with the concept of debits and credits and the interaction in the flow of transactions. The ten basic steps in the accounting cycle are applied to school business transactions in order to give a sense of sequence. Adoption of the principles to contemporary manual, automatic, or machine accounting results in very complex and rapid processing. Few if any school business administrators will have responsibility for actually operating such equipment. However, a knowledge of the accounting principles will enable him to read, analyze, and interpret the data and reports produced by such machines. In this way the school business administrator has the information he needs to initiate, design, and implement his plans in the school business sphere.

The accounting data generated provides the raw material for auditing and reporting. Audits are used internally (preaudits) to monitor financial affairs. Postaudits are conducted after the fact to determine the accuracy of the system and the propriety of the transactions. Both audits and reports are important in maintaining accountability and credibility in both the state and local communities.

SUGGESTED ACTIVITIES

1. Obtain a copy of your state system of classification of accounts and compare it with the accounting system being used by a local school system of your state. If there are variations between the two, try to account for them.

2. In many states the accounting responsibility is vested in an office other than that of the school business official. Find how this responsibility is designated in your state. How does this affect the responsibility of the school business administrator?

3. Obtain a copy of a monthly financial report of a board of

education. From it develop an interpretation which could be understood by a reasonably perceptive layman.

4. With the cooperation of an accountant in a local school system business office, select a given transaction and trace an audit trail on it from its initiation to its final disposition.

SUGGESTED READINGS

Adams, Bert K., Hill, Quentin M., Lichtenberger, Allan R., Perkins, Joseph A., Jr., and Shaw, Phillip S. *Principles of Public School Accounting.* State Educational Records and Reports Series: Handbook 11-B, Washington, D.C.: U.S. Government Printing Office, 1967.

Lanham, Frank W. *The Meaning of School Accounts,* 2d ed. Columbus, O.: The University Council for Educational Administration, 1964.

Lichtenberger, Allan R., and Penrod, Richard J. *Staff Accounting for Local and State School Systems.* Washington, D.C.: U.S. Department of Health, Education, and Welfare, 1965.

Mitchell, Herbert S. *Manual for School Accounting.* Danville, Ill.: The Interstate Printers & Publishers, Inc., 1961.

Mitchell, Herbert S. *School Accounting for Financial Management.* Danville, Ill.: The Interstate Printers & Publishers, Inc., 1964.

Reason, Paul L., and White, Alpheus L. *Financial Accounting for Local and State School Systems.* Washington, D.C.: U.S. Department of Health, Education, and Welfare, 1957.

Samuelson, Everett V., Tankard, George G., Jr., and Pope, Hoyt, W. *Financial Accounting for School Activities.* Washington, D.C.: U.S. Department of Health, Education, and Welfare, 1959.

Tidwell, Sam B. *Public School Fund Accounting.* New York: Harper and Brothers, 1960.

PLANNING FOR EDUCATIONAL CONTINUITY—PURCHASING, INVENTORY CONTROL, AND DISTRIBUTION

EDUCATIONAL MATERIAL ACQUISITION—PURCHASING

Purchasing—A Support Role

Purchasing is not an end in itself. Educational materials, supplies, and equipment are bought because they are needed in the educational process. Since purchasing has the primary purpose of implementing the work of other areas of the educational complex by procuring needed materials, it can be regarded as a service function. Purchasing can be carried on under this concept with partial effectiveness. The implication, however, is that purchasing considerations are subordinated to the aims, desires, and policies of those being served. This is to sacrifice, by default, the larger benefits and full potentialities of scientific purchasing policies and decisions.

The progressive view, which is gaining in acceptance, is that purchasing's role is coordinated with those of other phases of the school's activities, neither subordinate nor dominant, but working closely with other departments toward an optimal educational program. Purchasing involves the management of materials in flow, from the establishment of sources and shipping, through inventory and warehousing, to the ultimate delivery at educational stations. At every stage there are decisions to be made as to quality, quantity, timing, source, and cost. These decisions must be keyed to constantly changing educational, business, and economic conditions that alter the immediate objectives and policies of purchasing from month to month.

Relationship of Purchasing Agent to Educator

Ultimate responsibility for the type, quality, and quantity of materials to be bought must rest with those who use them and are responsible for results—the educators and support personnel. In this sense, the using departments are in the relation of customers to the purchasing department; and they must be satisfied. This does not place the responsibility or authority for selection in the hands of the educator or the support personnel. Rather, their responsibility is for an accurate definition or specification of the product in terms of formula or analysis, accepted commercial standards, blueprints or dimensional tolerances, the intended purpose of the material, or, in some cases, the identification of a product in the vendor's catalog. Most educational materials, supplies, and equipment are procurable in competitive markets from a variety of vendors; and it is the function of purchasing to select the particular material and source most advantageous to the school system, patronizing two or more alternative sources if it is desirable to stimulate competition or ensure continuity of supply, always remembering that the essential requirements, as defined, must be met. Sometimes it is believed that purchases must be made from local vendors as taxpayers. This should be discouraged unless local vendors meet competitive prices and other vendors are aware of this purchasing practice.

The request for materials involves a statement of quantity needed and the date or time when it should reach the user. The purchasing agent must check quantity ordered against need, particularly if an order deviates from past experience. It is part of his duty to avoid duplication, excessive stock, and unnecessary rush orders that may disrupt the procurement program and cause unnecessary expense.

When quantity and delivery requirements have been established, it is the responsibility of purchasing to decide whether the goods shall be bought in a single lot, in a series of smaller transactions over a time span, or in a single long-term contract with delivery schedules specified according to needs.

Commercial aspects of the transaction negotiations as to price, delivery, guarantees, terms and conditions of contract, and adjustments for over- and undershipments or deficiencies in quality are the responsibilities of purchasing. For most school systems, the purchasing function should include follow-up for delivery, reconciling receipts and vendor's invoices with the purchase order, and passing invoices for payment. Inspection and quality testing of purchases should be handled by the person or persons responsible for purchasing. This function could be contracted to an outside firm. The purchasing department should also be held responsible for storekeeping, warehousing, and complete accountability for materials until they are issued to the using department. With most purchases under the federal titles, this is not an easy task.

Legal Aspects of Purchasing

In an industrial setting the purchasing agent, as indicated by his title, is an agent authorized to make valid contracts of purchase for his company. Many vendors are aware of the role of the industrial purchasing agent and assume the same relationship exists within the educational setting. Because of this distinct difference in role and function, school administrators should develop comprehensive job descriptions for their purchasing personnel with definitive statements as to authority and responsibility.

A primary rule for purchasing personnel is to consult the school's legal counsel on any doubtful or controversial points, in the analysis of unusual or obscure legal terms in the vendor's forms, and in the phraseology of the clauses and conditions that are to be incorporated in purchase agreements. It is not enough that a purchase be economically sound; it must be legally sound as well, both in the agreement itself and the way it is carried out, because purchase orders issued or contracts signed are legal documents. Many governmental regulations directed at labor conditions, employment practices, ensuring fair competition, and those governing the price and distribution of goods have legal implications.

Unless a purchase order is issued in acceptance of a specific bid or offer by a vendor, it is not a contract; it is an offer and becomes a contract only when it is accepted by the vendor. This is the reason for "acknowledgment copies" of purchase orders, sent with the original order to be signed and returned by vendor. It has been held in various courts that a signed order given to a traveling salesman is not valid until accepted by his employer. Salesmen are not agents of the company and are generally legally allowed a degree of "puff" about their product. A contract, to be valid, must impose an obligation upon both parties. The obligation should be specific. Contracts may be void when there is no obligation on the buyer's part, when the demand is hypothetical, or the quantity to be delivered is conditioned solely by the will of one of the contracting parties. Date and time of delivery and price should be integral parts of the contract.

Warranties are of two types: express and implied. If, in the absence of express warranties of quality, fitness, or performance of a product by a seller, the buyer makes known to the seller the particular purposes for which the goods or equipment are required, relying on the seller's judgment and skill, there is an implied warranty that the goods shall be reasonably fit for that purpose. In invoking the warranty clauses of a contract, the purchaser is under obligation to take action as soon as the deficiency of goods or the breach of warranty is observed.

Making a purchase involves a transfer of title to the merchandise from vendor to buyer. If goods are sold and shipped f.o.b. (free on board) the vendor's location, the purchaser automatically takes legal title. By doing so, he assumes full responsibility for accidents, contingencies, damage, loss, delay, etc., by the carrier. He must determine the best route of shipping, suitable insurance, and installation or handling of materials upon arrival at destination. If goods are shipped f.o.b. buyer's location, title passes to the buyer when goods are delivered by carrier.

Legal fraud has been defined as any act, deed, or statement made by either the purchaser or vendor before the purchase contract is formalized, that is likely to deceive the other party. A vendor is not liable for fraud if the evidence proves (1) that the vendor or the salesman made a false statement after the contract was signed, (2) that the vendor or his salesman did not know that the quality of the merchandise was not as claimed in the contract, or (3) that the buyer did not rely on the vendor's statements concerning his product. If a buyer inspects merchandise before entering into the contract, he is put upon his guard and if experienced with the merchandise, is expected to practice good judgment in decision making.

If a contract agreement is made on the basis of fraudulent acts or statements, the contract is not valid. A delay in claiming fraud or making a payment after having discovered fraud may destroy the basis for rescission and damages.

There are many more aspects of law that affect purchasing. In planning the purchasing routine, the person responsible for purchasing should work very closely with the school board's attorney in preparing procedures, purchase forms, and contracts.

Relationship of Purchasing Role in Educational Budgeting to Roles of Other Administrative Divisions

The purchasing function is an integral part of the administrative complex. In the area of budget planning, whether short- or long-term, the purchasing group can be instrumental in costing out educational programs. The purchasing personnel, because of training, experience, and current understanding of costs, can be extremely beneficial in developing program budgets of one kind or another. The purchasing agent can assist educational personnel in exploring possible new instructional materials and media. In maintenance and capital outlay programs, purchasing personnel can perform the costing function. As cost benefit analysis and cost effectiveness analysis become common evaluative planning procedures in the educational world, purchasing personnel can give valuable operational inputs. In buying for a hospital, a university, a school system, or some governmental unit, when the profit motive and competitive factors are absent, the goal should be to get maximum value for the expenditure of a fixed budget appropriation. Purchasing efficiency in institutional and governmental administration seeks to make the materials dollar go farther, thereby either reducing the necessity of raising additional funds by taxation and appropriations or releasing available funds for an extension of services.

Purchasing—the Act

The fundamental objectives for purchasing may be summarized as follows:

1. Planning a program of educational materials and equipment procurement that will optimize the educational output of the system;

2. Maintaining continuity of supply to support the educational program, and doing so with the minimum in inventory, consistent with educational need, safety, and economic advantage;
3. Avoiding duplication, waste, and obsolescence of materials and equipment;
4. Maintaining standards of quality in relation to suitability of use;
5. Acquiring materials and equipment at the lowest cost consistent with quality and service required;
6. Helping the educational system maintain maximum instructional efficiency at all times.

Purchasing personnel must remember that they are serving a support function for the educational system. They must not become so enamored with the purchasing act that it becomes cumbersome.

The Right Quality

Quality must be defined. It is, specifically, the sum or composite of the properties inherent in a material or product. Every definition of quality is predicated on some unit of measurement understood by purchaser and vendor.

Chemical analysis is one method of measurement. The formula of a cleaning compound measures its usefulness and safety on various types of materials and its efficacy in removing various types of dirt or foreign matter. The sulfur, ash, and BTU content of coal tell whether a fuel is suitable for use in a particular power equipment installation and its measure of heat efficiency. The school system may need to employ outside testing agents for this type of quality control. Another possibility is to buy products meeting federal purchasing specifications; e.g., motor oil, floor waxes, ink, cleaning solutions, lunchroom detergents, etc.

Physical tests provide a measurement of quality in respect to such properties as tensile and shearing strength of metals and fibers, the bursting, folding, and tearing strength of paper, and elasticity, ductility, opacity, resistance to abrasion or shock, and resistance to sunlight or moisture of other materials. Performance or guaranteed output may be a basic measure of quality, and a proper description of intended use would make this the responsibility of the vendor.

If purchasing is done by brand name, "or equal" should be

added to the statement or one has the serious disadvantage of limiting procurement to a single vendor and thus eliminating the competitive element, except insofar as competition may exist in distribution.

The actual description or definition of quality is sometimes avoided by inviting prospective vendors to match a sample submitted by the purchaser. This practice is justified under certain conditions — in the case of special, nonrepetitive items when absolute quality requirements are not a significant factor, or when the size and importance of the purchase do not warrant the effort and expense of formulating a more definitive buying description.

In many commodity fields there are well-established grades or quality designations that are common to vendor and purchaser. Where this is the case, the commercial description of desired qualities is simplified by reference to the appropriate grade.

There are some items, usually of a technical nature, whose quality cannot be sufficiently defined by any of the preceding methods, so that formal bid specifications must be prepared. The specifications should state the means or basis for testing purchases so specified. Nonessential quality restrictions should be avoided because they can add to cost and difficulty of procurement without adding to utility or value. Definitions that unnecessarily restrict competition should be avoided. Conformation to established commercial and industrial standards should be encouraged. Analysis of function to be performed should receive primary consideration in preparing specifications. Minimum standards should be stressed so that anything meeting the standards may be considered.

In summary, it cannot be stressed too strongly that the quality requirements of purchased goods are properly determined and defined by those who are responsible for the utilization of the purchased materials.

Before an order is placed or a quotation is requested, the purchasing official must specify what is desired in order that prospective vendors may intelligently quote prices and fill orders. Specifications may be very simple or in considerable detail.

Example: *8d common wire nail* is a generally understood term and requires little explanation.

Example: *Smooth-on no. 4 plane or equal* is also generally understood.

Example: *Ink, writing, blue-black to meet federal specifications #TT-I-563b of October 1, 1968* is more detailed.

Items of office equipment may require a lengthy description of type, style, material, and sometimes method of construction.

In addition to the description, specifications should state, "or equivalent."

The Right Quantity

The second decision a purchaser must make, after determining the right quality to buy, is how much to buy. Purchase quantities must maintain a balance with current educational needs and with the advantages of volume buying, aided by the cushioning effect of an inventory reservoir of materials, to which current purchases are added and from which currently needed quantities are withdrawn.

The determination of optimum ordering quantity is a mathematical computation. Besides the basic purchase, there are many factors to be taken into consideration: the unit cost of items in various lot sizes, the average inventory resulting from purchasing in different quantities, the number and cost of negotiating and issuing a purchase order, and the cost of carrying materials and equipment in inventory. The utilization of computers in purchasing has expedited the determination of optimal orders. A school system with definitive cost accounting can use the following formula for determining optimum quantity:

$$E = \sqrt{\frac{2\,UP}{I}}$$

Where: E = Economic order quantity (in dollars)
U = Annual usage (in dollars)
P = Cost of issuing purchase order (in dollars)
I = Cost of carrying inventory (as a decimal percentage of inventory value).

Computers can implement an entire purchasing system so far as standard stock items are concerned. The key to its value and effectiveness is its ability to determine optimum ordering and stock quantities and to control reorder points and quantities once proper inventory standards and policies have been established.

Thus the automation of the mechanical features of purchasing procedure is valuable in itself. The role of the computer in purchasing has been greatly and effectively extended with added experience. Among the operations that are now performed electronically are:

1. Automatically reordering for stock replenishment, including the writing of the purchase order;
2. Follow-up of all open purchase orders, not only the "machine" orders for stock items, but also the manually written orders for nonstock, nonrepetitive, custom-made items;
3. Checking of invoices, and payment of invoices by automatic writing of the check;
4. Distributing changes to the proper account code;
5. Providing statistical data for quality control, vendor rating, and similar purposes, including the direct interpretation of such data by machines.

Factors influencing quantity are the time required for delivery from the time the order is issued and manufacturing costs per item if special items are ordered. There are quantity economics involved when considering the costs of transportation and storage facilities. Market trends can also influence optimum purchasing quantities. See figure 10.1.

The Right Price

Price is meaningless unless it is predicated on adequate quality and quantity, assured delivery, reliability and continuity of supply, maximum efficiency in educational utilization with minimum downtime because of service needs. To establish a right and realistic price, buyers properly insist upon firm bids (see figure 10.2 for sample notice to bidders). Competitive bids are almost mandatory in government purchasing because of the charges of favoritism and patronage and the need to conserve taxpayers' money. Negotiated prices are not necessarily incompatible with competition. In almost all cases negotiation starts with a firm bid, but many further modifications may be made before the optimum balance is achieved between quality, service, and cost.

There are three types of discounts which concern the buyer in his consideration of price. Trade discounts are set up on a graduated scale which are applicable according to the vendor's

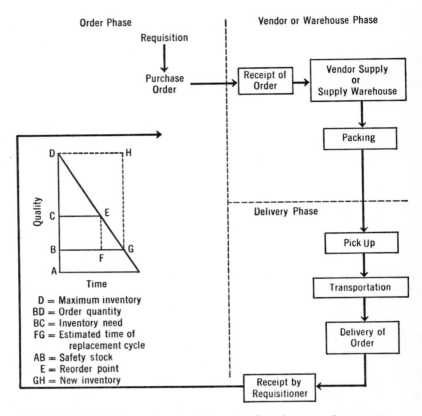

FIGURE 10.1   Three phases of planning for educational continuity.

classification of customers. The purchaser's responsibility is to see that the school system is in the most favorable customer classification possible. This is a proper subject for negotiation with the prime supplier, distributor, or both.

Quantity discounts offer lower unit prices on large quantity orders. The buyer's responsibility is to adjust his ordering practices to the most advantageous quantity price break (see figure 10.3 for sample price quotation).

Cash discounts are an inducement for prompt payment of invoice charges and are earned only when payment is made in accordance with stipulated terms. The purchaser's responsibility for this potential saving includes: (1) seeing that proper cash dis-

Board of Education of the Memphis City Schools
DIVISION OF PURCHASES
2597 Avery   Tel. 323-8311   Memphis, Tenn., 38112..19........

NOTICE TO BIDDERS
(NOT AN ORDER)

Please submit quotations on the items listed below. The right is reserved to reject any or all bids. If substitutions are offered, give full particulars. There will be a public opening of this bid not later than..19........
The right is reserved to accept the bid most advantageous to the Board of Education. Successful vendor shall be paid only when delivery is complete.

Item No.	Quantity	Board of Ed. Warehouse No.	Article and Description	Price	Unit	Total
Remarks						

Notice: Time, date, and nature of bid must be clearly marked on face of a sealed envelope.

The Board of Education of the Memphis City Schools:
We propose to furnish the items listed above at prices quoted and guarantee safe delivery F.O.B.
_____ and as specified.

Terms:_____

_____ (Name of Firm)

_____ (Address)

_____ (Telephone No.)   _____ (Authorized Representative)

FIGURE 10.2 Sample notice to bidders. (*Courtesy Memphis City School System.*)

BOARD OF EDUCATION
MEMPHIC CITY SCHOOLS
2597 Avery Avenue
Memphic, Tennessee 38112

Date May 1, 1973

TO John Smith Publishing Co.   QUOTATION DUE: May 9, 1973

    1111 First Avenue

    New York, New York

PRICE QUOTATION

THIS IS NOT AN ORDER--PLEASE QUOTE PRICE ON THIS FORM ONLY

QUANTITY	ARTICLE AND DESCRIPTION	UNIT	PRICE	TOTAL
1 ea.	MIDNIGHT SHADOW by Danny Charles			

REMARKS:

TERMS:_____   SIGNED_____

                                     TITLE _____
DELIVERY FOB:_____
                                     FROM E. P. Williams
FOR: Tech High School   TITLE Buyer
          School or Department

FIGURE 10.3   Sample price quotation. (*Courtesy Memphis City School System.*)

count terms are incorporated in the order, (2) securing invoices promptly from vendors, (3) processing invoices promptly and getting them to the proper paying agent, and (4) securing extended discount privileges when unavoidable delays are encountered.

The objective evaluation and rating of vendor performance has lagged behind the measurement of other factors in purchasing. The buyer is aware in a general way that some vendors require an excessive amount of expediting effort and are consistently late in deliveries and that rejections for inadequate quality are more numerous than with other vendors. Many times these same vendors are slow to assemble or service equipment or may do so incorrectly. A computer in which downtime due to lack of service is measured in days rather than hours can make the initial purchase price a rather insignificant portion of the total price. Purchasers should establish a system of vendor evaluation with the results being included in the determination of the lowest responsible bidder.

Purchasing—the Followup

The establishment of centralized purchasing is a reflection of overall school board philosophy and policy. It immediately entails a whole series of internal, interdepartmental policies relating to lines of authority, channels of procedure, and departmental relationships. These policies should be very carefully defined and made a matter of record, for they define the scope and responsibility of the purchaser. Policies include such matters as the authorization to make requisitions, permission for vendor representatives to contact school personnel, the final responsibility for specifications, and value analysis.

The Requisitioner

The first step in the chronology of procurement is to advise the purchasing department of a need, defining it in sufficient detail for ordering purposes and supporting the request with the necessary approvals to authorize a purchase. Definition of the need includes a description or code identification of the material wanted (this may be as simple as giving an item number in a specific vendor's catalog), the quantity requested, and the date by which it will be needed. School policy should explain carefully

Form 14634

Original (Retained by Purchasing Dept.)

BOARD OF EDUCATION OF THE MEMPHIS CITY SCHOOLS
Requisition For Supplies Materials or Service

_____ 19___

N⁰ 12404

School or
Department. _____

Delivery Address _____

Whse. No. _____ Fund _____ Location _____

For Use By Requisitioning Agency

Func.	Obj.	Quantity	Whse. Stock No.	Exact Description, Specifications and Nomenclature of Articles	Approx. Cost of Item	Purchasing Dept. Only						Purchase Order No.
9410	730	1 ea.		13" Typewriter, manual								
2210	400	1 ea.		Bates List Finder								
9410	730	1 ea.		Ten key adding machine, seven list – eight								
				total with credit balance								

Justification Of Need _____

Approved _____ Title _____ Signed _____ Title _____

Requisitioner

FIGURE 10.4 Sample requisition. (Courtesy Memphis City School System.)

the procedure for approving requisitions initiated at any place in the educational system. Some larger school systems develop a system catalog which will include all the standard items used in the educational systems. The teacher then lists the catalog and item number on requisition, thus simplifying the process (see figure 10.4 for sample requisition).

The Purchase Order

See figure 10.5 for sample purchase order. This is the instrument by which goods are procured to fill a requirement. The es-

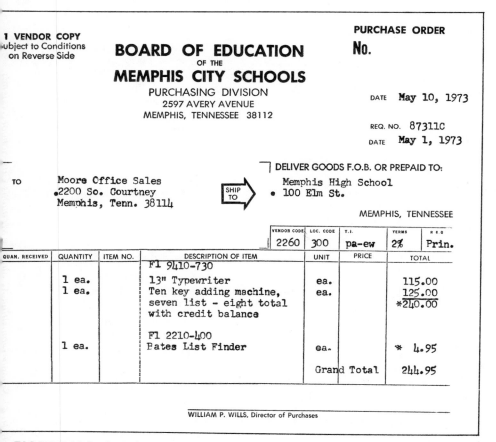

FIGURE 10.5   Sample purchase order. (*Courtesy Memphis City School System.*)

sential information on every purchase order should include: name and address of school system; identifying order number; date; name and address of vendor; general instructions (marking of shipment, special shipping informations, number of invoices required, etc.); delivery date required; shipping instructions (destination, type of carrier, traffic routing, packaging requirements, receiving hours); terms and conditions of the transaction; description of materials; quantity; price; appropriate discount information; and signature.

The purchase order should be prepared in multiple copies. The original copy should be sent to the vendor. A second should be sent to the vendor to be signed and returned as acknowledgment and acceptance of the order. Additional copies are useful for the following purposes:

1. Copy to the receiving department as notice that a shipment is expected and to facilitate identification;
2. Copy to the accounting department as notice of the commitment, to be later reconciled with the invoice and receiving reports as authorization for payment;
3. Copy to the requisitioning department as confirmation;
4. Copy for follow-up or expediting purposes (see figure 10.6 for sample purchase expediter).

Color coding will facilitate routing and processing.

The Warehouse

The warehouse department is responsible for receiving incoming goods, signing and checking carrier's delivery notice, identifying and recording incoming goods, reporting receipt to purchasing, to inventory control, and quality control personnel, and making prompt disposition to the appropriate department.

Accounting

The purchasing department's copy of the invoice is checked against the purchase order number to identify shipment and avoid duplication. Prices and terms, f.o.b. point and transportation charges, and quantity and quality are verified, and prices are extended. When all this is done, the invoice is passed along from

BOARD OF EDUCATION
MEMPHIS CITY SCHOOLS
PURCHASING DIVISION
2597 AVERY AVE.
MEMPHIS, TENN. 38112

Purchase Expediter

PLEASE REPLY IMMEDIATELY

☐ BY PHONE

☐ BY WIRE

☐ ON THIS FORM

PLEASE SAVE YOUR TIME AND OURS, BY COMPLETING THIS
FORM RATHER THAN WRITING A LETTER. FORM MAY BE
RETURNED IN A #10 WINDOW ENVELOPE. FOLD AS
INDICATED AT UPPER LEFT.

To
John Smith Publishing Co.
1111 First Avenue
New York, New York

DATE May 1, 1973

OUR PURCHASE ORDER NO.	YOUR INVOICE NO.	YOUR ORDER NO.	INVOICE DATE	INVOICE AMOUNT	REFERENCE
120120	B7702	W2871	4-6-73	$159.50	

ORDER INFORMATION

1. ( ) Please rush PRICES.
2. ( ) Acknowledge our order and give SHIPPING DATE.
3. ( ) Please mail us ACCEPTANCE COPY of our Purchase Order.
4. ( ) Is this order considered COMPLETE?
5. ( ) Please inform us about items BACK ORDERED.
6. ( ) CHANGE made on above order. Please acknowledge.

SHIPPING INFORMATION

7. ( ) RUSH shipment. ADVISE earliest shipping date.
8. ( ) Will you SHIP on date requested?
9. ( ) WHY did you not ship as promised? WHEN will you ship?
10. ( ) IF SHIPPED advise method.
11. ( ) What PARTIAL shipment can you make and WHEN?
12. ( ) When can BALANCE of order be shipped?
13. ( ) Please make certain order is SHIPPED VIA_____
14. ( ) Please make SHIPMENT RELEASES as shown under Remarks.

ACCOUNTING INFORMATION

15. ( ) We require_____INVOICE COPIES.
16. ( ) INVOICE enclosed RECEIVED IN ERROR.
17. ( ) We are RETURNING attached invoice.
18. ( ) PURCHASE ORDER NO. incorrect or missing.
19. ( ) PRICE ☐ TERMS ☐ DISCOUNT ☐ do not agree with quotation.
20. ( ) Please forward CORRECTED INVOICE or CREDIT MEMO for following reason:

( ) Quantity incorrect.   ( ) Extension incorrect.
( ) Should be F. O. B. destination. ( ) Unit price incorrect.
( ) Material wrong or defective.

21. ( ) SALES TAX not applicable. Exemption No. is_____.
22. ( ) We have no record of RECEIVING INVOICE NO._____
shown on your statement. Please send duplicate invoice.

SERVICE AND OTHER INFORMATION

23. ( ) If order has been shipped, MAIL INVOICE today.
24. ( ) Please forward CERTIFIED WEIGHT slip.
25. ( ) Please forward SHIPPING NOTICE.
26. ( ) Please show PURCHASE ORDER NUMBER on papers referred to or attached.
27. ( ) Material not received. TRACE AND ADVISE.
28. ( ) Please forward receipted FREIGHT BILL.
29. ( ) We have NO RECORD of transaction covered by your invoice. Advise date of shipment, name of person placing order and furnish signed delivery receipt.
30. ( ) Please complete and return our REQUEST FOR QUOTATION dated_____.

REMARKS

SIGNED

Reply

Balance will be shipped from our warehouse May 15.

DATE   SIGNED

· PLEASE RETURN THIS COPY TO SENDER WITH REPLY
PINK COPY IS FOR YOUR RECORDS

FIGURE 10.6   Sample purchase expediter. (Courtesy Memphis City School System.)

the purchasing to the accounting department and serves as a voucher for payment through the disbursing office.

EDUCATIONAL MATERIALS AT REST—INVENTORY

There has, for some time, been a growing awareness of the importance of inventory control as a planning and policy function of the school administrator. The school administrator must strive for maximum utilization of school equipment and supplies and prevent the breakdown of the educational process from lack of school supplies. The size of the school system's inventory will depend upon the delivery service of vendors. When vendors carry complete inventories, this negates the need for large inventories by school systems.

Flow of Materials

Having a current and a long-range storage plan is one key to consistent and efficient warehouse operation. Some questions that must be asked in planning proper warehousing and flow of material are as follows:

1. How much space is required to store items properly?
2. How many units are normally withdrawn as an order?
3. What is maximum number of items to be stored at any one time?
4. What type of storage is best (considering weight, shape, and handling)?
5. What handling equipment is necessary to transport the item?
6. How often is the item withdrawn from stores?
7. Where is the item most frequently used in the education process?

Storeroom Layout

Good storeroom layout attempts to achieve eight objectives:

1. A straight-line flow of activity through the warehouse
2. Minimum handling and transportation of materials
3. Minimum travel and waste motion of personnel
4. Efficient use of space

5. Provision for flexibility and expansion of layout
6. Security against pilferage
7. Ease of physical counting
8. Minimization of material deterioration

Control

Efficiency and economy in inventory control can enhance the educational program to a great degree. As individual learning processes require greater and more complex planning, the acquisition, storing, and delivery of educational materials and equipment become more important. Some advantages of inventory control are as follows:

1. Expedites educational planning throughout the system.
2. Promotes buying economies by determining needs scientifically.
3. Prevents duplication in ordering because it offers a clear picture of present materials available throughout the system.
4. Facilitates the exchange of materials and equipment throughout the system.
5. Minimizes losses from damage due to transit.
6. Reduces losses from mishandling and theft.
7. Aids cost accounting and the development of a program budgeting system.
8. Aids in cost comparison between and among programs and departments.
9. Provides data for perpetual inventories and therefore can lead to reduced insurance costs.
10. Minimizes the investment in inventory.

Inventory control may be expedited through the utilization of a computer. All material receipts and issues for each stock item are fed to the computer daily from keypunched records. There is no hand posting of stock records. The computer performs all the additions and subtractions so as to show the current inventory status of each item at all times, and automatically compares this figure with a previously established reorder point, signalling whenever an item reaches reordering status so that purchasing action is required to replenish stock in accordance with predetermined inventory and ordering quantities (see figure 10.7).

The ordering quantity in this system is fixed in the machine memory. It is possible to program a system for (a) fixed ordering

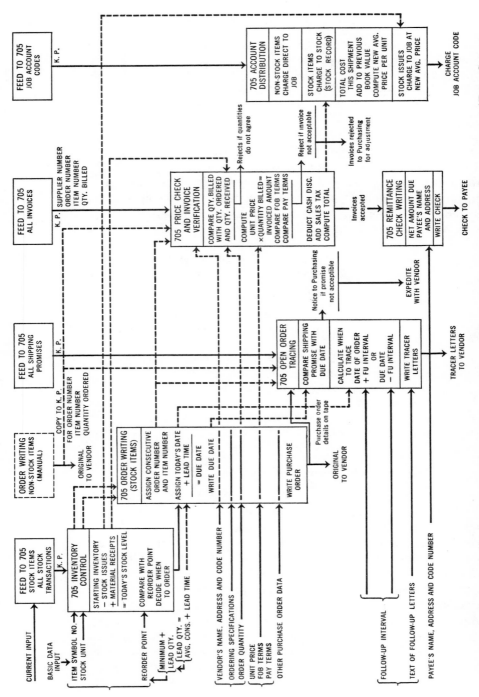

FIGURE 10.7   Flow diagram of a computer system for automated inventory control and procurement. (From Stuart E. Heinritz, Principles and Applications, 3rd ed. [Englewood Cliffs, N.J.: Prentice-Hall, Inc. © 1959], p. 327, re-

quantity with variable ordering frequency, (b) fixed ordering frequency with variable ordering quantity, or (c) at the expense of some additional computations and running time, variable ordering quantity and variable ordering frequency. The first system is deemed advisable since the fixed ordering quantity achieves the advantages of ordering in full package lots rather than broken package quantities, in the most favorable quantity discount brackets, and in lots conforming to full pallet loads.

If the reorder point and quantity have been set with accurate consideration of lead time and safety stock requirements, and if all vendors keep their delivery promises, the system is completely automatic. If an emergency situation arises, due to failure in delivery or because of abnormally heavy usage of an item, the machine signals the emergency and the buyer handles it manually either by expediting an open order or by placing an emergency order to supplement the normal flow of material.

Provision is also made for automatic consideration of stock status within "families" of items—related items procured from one source. Thus, stock items frequently go on order without manual assistance of any kind.

Salvage

The first responsibility in any surplus and scrap disposal is to avoid, so far as possible, the generation of surplus and scrap items. Requisitions must be screened carefully to avoid overbuying. Through centralized purchasing for a school system, the needs of one particular school may be met through the salvage from another school.

Selling

In disposing of surplus or salvage one should first consider the original vendor. Many times he may have an outlet for your materials or equipment. Secondly, there is an established trade of surplus and used equipment dealers. If the surplus items have any general utility and marketable value, such dealers constitute a logical outlet. Another possibility is direct sale to other possible users. Many business publications and association bulletins have sections devoted to the listing of surplus materials and equipment.

Leasing

An alternative method of procuring equipment whereby the salvage problem is circumvented is by leasing instead of outright purchasing. This is particularly beneficial in the areas of equipment development that are showing great technological advancement; e.g., computer hardware. When leasing is done, advantages can be taken of recent innovations without the problem of surplus or salvage sale. Advantages of leasing are as follows:

1. It postpones large capital outlay but permits the use of modern equipment at low initial cost.
2. Equipment can be tested in actual use, bypassing the risk of buying the wrong machine or equipment.
3. Maintenance costs are minimized or can be included as a part of the leasing arrangement, thus reducing the need for highly specialized personnel within the system.

Destroying

Almost every school system has had, at some time, sad experience with destroying obsolete texts, library books, equipment, or educational materials. Before considering destruction as a solution, all possibilities suggested under salvage should be considered as alternatives. If these alternatives have been considered and costs are prohibitive, then destruction may be a possible answer. However, even though economically sound, from a public relations standpoint it may be a poor alternative.

EDUCATIONAL MATERIALS ENROUTE — DISTRIBUTION

Distribution of educational materials is concerned with how teaching materials and equipment move from one place of need to another. A steady, constant flow of materials between learning stations is very important. Time spent in transit is wasted as far as optimal use in the learning process is concerned. Using teachers or school administrators to deliver materials to the next point of use is very inefficient utilization of high-cost professional personnel. Clerical or hourly employees can perform this function efficiently and economically.

By Request

In smaller school systems, materials and equipment may need to be moved throughout the system upon request. Some of this service may be done during the hours when schools are not in session. Directions must be explicit so that the messenger will pick up materials at the correct location and deliver to the proper locations for tomorrow's optimal utilization.

Routing

Larger school systems may have regular delivery routing between schools within the system. Studies should be made to determine priorities of deliveries. General supply deliveries can be scheduled to avoid peak periods of educational materials movement. Flow charts and linear programming techniques can be used in planning optimal distribution of educational supplies and materials (see figure 10.8).

Central vs. Decentralized Storage

Many authorities advocate the decentralization of supply storage. They suggest that this gives a degree of autonomy to the individual schools. In essence it adds to the supply management problem. It is much more difficult to keep accurate inventory records. Accurate costing of supplies to various departments is much more difficult. This also adds to the problem of keeping supplies current and fresh. Supplies tend to become the sole property of that particular building and are not moved to meet needs throughout the system. Pilferage is much more difficult to protect against under the decentralized system. If the school system has centralized storage space and a delivery system there are many advantages to centralized storage.

Conclusion

The procurement program must follow the budget planning and adoption phase of the financial cycle. The purchasing function requires a high level of commitment to the school system and a high code of ethics, keeping constantly in mind that it is public not personal money being spent. All purchasing should be done

VEHICLE LOG FOR MAIL AND DISTRIBUTION AND WAREHOUSING

DATE: _____

DRIVER'S NAME	TRUCK NO.	DESTINATION	TIME OUT	TIME IN

FIGURE 10.8   Vehicle log for mail and distribution and warehousing. (Courtesy Memphis City School System.)

openly and aboveboard without resorting to secrecy or favoritism. Some administrators enjoy a certain amount of secrecy and quickly rationalize this practice. This approach to the problem will ultimately result in a weakening of confidence of teachers, other personnel, vendors, and the public in general. This in time will destroy the effectiveness of a purchasing program.

The purchasing group must remember that their function is to support the teachers and other educational personnel. Educational usage of supplies, materials, and equipment must first meet the educational criterion for best utilization. Decisions of the purchasing group must not impede the efficiency of the educational team. The purchasing function must have as its primary objective the provision of quality materials, supplies, and equipment of the right quantity needed by the user at the time he needs it. If this objective is not accomplished, various economies and technical efficiencies become worthless. On the other hand, the necessity of accomplishing this objective does not mean that the purchasing function should be carried out without giving consideration to economical methods of purchasing and distribution. It should be recognized that through effective and economical procurement more and better equipment and supplies are provided. This is highly significant, as there are very few school systems that have all the instructional supplies, materials, and equipment of the proper quality that they need.

SUMMARY

Every principle of good procurement applies to purchasing, inventory control, warehousing, and salvage in all types of institutions. Good purchasing follows the same guidelines for industry, government, and institutions. However, institutions often lack the motivation for cost-control efficiencies that may exist in competitive industries. Institution budgets, therefore, tend to be harder to control.

Schools deal with a much broader spectrum of materials and services than the average industrial firm. Challenging specifications are especially important and fruitful. A researcher's or teacher's knowledge of his field does not entail knowledge of economics and market availability of equipment and supplies needed to conduct teaching and research. The purchasing manager, by working with the academician well "upstream," can save him time and needless worry as well as save the institution money.

Ethics in educational purchasing are probably more critical than they are in industry. This is especially true because of increasing interrelationships among business, government, and institutions. Controlling salesmen and their attempts at backdoor selling is frequently more difficult in institutions than it is in industry. In theory, reciprocity should be easier to control in schools and hospitals than it is in industry; in practice, this is often not the case. Trustees, donors, board members, and alumni on occasion bring great pressure on institutions for the purchase of their companies' products. Normally, such purchases (if made on any basis other than quality, service, and price) should be resisted as being an expense, rather than a benefit.

Institutions have the same two reasons for carrying items in stores as an industry—economy and service. However, institutions also have a third—campus congestion. Supply reserves, however, do not have to be stored in the institution itself. They can be stored in the vendor's storeroom. This concept of the vendor being an extension of the institution's stores system can free funds for other purposes. All these factors will increase procurement efficiency.

SUGGESTED ACTIVITIES

1.   Explain why reciprocity can take on a different form in institutions than in industry.

2.   Explain in some detail why purchasing goods and services for large institutions requires special abilities.

3.   Diagram an automated purchasing and inventory system.

4.   The uninformed person sometimes envisions an automated purchasing system as one in which most purchasing personnel are simply replaced by a huge computer. This is not true. What jobs do people perform in operating an automated purchasing system? Discuss the importance of these jobs.

5.   Explain how a computer can calculate the economic order quantity for a particular material. From a buyer's point of view, what problems might you anticipate regarding the computer's ability to calculate accurate and valid EOQ values? Explain.

6. When a purchase (or sales) contract is created, what specific actions constitute the "offer" and the "acceptance"?

7. List and discuss the essential elements of a contract.

8. Discuss the warranty protection a purchaser has when he makes a purchase.

9. How can a purchaser infringe the rights of a patent holder?

SUGGESTED READINGS

Aljian, George W. *Purchasing Handbook: Standard Reference Book on Purchasing Policies, Practices, Procedures, Contracts, and Forms.* 2d ed. New York: McGraw-Hill Book Company, 1966.

Barlow, C. Wayne. *Purchasing for the Newly Appointed Buyer.* New York: American Management Association, 1970.

Cantor, Jeremiah. *Evaluating Purchasing Systems.* New York: American Management Association, 1970.

Harris, Douglas H., and Chaney, Frederick B. *Human Factors In Quality Assurance.* New York: John Wiley & Sons, Inc., 1969.

Heinritz, Stuart F., and Farrell, Paul V. *Purchasing: Principles and Applications.* 5th ed. Englewood Cliffs, N.J.: Prentice-Hall, Inc., 1971.

Killeen, Louis M. *Techniques of Inventory Management.* New York: American Management Association, 1969.

Lee, Lamar, and Dobler, Donald W. *Purchasing and Materials Management.* 2d ed. New York: McGraw-Hill Book Company, 1971.

Naddar, Eliezer. *Inventory Systems.* New York: John Wiley & Sons, Inc., 1966.

Stockton, Robert S. *Basic Inventory Systems: Concepts and Analysis.* Boston: Allyn and Bacon, Inc., 1965.

MAINTENANCE AND OPERATION

INTRODUCTION

One of the key planning roles of the school business administrator is in the operation and maintenance of the school plant, equipment, and service facilities. Billions of dollars have been spent for constructing and equipping currently operating school plants in the United States. Additional amounts have been spent on rehabilitating older facilities, adding much-needed equipment to meet current demands of such instructional programs as vocational-technical education and science, and providing more comfortable facilities in terms of thermal environment, lighting, and noise control. These facilities and vast amounts of complex equipment must be maintained and kept in current operational status. The school business administrator's role in maintenance is to oversee the functions associated with repair, replacement, and upkeep of all school facilities. His role in operations is to oversee the housekeeping functions, the performance of scheduled upkeep procedures, and plant security for the entire system. As a part of the administrative team, the school business administrator should join with other staff members in determining a philosophy of maintenance and operations and push for its adoption by the board. This philosophy should allow for the development of policies for maintenance and operations and provide the machinery for developing procedures to execute these policies. Detailed examples of policies are included in each section of this chapter.

It is important for the school business administrator, especially in urban centers, to be aware of those areas considered "maintenance" and those areas considered "operations" under local union agreements. The union agreement will spell out in great detail what can be done by the maintenance staff and what can be accomplished by operations personnel. The importance of this role differentiation should not be overlooked in planning for both the selection of personnel and for budget considerations by the total school system. Day-to-day operations of schools can be impacted by the school business administrator's success or failure in dealing with operations and maintenance union demands. Many school districts do not have union representation for maintenance and operations personnel; but the difficulties of selection, evaluation, and retention still face the local district. Whether professional negotiations are a part of the school business administrator's role or not, he is often directly responsible for the use of major portions of the budget as it relates to maintenance and operation of school facilities. The necessity to plan with other key members of the administrative team, therefore, assumes major importance.

MAINTENANCE

Maintenance is that function of the school system associated with repairs and replacements to ensure continuous usability of the physical plant, equipment, and service facilities. Availability for continuous use is the key item in any maintenance program and is the essential point undergirding the need for the planning role of the school business administrator. The development of the system's philosophy regarding maintenance and the establishment of policies necessary to implement this philosophy in day-to-day operations is the key to a successful maintenance program. Beyond the philosophy of maintenance developed by the district are those legal responsibilities of the state and the local governmental unit, ranging from worker accident laws to observance of local building codes. In many instances, certain worker accident laws do not apply directly to school districts but are a part of the overall operational policies of a district. The school business administrator should insist that at least these minimum standards be observed. These laws cover such items as employment of minors in hazardous jobs, the weight females are allowed to lift, and minimum safety regulations relative to activities at building sites and in capital improvement projects.

Obviously the effective organization of the maintenance program is essential to the success of the day-to-day operation of the local schools. It is through this function, for example, that school buses run on schedule and that heat is available for use in a building on a given day. The overall philosophy of maintenance should consider a number of points. A major item of consideration has to do with initial facility planning in terms of maintenance. Other major considerations include the concept of educational obsolescence versus physical obsolescence, the practice of preventive maintenance, contingency planning in the event of budget reductions, the role of the maintenance staff in capital projects, contract versus local staff maintenance considerations, priority of maintenance functions, and cost analysis. It is a recognized fact that in most situations the success and cost of maintenance of buildings and equipment is tied to the initial planning and construction of the facility. Low-cost, high-success maintenance can often be ensured with proper advance planning. This can be illustrated in terms of the choice of materials used in the construction of buildings; selection of equipment for heating/cooling, student work stations, laboratories, shops, and cafeterias; and purchase of consumable supplies impacting equipment, plant, or grounds.

It is apparent that initial low-cost construction is not always the answer when it is recognized that many school buildings have an expected life span in excess of fifty years. The actual construction cost of a building is generally considered inversely proportional to the cost of maintenance of that facility. For example, it is expected that a poorly constructed or an improperly constructed building will cost a great deal more than the average 1.5 to 2 percent maintenance figure generally accepted for overall school building maintenance. Maintenance costs are often in excess of 7 percent for buildings which were very poorly constructed.

The next area for serious consideration by the school business administrator as he participates in team planning is decision-making relative to educational obsolescence versus physical obsolescence of school plants. This question is concerned with the point at which, regardless of the effectiveness of continued maintenance programs, the building ceases to be a viable factor in the instructional program of the school district. The functionality rather than the maintenance of the facility becomes the issue. Considerations of structural alterations, program changes, and so forth, will be an integral part of all such considerations; but the ultimate decision to dispose of a property must be made on a programmatic basis, not on a maintenance-operations consideration. It is here that the role of the school business administrator again meshes with those of other members of the administrative team in planning relative to the overall school program. Decisions to abandon well-maintained buildings are hard; but an objective look by *all* members of the team allows for the proper interchange of data which can facilitate a consensus decision.

It is generally false economy on the part of a school board to reduce outlays for maintenance programs when a budget squeeze comes since deterioration of a building improperly maintained is potentially more costly than a current expenditure necessary to maintain it at an acceptable and usable level. Occasionally budget considerations do require that maintenance programs be curtailed or even halted in certain areas. The key to doing this without major implications centers in the time lapse and the selectivity of items to be curtailed. For example, it is generally conceded that plans calling for roof replacement on a fifteen-year cycle can be altered to allow for a seventeen-year cycle without major damage to the buildings. However, to go beyond the maximum safety period often creates additional problems. In the above illustration, leaks through a weathered roof could cause internal damage to ceilings, floors, walls, and equipment far in excess of the cost of the roof replacement. The planning function and team consultation will key these decisions.

In the same area, most maintenance persons would agree that a cut in a program such as roof replacement would be desired rather than a general across-the-board reduction of 15 percent in the total maintenance budget. The rationale supporting this is simple. It is far easier to convince a school board to reinstate a total program, i.e., roof replacement, than to replace a 15 percent cut in the total maintenance budget.

One overall consideration should be paramount in the maintenance program—it is difficult to convince the general public that a quality educational program can be or is being carried out in poorly maintained buildings.

Organization of Maintenance

All maintenance programs are concerned with the basic elements of safety, serviceability, and economy. There are basically three plans of maintenance for school district consideration: (1) the local system maintenance program, (2) the contracted maintenance program, or (3) a combination of these. For example, some districts elect to assume responsibility for the operation of a bus fleet, while other districts contract with individuals for buses, and still other districts operate no bus system at all. Some districts service their own office machines (both for staff use and instructional purposes), while others contract with outside vendors for the service.

In examination of the school district-operated maintenance system, there are a number of relevant factors to be considered. If a school district operates its own maintenance program, it can avoid such delays and costs as are associated with taking bids, opening them, and perhaps negotiating for services or materials of equal quality. Overhead costs which are charged by concerns performing maintenance functions can be eliminated. An additional factor which might influence the decision on contractual versus noncontractual services is that there need be no time delay with a local (i.e., "in-house") maintenance system as opposed to a contractual arrangement, although time delays do occur locally and must be a part of local contingency planning. It may be possible to make more efficient use of personnel in terms of scheduling peak-load, peak-time operations, if the maintenance staff reports directly to an employee of the local school district. Also, local district employees often can be required to provide higher standards of workmanship than can the contractor working for a profit.

However, there are some problems that are associated with implementing an in-house maintenance operation. Many maintenance functions require a very specialized type of procedure which may not be needed more than two or three times a year, and the skillful employee necessary to accomplish this work may be too expensive to maintain on a local school staff. Another factor involved in certain types of maintenance is associated with the use of very specialized equipment or tools in combination with very specialized requirements in terms of physical structure or materials which are not generally associated with a local school district maintenance program. Yet another factor is that of maintenance scheduling which can work both as a positive and as a negative consideration for a school district-operated maintenance system. For example, it may be noted that certain types of school repairs cannot be accomplished while school is in session, nor can they be accomplished when certain weather conditions exist. This can necessitate peak work loads within very finely distributed periods of time, causing a very difficult scheduling situation if a large maintenance staff were maintained locally. An additional factor to be considered in the local-versus-contracted services area is that while time and money may be saved at the bid phase of work by having local personnel perform the job, often costs related to equipment, depreciation of maintenance buildings, special insurance, sick leave pay, and so forth, are not considered. The scheduling of needed seasonal work may also require that a district consider contracted services for periods such as summer vacations. This additional need may be dictated by workload and local vacation schedules.

One major policy decision relative to contracted-versus-noncontracted services centers on the use of local maintenance personnel on capital outlay projects. To use maintenance crews to build bookcases or lay sidewalks may cause the routine maintenance program to be neglected. Again, if the school business administrator uses the planning function in a proper manner, he will be able to determine the approximate amounts of time when crews can be used on these capital projects and when they are to be on schedule or emergency requests.

Regardless of the organization of the maintenance program in the district, an individual plan for each structure and/or item of equipment must be established. A replacement schedule for bus engines, a plan for roof upkeep on each building (including a replacement cycle), and a painting plan for each building is a *must* for effective planning and allocation of scarce resources.

Cost Analysis

A competent school business administrator should be able to predict, within an acceptable range, the year-end balance for maintenance projects. Cost data for each job for which funds are encumbered should be compiled for the current year and used in making budget projections. Records for several years should be maintained for use in long-range planning. Accounting problems often occur in unfinished jobs when, for example, on-hand materials are used without appropriate requisition records or materials to be purchased cost more than estimated. Funds for maintenance should be allocated on a system-wide basis rather than on a building basis. This provides for flexibility in the use of funds and does not allow needed services to be omitted at one site while "make-work" projects are being accomplished at another. The use of electronic data processing can be invaluable in providing the data for predictions of budget figures and for use in the planning function.

Types of Maintenance

The key element in any maintenance program is not its complexity, its cost, or its organizational scheme, but simply its effectiveness. This effectiveness is measured each day in thousands of ways in countless locations from central office to athletic dressing rooms to laboratories. The major types of maintenance fall into four classifications: (1) preventive, (2) periodic, (3) recurring, and (4) emergency. The divisions overlap to a degree, but each has a separate function. Often a combination of two or more of the options below must be made to ensure adequate service.

Preventive Maintenance

Preventive maintenance is that program for servicing machines, systems, and structures devised to prevent a breakdown of the total system or any one of its component parts. For example, a preventive maintenance plan is set up for all parts of a lathe or band saw in a shop to inspect specific points for stress or wear which indicate possible failure at future points in time. The checking of belts and the checking of springs for tension, for example, on various machines are examples of preventive maintenance procedures. The purpose of preventive maintenance schedules is to maximize the useful life of and preclude or at least delay a breakdown of any sort which could render a piece of equipment, a structure, or an operating system unusable. It is generally accepted that the cost of a preventive maintenance program is, when properly planned, one of the most worthwhile items, in terms of cost return, in a school budget.

Preventive maintenance has not been practiced in many schools because manpower needs are so acute in other areas that there is no time for this function. Secondly, preventive maintenance has not been practical due to a lack of an easily administered inspection service. The planning function which provides for accurate control records and schedules is a necessary part of a successful preventive maintenance program. Record-keeping is discussed later in this section.

Periodic Maintenance

Periodic maintenance is scheduled on an occurring or a contractual basis for equipment and facilities for predetermined times. Generally speaking, periodic maintenance schedules are set up to be accomplished on specific days or at specific times. This type of program is often associated with the maintenance of school office equipment and with the maintenance of equipment in such teaching areas as business education, home economics, or trade and industrial programs. However, such building maintenance functions as painting can be scheduled on a periodic basis.

Recurring Maintenance

Recurring maintenance is more closely related to the day-to-day operation of facilities and use of equipment. Where periodic maintenance schedules are not in force or where the need to have repairs made in a short period of time is important, a recurring maintenance plan is needed. This plan allows for servicing equipment until it is restored to full operational status regardless of the number of service calls needed.

Emergency Maintenance

Emergency maintenance is, of course, that function of the maintenance operation which is to fix or repair equipment or systems which have ceased to function at a particular time. The basic differences in recurring and emergency maintenance are the time frames in which they occur and the cost factor. For example, an emergency maintenance plan on a system such as a computer system which is in operation twenty-four hours a day would be in effect at any hour of the day or night. On the other hand, in a recurring maintenance program several hours might elapse between the breakdown of the item and the arrival of maintenance personnel.

Many useful references are available which detail school building maintenance procedures. These sources provide reference lists and explanations beyond the scope of this chapter and should be examined carefully by the school business administrator for use in his system. An illustration from one of these sources appears in figure 11.1.

Selection and Training of Personnel

As is true with any other function of the school operation, the selection and training of personnel for the maintenance function have a significant impact upon the success of the maintenance program. Different patterns of selection and training emerge in school districts, with size and geographic location being the two major determining factors in most instances. As was noted in a previous section, larger school systems often have union agreements covering both maintenance and operations personnel. Under these circumstances, some of the elements of training and selection may be covered by union stipulations as to assignment based on union membership, journeyman worker status, etc. Stipulations of most, if not all, union agreements will detail specific competencies to be expected from each employee; at the same time the scope of each position is defined. Actual selection will generally be left to local systems, but qualifications will be spelled out. An orientation program may be required, but actual technical competence and desirable personal qualifications will be expected and can be demanded upon application of the prospective employee.

Where the size of the school district warrants, a supervisor should be employed to direct the maintenance program. He should report directly to the school business administrator and/or the assistant superintendent for buildings and grounds. The supervisor's responsibilities would include making recommendations concerning personnel selection, evaluation, and retention, and conducting training for all maintenance personnel.

In a small district the school business administrator may be charged with planning the maintenance function and, in addition,

BUILDING MAINTENANCE SURVEY

School _____

Date of Construction _____ Number of Teachers _____

Enrollment _____ Type of School: Grades _____

Number of Classrooms _____ Size of Site_____

Pupil Capacity _____ Type of Construction:

                                          Exterior _____

                                          Interior _____

Additions: Date _____ Type (size and type wall

construction) and/or Renovations _____

Number and Size of Regular Classrooms

_____ Classrooms @ _____ sq. ft. with _____ floor covering

_____ Classrooms @ _____ sq. ft. with _____ floor covering

_____ Classrooms @ _____ sq. ft. with _____ floor covering

Special Areas (in square feet) such as Science, Commercial, Home
Making, Health, Art, Music, Shop, others

_____ _____ sq. ft. _____ sq. ft.

_____ _____ sq. ft. _____ sq. ft.

_____ _____ sq. ft. _____ sq. ft.

FIGURE 11.1 Building maintenance survey sample.

be the direct supervisor. In small districts the problems of personnel selection may be compounded by the scarcity of competent persons available locally. If this is the case, extensive training programs may be needed to gain the level of competence necessary to handle the maintenance of expensive and highly technical equipment often found in many school laboratories, electronic shops, etc. Factors such as cost, time, staff turnover, and so forth, make extensive individual training impractical. The type of maintenance service in terms of local-versus-contracted service established by the local district impacts the role of the school business administrator and the nature of the maintenance staff.

Maintenance Records

One of the most important parts of any maintenance program is keeping adequate and complete records. It is imperative that an exact record of all maintenance functions within a school district be kept and that this information be available to the proper personnel within the district. Only through the proper selection of maintenance forms and the proper completion of these forms can one determine with any degree of accuracy the cost effectiveness of a maintenance program. No day-to-day record of the maintenance of each building within the district and each item of material used can be kept without these data. These facts are important for the determination of the cost-effectiveness factors noted above for determination of current maintenance fund balances, as well as for advanced planning within the school district.

Effective use of the system's data processing facility is mandatory in providing the data for complete records and for planning purposes. The combinations of data which the machine is able to analyze provide a basis for making sound administrative decisions and for recommending educationally sound policies to the school board.

When proper maintenance records are kept, it is possible to produce actual and predicted expenditures for each facility and/or equipment item within the district. These records should be maintained in a manner to fit directly into the accounting system of the district as would a payroll record or an attendance summary card.

The use of PERT charts or automated maintenance schedules in large systems can facilitate the necessary flow of staff and materials. Even small districts could use the PERT techniques in part to provide an overall plan for maintenance services.

PLANT OPERATION

Plant operation is concerned with such day-to-day activities of schools as cleaning, heating, and grounds maintenance. Generally, the term "plant operation" is limited to a specific building (or set of buildings) located on one site. Certain key elements emerge in any operational program, but the basic one is that of the cost of an effective operational plan.

As was discussed in the section on maintenance, a school district's philosophy for operations is a determining factor in the success of the program. Establishing an acceptable level of cleanliness, delineating staff responsibilities, developing personnel policies, and describing the role of the custodian are all board-level decisions. Legal requirements relative to activities of custodians and other operations staff members must also be understood and supported by the board.

The decision to provide the necessary funds for the operation of buildings is a key consideration for boards of education. Since each school building represents several hundred thousands of dollars in construction costs plus a comparable amount in furnishings and equipment, funds expended on the day-to-day operations should not be allocated to provide for only low-quality plant care. Funds expended for custodial services on each building should be allocated to provide a level of building maintenance appropriate to its effective and efficient operation. Good business practices have long since shown the value of adequate day-to-day custodial services in increasing the useful life of a school building.

Organization of the Custodial Department

The custodial department can best function under a centralized head. Individual school building operations may be a part of a system-wide program of operation and maintenance services, or the role of the central staff person may be only to allocate the position. This role difference is basically dependent on district size or philosophy as to whether services are provided on a district-wide or an individual school basis. When a system-wide plan of providing custodial services is used, the director of operations (and/or maintenance) is charged with the responsibility of providing services for all schools in the district. The use of head custodians or foremen is a necessary part of this program and any other plan where several employees work in the same building. Proponents of this plan say better use of staff can be accomplished, while opponents say it violates the basic management theory which says the principal is responsible for his building. Both plans have merit, and consideration should be given each as it should be with all possible centralized services.

The association between maintenance and operation is, of course, close. Because of this factor and related ones of cost, storage, and training, a single director of maintenance and operations may serve a school district. The size of a district will influence the organizational scheme best suited for implementation, but policies related to control are key elements in whatever organizational plan is followed. The person(s) responsible for maintenance and operations may report to the assistant superintendent for business or (in a small district) to the superintendent. Whatever the plan, the centralization of services, materials, procurement, and personnel selection is essential to the effective operation of a school district.

No single group of activities is as important to the success of the overall operations program as the selection, training, assignment, and supervision of staff. As was discussed in the introductory section of this chapter, union agreements in the area of operational and custodial personnel often determine the qualifications of persons to be selected, job definitions, and the scope of assignments. Thus, responsibility as an operations function or as a maintenance function is fixed. Again, the size and the geographic location of the system play significant roles in determining these requirements.

Selection

All staff members in the operations areas should be selected according to criteria established by the board of education and administered through the superintendent's office. The selection process should be inclusive enough to ensure that the school district gets "its money's worth." Factors such as age, health, skills or competencies, character, and attitude should serve as bases for establishing selection criteria. Figure 11.2 provides an illustration of the duties, features of the job, examples of work, required knowledge, skills and abilities, and acceptable experience and training for a custodian.

Under no circumstances should the awarding of custodial positions be viewed as a personal-type "reward" or established on a patronage system. However, the need to establish criteria should not be viewed by the board as a mandate to interview all potential employees at any level. The actual selection should be recommended to the board by a member of the superintendent's staff with this assigned responsibility. In many districts, a supervisor will be charged with the responsibility of administering the total program of maintenance and operations.

Since buildings need to be maintained twelve months per year, building custodians and maintenance personnel need to be employed for twelve months each year. Some reassignment to other operations areas is a possibility, but twelve-month employment is necessary to attract and keep quality personnel. A reasonable package of fringe benefits would also serve as a plus factor in attracting competent personnel. A high turnover rate among personnel at this level is as costly as high turnover in teaching staff. This cost may be even more pronounced if key skills are involved.

Training

Even though staff members are hired with a certain skill level, the need to provide in-service training is ever present. The establishment of a regular plan of in-service training affords the opportunity to sharpen general skills in building operations as well as to introduce new techniques and products to a large group. Group activity training and demonstration is a most effective method of providing necessary and useful information. Preschool workshops at which a wide range of activities are discussed serve a valuable function in a school district. At these sessions the entire operations plan for the year can be reviewed, questions answered, and new techniques or refinements of old ones introduced. Care should be taken to secure input from present custodial and maintenance personnel for use in planning future training programs.

DUTIES OF THE CUSTODIAN

GENERAL STATEMENT OF DUTIES:

Performs routine building cleaning and semi-skilled maintenance
tasks and related work as required.

EXAMPLES OF WORK: (Illustrative only)

Sweeps and mops floors and stairs;
Dusts desks, woodwork, furniture, and other equipment;
Washes windows, walls, blackboards, sinks, and other fixtures;
Polishes furniture and metal furnishings;
Empties waste baskets, collects and disposes of rubbish;
Clears snow and ice from walks and driveways;
Mows lawns, trims shrubs, rakes leaves, and performs a variety of
      other grounds-keeping tasks;
Operates a coal or oil low-pressure heating system, including fir-
      ing and removing ashes;
Delivers packages and messages;
Checks operation of clocks and bells;
Puts out and takes in traffic safety signs;
Arranges chairs and tables and other equipment for special use of
      school buildings;
Repairs window shades, replaces light bulbs, soap and towels;
Paints rooms and equipment, repairs furniture and makes minor
      plumbing, electrical, and carpentry repairs;
Prepares and maintains a variety of records and reports.

REQUIREMENTS: (Illustrative only)

Knowledge of building cleaning practices, supplies, and equipment; working knowledge of the operation and maintenance of heating equipment and ability to make minor plumbing, electrical,
carpentry, and mechanical repairs. Ability to follow oral and
written directions; willingness to do custodial and other manual
tasks; good physical condition.

DESIRABLE EXPERIENCE AND TRAINING:

One year of maintenance experience, or equivalent training.

FIGURE 11.2   Duties of the custodian.

Assignment

The assignment of custodial staff to individual schools should be made in accordance with established board policies. The determination of criteria for assignment should be made by members of the superintendent's staff as recommendations to the board. These professional staff members are better able to provide the specialized inputs necessary to this area and to apply general personnel criteria useful in avoiding charges of patronage or favoritism at certain schools or with certain persons.

An appropriate number of custodial persons should be assigned to each building to maintain that building at an acceptable level according to board policy. Figure 11.3 provides a custodial analysis for an elementary school. As was noted previously, it is inappropriate to build and not maintain a building at an acceptable level. This previously determined acceptable level will dictate the number of custodial staff necessary for that building and also indicate what central office maintenance services will need to be allocated for this structure. Through these activities the proper cost factor may be projected for long-term budget work in areas of personnel, purchase of supplies, and maintenance scheduling.

Assignments are determined in a number of ways; one of the more common ways involves some type of square footage measure. It is important for the school business administrator or his supervisor to give some consideration to a factor-weighting scheme based on the type and use of the facility rather than on size. Laboratories, auditoriums, gymnasiums, home economics rooms, and athletic dressing rooms all have unique cleaning problems; and size may not be an effective common denominator in assigning work to a group of custodians.

Supervision

The day-to-day supervision of a custodial staff will be at the system or at the building level depending on the plan for operating adopted by the board. As was previously discussed, if the principal has direct responsibility for the condition and maintenance of his facility, it is necessary that the custodial staff be responsible to him. If this responsibility is assumed at the system level, an operations manager is responsible. If more than one custodian is working at a single facility, one should be designated

CUSTODIAL ANALYSIS

Name of school. . . . .   Jones Elementary School

Number of custodians. 3½

Total square feet of floor space.   49,295

Square feet per custodian   14,084

Type(s) of floor:

Vinyl asbestos tile	AREA:	Classrooms and halls
Ceramic tile	"	Restrooms
Quarry tile	"	Kitchen
Concrete	"	Basement halls, stairways
Asbestos tile	"	Classrooms, halls, cafe-teria, and gymnasium

Salary per custodian (monthly):

Full-time custodian	$230 (10 months)
Part-time custodian	$115 (10 months)

Number of students enrolled.   1035

Equipment:

floor brushes	wet mops
corn brooms	deck or stock mops
dust pans	wringer buckets with rollers and casters
dust mops, hall mops	force cup
waste paper baskets	electric scrubbing and polishing machine
step ladders	toilet bowl brushes

Remarks:

FIGURE 11.3 *Sample custodial analysis.*

as head custodian. This person, the principal, the general maintenance and operations supervisor, and other appropriate staff should plan work schedules on a short-range and long-range basis. Whenever possible, each staff member should be involved in evaluation of his own competence. This facilitates explanation of work expectations and assists in producing a sense of accomplishment in the day-to-day work assignment. Plans should be made for "exception" custodial requirements, since special cases do arise for additional services; however, board policy should provide for such contingencies, rather than have to rely on one person's decision.

Continuous evaluation should be made for all maintenance and operations personnel in the district. Annual efficiency reports should be prepared on each person by his immediate supervisor. General supervisory evaluations should be made where appropriate, and the sum of all ratings should serve as the basis for retention, transfer, and/or merit salary adjustments.

Inspection

Safety inspections should be planned as a regular part of the maintenance and operations schedule of a school district. A detailed plan for this procedure should be established for each building in the district and coordinated with manufacturer recommendations on items of equipment so as to comply with local fire, disaster, and civil defense regulations. Inspection teams should be established, trained, and allowed to function in terms of being granted adequate fiscal resources and time. The use of manufacturer representatives, local governmental personnel, and/or community members should be encouraged; but the supervision of these persons should be handled by the responsible representative of the local school district.

Inspections of potential safety hazards noted by parents, school personnel, students, and/or others should be made promptly. Necessary corrections should follow or adequate warning procedures should be initiated until such time as proper repair or removal of the hazard can be made. General health inspections procedures may fall in the area of maintenance and operations, but adequately trained personnel must augment the general staff if these inspections are to be effectively made.

Plant Security

The security of the physical plant and equipment is a major concern of local boards of education and directors of maintenance and operations, as well as local law enforcement agencies and the general public. Damages to school buildings are increasing each year. The incidence of window breakage, paint smearing, destruction of toilet facilities, forced door locks, etc., are reported daily in the local papers and are discussion points at all gatherings of school administrators and business managers. Since few school systems are capable of providing security guards for their facilities, it is more important than ever that proper security measures be exercised from the board of education down to the local school custodian. Detailed descriptions of what areas are to be secured and how these are to be secured must be determined for each building in the district. Proper locking devices, alarm systems, and surveillance systems must be decided upon by the local boards and installed at appropriate locations.

A goal of each system should be an antivandalism program. Whether this is an educational program, a community assistance program, or a combination of a number of programs, the entire administrative team should assume shared responsibility. Inputs from various sources should be welcomed and no avenues should be closed that could lead to a reduction in vandalism in the school district.

Scheduling of Custodial and Maintenance Services

During the School Year

Routine custodial services and certain types of maintenance are generally performed during the school year. Housekeeping chores, small repair projects, and selective replacement work can take place without disrupting the instructional program. Figure 11.4 shows the schedule for one custodian for one day. Some major capital projects may be undertaken or finished during the school year if the proper safety standards can be met and if the proper combinations of production and noise control can be established to allow for the normal continuation of classes. Of course, emergency repairs may need to be made at any time during the school year, with a certain amount of inconvenience resulting.

CUSTODIAL SCHEDULE

7:00-7:15   Put up flag, unlock doors, turn on lights in all areas.

7:15-8:00   Check on rest rooms. Clean administrative and guidance offices.

8:00-8:30   Clear student activity center and corridor around this area.

8:30-9:00   Clean dressing room areas.

9:00-11:30   Clean foyer and lobby and take care of preventative maintenance as noted on repair list.

11:30-12:30 Assist in the feeding operation.

12:30-1:00   Lunch.

1:00-1:30   Clean walk-off mats after children have come in from recess.

1:30-2:30   Clean the following rooms now vacated due to dismissal: kindergarten, EMR* #1, EMR #2, SMR,† rest room in student activity center.

2:30-3:00   Clean the gym and state area.

             *Educable Mentally Retarded
             †Severely Mentally Retarded

FIGURE 11.4   Sample custodial schedule.

In many instances, a one-day interruption of classes is not beyond question to accomplish an inside task such as ceiling repair or lighting corrections. These activities could not be accomplished by the staff available to the system if all such tasks were left to those periods when school was not in session. Even if additional personnel were available, the cost could prove prohibitive. An additional factor for consideration is that staff members under full-time contract must be continuously utilized.

During Closed Periods

Those activities from the total plan not accomplished during the school year must be accomplished, of course, during periods when schools are closed. These activities would center around areas of major disruption as well as items requiring that utilities be suspended or that no persons be allowed to use the facilities for an extended period of time. Such work as sanitary facility replacement, replacement of water systems, or the paving of access roads needs to be scheduled during periods when school is not in session.

SUMMARY

Advanced planning and scheduling by the system's administrative team holds the key to an effective maintenance and operations program as it does with all system activities.

A philosophy of maintenance and operations must be established by the board, and policies to implement these philosophies in the day-to-day school setting must be established. Decisions relative to contracted services versus system-provided services, procedure for selection, training, and retention of staff, budget priorities, etc., are all related to a successful maintenance and operations program. The school business administrator should supply cost analysis data representing many facets of maintenence and operations needed for effective decision making. Planning is the key for the successful merger of these needs with others throughout the district.

SUGGESTED ACTIVITIES

1. How can the school business administrator ensure that he is operating a cost-effective program?

2. How should decisions be reached regarding use of contract versus system-supplied maintenance services?

3. What is the value of in-service training for school custodial personnel? How should this training be organized?

4. Develop a plan for the maintenance of the school buildings in your district. How could this plan be computerized?

5. How would PERT charts be utilized in a system-wide maintenance program?

SUGGESTED READINGS

American Association of School Administrators. *Profiles of the Administrative Team.* Washington, D.C.: The Association, 1971.

Baker, Joseph J., and Peters, Jon S. *School Maintenance and Operation.* Danville, Ill.: The Interstate Printers and Publishers, 1963.

Educational Facilities Laboratories, Inc. *The Cost of a Schoolhouse.* New York: The Laboratories, 1960.

Finchum, R. N. *Administering the Custodial Program,* OE-21005 Bulletin 1961, No. 4 Washington, D.C.: U.S. Department of Health, Education, and Welfare, 1961.

Finchum, R. N. *Organizing the Maintenance Program* OE-21002 Bulletin 1960, No. 15 Washington, D.C.: U.S. Department of Health, Education, and Welfare, 1960.

Johns, Roe L., and Mophet, Edgar L. *The Economics and Financing of Education.* Englewood Cliffs, N.J.: Prentice-Hall, Inc., 1969.

Knezevich, Stephen J., and Fowlkes, John Guy. *Business Management of Local School Systems.* New York: Harper and Row, Publishers, 1960.

Linn, Henry H., ed. *School Business Administration.* New York: The Ronald Press Company, 1956.

Nelson, D. Lloyd, and Purdy, William M. *School Business Administration.* Lexington, Mass.: D. C. Heath and Company, 1971.

INSURANCE PLANNING

For the practical purpose of presenting the mechanism that gives effect to insurance, it may be said that insurance is a promise by an insurer to an insured of protection and/or service. By "protection" is meant making good a financial loss; and by "service," rendering aid of various sorts in connection with the promise of protection. The promise is made only to the extent that the loss may be caused by fortuitous events, and, with certain exceptions, promised protection is legally enforceable only to the extent of actual loss. The insurer is the person or organization making the promise; the insured, the person or organization subject to loss to whom the promise is made.

To clarify further the concept of insurance a discussion of insurable risks is appropriate. There are many risks of economic loss that no insurance company would be willing to accept. Conversely, there are a number of conditions that make a risk insurable. While some kinds of insurance are written where one or more of these conditions is not present, its absence acts as a danger signal to the insurance company, which then must take extra precautions to protect itself.

The conditions that make a risk insurable are:

1. The peril insured against must produce a definite, fortuitous loss not under the control of the insured:
2. There must be a large number of homogeneous exposures subject to the same peril;
3. The loss must be calculable and the cost of insuring it must be economically feasible;
4. The peril must be unlikely to affect all insureds simultaneously;
5. The loss, when it occurs, must be financially serious.

Insurance Contract

Fortunately for the consumer, insurance contracts are highly standardized as a result of statutory or administrative directives, voluntary agreement, or customary practice. Otherwise, choosing among the policies issued by thousands of insurers would be extremely difficult.

For example, in most states the standard fire policy is prescribed word for word by statute. All insurers, domestic or foreign, writing fire insurance in those states must use the prescribed policy. Consequently, (1) the insured need not consider differences in policy language when selecting an insurer, (2) all insureds are subject to the same treatment, (3) policy conflicts do not arise when two or more insurers are required to provide the necessary protection or become involved in the same loss, (4) court interpretations of the contract become more meaningful, (5) insureds and insurance agents save time and energy in contract analysis, and (6) loss experience can be pooled for rate-making purposes.

Structure of the Insurance Contract

All insurance contracts, whether consisting of policies plus forms or policies only, contain certain provisions that can be classified as (1) declarations, (2) insuring agreements, (3) exclusions or (4) conditions, (5) endorsements. In many property or liability insurance contracts the provisions are grouped into these five categories and labeled accordingly, but in other lines the provisions must be rearranged to achieve this grouping.

Declarations

These are statements by the insured, on the basis of which the insurer issues its contract. In life insurance they cover such matters as the age of the insured, his present and past state of health, his occupation, and his intentions as to certain specified activities. The purpose of the declarations is to give the insurer sufficient information to enable it, with information from other sources, to issue an appropriate contract at a proper price.

Insuring Agreements

These are the provisions distinguishing one contract from another. They comprise the insuring agreements defining the perils insured against, the services promised, the losses covered, the amount (limits of liability) of the insurance, the parties to the contract (insurer and insured), the interest or property insured, the term of the contract, and the rights of third parties not named as insureds.

Exclusions

Many exclusions may be nullified by endorsement, though some are absolute. Exclusions of perils, persons, property, or situations not covered by the insurance contracts may have any one or more of three purposes: (1) drawing lines between the coverage of the contract and that afforded by other contracts, (2) making exceptions that may be covered under the contract but only after consideration by the insurer and/or on payment of additional premium, or (3) making exceptions that the insurer regards as uninsurable. Among the most common exclusions are those due to hostilities or warlike action; nuclear-energy hazards in general; insurrections; and civil disorders.

Conditions

A condition is a provision in the contract, compliance with which by the insured is essential to enforcing his rights under the contract. Failure to observe conditions may deprive the insured of the insurance on which he relies. A typical condition is a warranty that a device protecting against loss will be properly maintained (building sprinkler system), or a provision that the insurance will be suspended if the premises are vacant or unoccupied beyond a specified period.

Endorsements

If these are added to the basic contract they supersede any provisions in the contract with which they are in conflict. Endorsements serve many purposes. They may increase or decrease the scope of protection, transfer the protection to a different insured, change the location of insured property, excuse the insured from some condition in the contract, change the amount of insurance, change the rate, or, as in the fire insurance contract, be necessary to complete the contract.

Planning Insurance Acquisition

The insurance buyer for a school system has direct touch with the insurance field and its limitations. In selecting an agent to handle the business for the schools, he must investigate the facilities of the possible agents with a view to determining to what extent his school's needs can be met. Familiarity with the market and ability to cover unusual risks are evidences that the agent or broker is well informed and keeping abreast of developments in his field.

Many school districts have made it a practice to award school insurance business to local agents regardless of the cost. The basis for this practice has been that the local board should do business with local taxpayers. Since substantial amounts of local district revenue come from state and/or federal sources, the board has no obligation to subsidize local businessmen. Thus, local boards should examine the possibility of using the competitive bidding process in insurance acquisition as it does in securing supplies and materials. Several bids should be received, since the same coverage is not provided at the same rate by all companies. Care should be taken in using the sealed-bid approach, since this procedure may obligate the district to awarding a contract to the lowest bidder. Informal bids can allow for more flexibility in determination of quality and extent of insurance services.

Property Insurance

The term property insurance encompasses such lines as fire and marine insurance, liability insurance such as automobile and aviation insurance, workmen's compensation, theft insurance, fidelity and surety bond, and title and mortgage insurance, as well as many other types.

Until 1949 there were two distinct types of property insurers: fire and marine companies and casualty insurance companies. Even though some fire insurance companies own casualty subsidiaries and vice versa, state insurance laws required that the two classes of property insurance be written by separate corporations. Since that date the same company can write all lines of insurance but vestiges of the artificial pre-1949 schism between casualty and fire companies are still noted through different ways of doing business. These are different methods of rate-making and in some cases different attitudes toward customers. The large losses sustained in recent years in some lines of casualty insurance, particularly auto insurance, have deterred some fire companies from expanding into the other phases of insurance. Many casualty companies have entered the more profitable fire insurance field.

Fire and Casualty Insurers

In the United States property insurance is written by four types of insurers: stock companies, mutual companies, reciprocals, and Lloyd's. Stock companies have a major share of the business; they hold 75 percent of the total assets of all property insurers, write 70 percent of the premium volume and have 85 percent of the total capital and surplus available for protection of policy holders.

Stock Companies

A stock life insurance company is, like any other corporation, owned by its stockholders, who are desirous of profit. It is managed by a board of directors elected by the stockholders and by officers chosen by the board. If the company realizes a profit, the stockholders receive dividends; if business is unprofitable, reserves are depleted. Many stock insurance companies issue nonparticipating policies; these companies charge a fixed, definite premium and the policyholders have no financial interest in the company (provided it remains solvent). Other companies issue participating policies which allow the policyholder to share, through dividends, in the profits of the company.

Although there are some property insurers who specialize in one or two lines of insurance, most stock carriers write all, or nearly all, lines of fire or casualty insurance. They also operate in a large geographic area comprised of several states. Some, particularly those companies writing marine insurance, conduct an international business. Stock companies can be divided into two types: "bureau companies" and "independents." Bureau companies belong to rating bureaus organized and managed by the member companies, and make premium rates in concert. Independent companies calculate their own premium rates and compete in price with bureau companies.

Bureau companies usually write business through the "American Agency System," a countrywide network of insurance agents, each an independent who may represent as many as ten or twenty bureau companies. Since all charge the same premium rates they compete primarily on the basis of service.

Mutual Companies

There are four types of mutual companies: assessment mutuals, advance-premium mutuals, factory mutuals, and "specialty" and "class" mutuals. Many write only fire insurance and allied lines; in some companies all members participate in the management of the company. Many advance-premium mutuals charge a lower initial premium than do stock companies, but others pay out the profits from their lower operating expense in the form of policyholder dividends. Though he receives dividends in profitable years, the policyholder cannot be asked to pay anything additional in years when operating results are poor. Any losses are absorbed by the company's surplus funds.

Reciprocals

A reciprocal or interinsurance exchange is an insurance carrier without any corporate existence. The members pay an advanced premium and are also liable for assessments of a stipulated amount. Theoretically, a reciprocal should be able to provide low cost insurance for its members, since its cost of acquiring business, a major expense of most insurers, is so low. This may be an excellent form of insurance coverage for school districts.

Lloyd's of London

This is a unique organization of individual underwriters. When a Lloyd's broker has a risk to place he enters the "Room" and presents his proposal to the underwriting manager of one of the syndicates represented there. When he has obtained the participation of enough syndicates to insure the risk, he draws up the policy. Each member of the syndicate is personally responsible for his share of each loss, and his entire fortune is available to meet claims against him; his liability is unlimited.

State Insurance

A few states have state-operated school insurance programs. North Carolina covers elementary and secondary schools. Some of the state programs are handled through the state department of education while others are handled through the state insurance department. Many programs parallel self-insurance in that the local districts do not pay premiums. If administered correctly these programs are much more economical than insuring through private agencies because of the lack of high overhead common to many insurance firms. This practice has not spread primarily due to the strong insurance lobbies in most states.

The North Carolina state insurance program for public school buildings was developed as a school insurance program and was not an internal adjunct of another program, as was true of all other states with state property insurance. The North Carolina program is different in one other way. It is administered by a division under the State Board of Education. The event which precipitated the establishment of this fund was a 1948 decision of the insurance commissioner of North Carolina. He approved a 25 percent increase in fire insurance rates for public schools without any public hearings. The State Board of Education protested the increase but to no avail. The commissioner refused to cancel or modify the increase.

The State Board of Education then sought from the 1949 General Assembly authority to set up and operate a school building insurance fund. The insurance interests, including the companies and the agents, opposed the legislation most vigorously. The State Board of Education, however, managed to obtain favorable action from the General Assembly, and the Public School Insurance Fund began operation July 1, 1949.

One of the first tangible results of the establishment of the fund was a slash in the rates charged by the insurance companies. Within a few months after the establishment of the fund, the insurance companies petitioned the insurance commissioner to reduce the fire insurance rates on public schools. Since then these rates have been further decreased. The State Board of Education is convinced that no such relief would have been granted if the insurance companies had not been forced to compete for business.

The state program coverage is optional with local school boards. In 1969, it was estimated that the fund coverage included about 65 percent of the school value of the state. Under the state program the coverage on each property is supposed to be not less than 75 percent nor more than 100 percent of the insurable value. Insurance contracts are standard-type policies issued on a one-year basis. Coverage may be cancelled for poor housekeeping or other hazardous conditions.

The Division of Insurance rates the properties insured using its own engineers who make annual inspections. Rating is done in classes according to the National Board of Fire Underwriters' city classification, the building protection, and the type of construction. The division classifies buildings into one of eight classes for the purpose of obtaining a base rate.

Rates of the fund have averaged approximately 54 percent of standard rates. According to statute, the fund will decrease insurance rates as the reserve fund increases. When the fund accumulates a balance equal to 5 percent of the total insurance in force, the board shall decrease the premiums collected to an amount that will maintain the reserves at this 5 percent level.

The total premium-loss ratio of the fund, since its inception, has been 65.45 percent of premium income. These premiums average more than 40 percent less than commercial rates. The average annual cost of administration of the fund has been 8 percent. The fund has earned approximately 5 percent annually on all monies reinvested.

Self-insurance

Many large school systems recognize that because of their size they already have spread considerable risk and thus might save money by a program of self-insurance rather than buying insurance from commercial companies. Normally, the school system sets up a self-insurance fund, makes small annual appropriations into the fund, invests the accumulated reserve, and adds the earned interest to the reserve. As the accumulated reserve increases through adding the annual appropriation and interest, the system gradually phases out policies held in commercial companies. Ordinarily, the first buildings phased out of the commercial policies are the relatively low-risk units, and, conversely, high-risk buildings are the last to have commercial policies dropped. Only when the business administrator and the school board are convinced they have adequate reserve to cover the reasonable probability of loss should the school system become completely self-insured.

Since there is never complete assurance that this point of probability has been reached, boards and business administrators must exercise considerable judgment. Considerations which must be entertained in making this decision are:

1. The magnitude of the spread of risk.
2. The general comparability of *value* of the several buildings in the system so as to prevent distortion in the spread of risk.
3. The general comparability of *risk* of the several buildings of the system so as to prevent distortion in the amount of risk.
4. The geographic separation of buildings to avoid multiple loss from a single conflagration.
5. Transition of coverage from commercial companies to self-insurance in the low-risk to high-risk sequence.
6. The probabilities and magnitude of future expected losses, based on current risk exposure rather than on past loss records.
7. The fiscal alternatives available to the school system to replace a loss exceeding the revenue available in the self-insurance fund.
8. The ability of the school system to maintain the self-insurance fund at the level necessary to provide adequate protection.

No Insurance

This is a possibility for the very large district or state which has a good reserve of bonding power. Many states use this system for state buildings throughout the state, including higher education facilities which are a part of the state system.

Agents and Brokers

An agent is an individual, or sometimes a partnership or corporation, licensed to represent a particular insurance company in a certain area. He may be a general agent, allowed to hire and supervise other agents, or a soliciting agent, responsible only for his own production. An agent may represent more than one company, particularly in the property insurance field, but he holds a specific agent's contract with each company. As the company's representative he frequently has the authority to "find" risks for the company (except in life insurance), to collect premiums, and sometimes to investigate and settle small claims.

When a school system places business with several agents throughout the district, coordination of the insurance program can become rather cumbersome. Under these circumstances the district may appoint an agent of record who will then assume the coordinating role with all the other agents involved. This can be a tremendous time saver for the district.

When buying property insurance, particularly, it is sometimes better to deal with a broker. A broker is the representative of the insured, whose job it is to place the insurance on the most advantageous terms for his client. Brokers may do business with any company licensed in the state and try to obtain the maximum protection of the client's property for the lowest premium.

Although a broker represents the insured rather than the insurer, he is compensated, on a commission basis, by the insurer. Despite the possible conflict of interest that this entails, brokers are very useful to buyers of large amounts of insurance, since they are expert in fitting the various types of available insurance policies to the needs of the buyer and they know which company's policy is most appropriate in a given situation. In nearly all states, the law does not recognize the existence of life insurance or health insurance brokers, though many property insurance brokers also hold life insurance agent's licenses.

Valuation

The value for which any structure should be insured is the sound replacement cost after such items as depreciation, site acquisition and architects' fees are removed. Since costs of construction and general replacement costs for furnishings and equipment change frequently, a district must make every effort to keep its records up to date. Accurate and frequent appraisals are the surest method of having the proper information available for determining the proper insurance program. The selection of a commercial appraisal firm or the employment of a staff member with proper appraisal credentials will be money well spent. Insurance companies often take local appraisal at purchase but reserve the right to have commercial appraisal when a claim is filed. For the same reason, overinsuring is a needless expenditure of district funds. Replacement cost insurance for buildings should be considered where appropriate, especially in the case of relatively old buildings.

In summary, a district is foolish to take "hit-or-miss" guesses on the value of buildings, to not cover adequately the replacement cost of equipment and furnishings, and/or to purchase amounts of insurance far in excess of what will be an acceptable replacement cost.

Insurance Records, Maintenance, and Protection

It is imperative that all school district records be maintained in a safe and yet accessible manner. Insurance records and all other records within the school district must be protected to the degree that the value of the document warrants. For example, there are crucial, important, useful, and nonessential insurance records. It is imperative that each type of record be classified by category and that the appropriate procedures be established to be certain that vital records are protected. Proper security measures must also be maintained to ensure that these data are transported to and from the vaults so that they may be used but that their safety will be maintained. As is true with most other records in today's society, insurance records can be maintained on microfilm or microfiche with a relatively small expense and stored at a distant location so that there is always a retrievable copy in the event of a natural disaster or a civil disorder.

The maintenance of insurance records, as was indicated in other sections of this book, is as essential as the maintenance of any other record. To be efficient and effective, a school district must maintain proper and adequate records in an up-to-date manner. It is also important that insurance records be designed to feed back into the fiscal accounting procedures so that the school business administrator can direct these materials into the day-to-day flow. This will allow for the use of particular items of information for projections relative to system costs or bid and contract lettings.

Liability Insurance

Liability insurance is written to cover any insured party's responsibility for damages due to bodily injury, death, etc. Two areas of liability—general liability and vehicle liability—are covered in most school district policies. Vehicle liability is covered in another section of this chapter.

The area of liability insurance is a complex one for any school district and should be closely studied by the administrative team. An overall, comprehensive insurance plan to cover the district is to be recommended over scheduled plans. Workmen's compensation (see next section) is designed to cover injuries to school employees, and such injuries are generally not covered in liability programs. Liability insurance is not an accident policy and payment need not be made until damages are awarded by a court. State statutes and the determination of what constitutes neglect affect decisions to such a degree that a board must insure for self-protection. In most states, school districts may not be held liable for injuries to pupils or other persons. This legal position has led to the establishment of nominally priced pupil accident insurance plans where coverage is purchased by parents. Group rates apply and coverage is usually restricted to the school day and that time spent traveling to and from school. Competition in interscholastic athletic events is usually excluded in these policies. Insurance covering these athletic events is purchased by athletic departments and/or parents for the specific sport in which the pupil participates. Teachers, administrators, and other school personnel are turning to personal liability insurance at a rapid rate.

Employee Insurance

Employee insurance programs constitute one of the major insurance items for a school district. Workmen's compensation and medical insurance constitute the two major items of employee-related expense and will prove to be major items for consideration in the planning role of the school business administrator.

Workmen's Compensation

No benefits are payable in the case of injury resulting from willful intent. Specific injuries, medical expenses, disability, and death are covered in workmen's compensation programs. In several states, workmen's compensation is required for all public employees, while in others the school districts may elect to assume the risk. Rates for workmen's compensation are based on employee compensation and the risk value associated with specific jobs within the district. Special cases or situations may be covered by adjusted rates for the specific district. A good accident prevention program, coupled with regular physical examinations and strict adherence to safety rules, is an effective method of reducing workmen's compensation claims for any school district.

Medical Insurance

Group medical insurance programs with options to cover both the employee and his family (spouse and children) are features of virtually all plans. This coverage is often an integral part of union agreements or other negotiated packages. Coverage has increased in recent years to include major medical and disability or income protection programs as well as death benefits. Many programs are built on a plan of employer-employee contributions based on a percentage distribution. The selection of the insurer should always be made on a bid basis. Generally, the more employees covered by a group policy, the cheaper the rate. Group medical programs should be examined on a yearly basis and consideration should be given to needed improvements.

Surety Bonds

A surety is a person, group of persons, or company guaranteeing that other persons will fulfill a valid obligation to the school district. There are several kinds of surety bonds available to public school districts and to the school business administrator. These include statutory public official bonds, public official dishonesty bonds, contract bonds including bid performance payments and supply type bonds, and fidelity bonds. Each of these bonds guarantees that under a particular situation, such as a performance contract, failure to perform a certain activity or produce a certain acceptable level of work will be covered for the completion of that contract in accordance with its terms. Contract bonds help to eliminate incompetent and/or dishonest contractors from bidding since a contractor without a good reputation is unlikely to be able to secure a bond. The advantages of bonding in general include the district's knowing its contract will be completed or that the surety company will have the contract completed, that incompetent or dishonest contractors will have difficulty in obtaining contract bonds, and that construction progress will be aided since payment of bills is guaranteed in a performance bond or in a separate payment bond. Bonds affecting individuals are aimed at ensuring the performance or faithfulness of another party under an "honesty of the employee" bond. Under such a bond, if a public employee is careless or dishonest any losses incurred by this activity will be covered.

Vehicle Insurance

Insurance coverage associated with school transportation is a many-faceted aspect of the school district's total insurance program. Planning on the part of the school business administrator as to recommended coverage requires inputs from many sources, including the district's legal counsel, the personnel supervisor, union representatives, the purchasing agent, and the transportation director. Areas for consideration in a district's vehicle insurance program include, among others, comprehensive, collision, fire, theft, liability, and medical coverage.

Additionally, the school business administrator as part of the administrative team has a responsibility for providing information to all affected in the use of private automobiles for school-related functions. It may logically fall to the school business administrator to keep abreast of the latest legal decisions in this area and to advise appropriate administrators, parent groups, coaches, and teachers of current laws. He may also be expected to give suggestions as to types of insurance coverage needed or additions to existing private coverage necessary to provide adequate protection.

Drivers of school buses are, of course, liable for negligence which causes personal injury or property damage. Questions must be answered as to the extent of coverage permitted or required by the state. Additional questions must be answered about the extent of coverage provided for drivers, passengers, and property. Safety training programs for drivers as they relate to a reduction of insurance premiums, efforts to regulate pupil conduct for the protection of equipment, and other safety considerations may well be a partial responsibility of the school business administrator.

Other Insurance

All school districts are faced with a multitude of insurance needs other than those previously noted. Burglary, robbery, theft, glass, and boiler and machinery insurance are other needs of the district. Limited coverage and broad coverage are available for boilers, the difference being the extent of coverage. Specifics will be determined by state and local regulations. Glass insurance is generally restricted to the plate type and/or other special types. Coverage for burglary, robbery, and theft is determined by the legal definitions of each of these items. The all-risk type of insurance may be used rather than certain specific coverage.

SUMMARY

This chapter discusses the major planning responsibilities of the school business administrator in the insurance program of a school district. Insurance contracting, including such facets as declarations, exclusions, conditions, and endorsements, is discussed; and material is presented on insurance acquisition, property insurance, fire and casualty insurance, state insurance, self-insurance, and their interrelationship. Information on insurance record-keeping and valuation, and discussions of employee insurance, surety bonds, vehicle insurance, and other insurance types are provided.

It is clear that since one of the special purposes of the school business administrator's role is to maximize returns on educational dollars spent, protection of school funds, persons, and property is an integral part of this function. It is also pointed out that protection involves expenditures; wise protection, however, is a vital part of effective planning.

SUGGESTED ACTIVITIES

1. Under what circumstances could competitive bidding for insurance *not* be desirable?

2. What are the major functions of insurance for a school system?

3. What are the conditions in your school which could make a risk insurable?

4. How is insurable value found?

5. Would self-insurance be suited to the district in which you work or last worked? If so, how? If not, why?

SUGGESTED READINGS

Allen, Clifford H. *School Insurance Administration.* New York: The Macmillan Company, 1965.

Athearn, James L. *Risk and Insurance.* 2d ed. New York: Appleton-Century-Crofts, 1969.

Bickelhaupt, David L. *General Insurance.* 8th ed. Homewood, Ill.: R. D. Irwin, Inc., 1970.

Chernick. Vladimir P. *The Consumer's Guide to Insurance Buying.* Los Angeles: Sherbourne Press, 1970.

Dickerson, Oliver D. *Health Insurance.* Homewood, Ill.: R. D. Irwin, Inc., 1968.

Haber, William, and Murray, Merrill G. *Unemployment Insurance in the American Economy; An Historical Review and Analysis.* Homewood, Ill.: R. D. Irwin, Inc., 1966.

Huebner, Solomon S., Black, Kenneth, Jr., and Cline, Robert S. *Property and Liability Insurance.* New York: Appleton-Century-Crofts, 1968.

Kulp, Clarence A., and Hall, John W. *Casualty Insurance.* 4th ed. New York: The Ronald Press Company, 1968.

Sullivan, Eugene. *Where Did the $13 Billion Go?* Englewood Cliffs, N.J.: Prentice-Hall, Inc., 1971.

AUXILIARY SERVICES PLANNING

Auxiliary services generally provide the school business administrator most of the severe day-to-day problems encountered in the average school system. While these services are not directly related to the teaching-learning situation, their absence makes it impossible for the primary function of the school to continue. Because auxiliary services are so important to the normal operation of a school system and because the efficient performance of these services enables the educational process to proceed with a minimum of distraction and disruption, considerable planning effort must be devoted to their appropriate injection into the total operations of the school system.

In planning auxiliary services, the school business administrator must first adopt the premise that these services are support services to the teacher-learner situation and not ends in and of themselves. Additionally, the function of the auxiliary service is to enhance the educational environment and to make possible the most efficient learning situation possible. Therefore, the auxiliary services personnel must see themselves as support personnel and must have the capacity to make adjustments as they are needed to accommodate the learning process.

Since auxiliary services often involve the provision of a

specific service at a specific time, e.g., food services and/or transportation, careful planning of the logistical details is crucial to success. Optimum use of expensive equipment also requires careful attention to logistics.

While auxiliary services include such items as attendance services, health services, student activities, and community services, among others, those services which most often tend to become a part of the school business administrator's direct responsibility are the food services and the transportation programs. These are services over which the business administrator is quite apt to have line responsibility, as opposed to the staff relationships pertaining in the aforementioned services. It is therefore appropriate for this work to deal in some depth with the planning of the food services and transportation programs. The authors examine these areas with complete awareness that the nuances of regionality and geography and the variables of local and state policies do make generalizations hazardous.

TRANSPORTATION SERVICES

Historical Perspectives

What was once a rural phenomenon has become an accepted service provided to over half of the public school children in America. In addition, a sizeable proportion of the parochial school pupils are provided transportation services. The transportation of school children began at a time when the country entered the automotive age and was a real stimulus to the development of consolidated school systems. The breakthrough in transportation led to the elimination of small, inefficient school systems and greatly assisted in the establishment of the comprehensive school systems of modern America. As paved highways and improved vehicles were developed, the service area of a school system could be expanded until today it is not unusual for children to be transported many miles to schools suited to their educational needs. Indeed, in some of the more sparsely populated sections of the country it is quite common for children to be transported over fifty miles to school. The sight of fifty, one hundred, even two hundred school buses parked on a school transportation site is no longer unusual. The big yellow vehicle going down the road has become a common scene to most American drivers.

As the nation's highways became more highly developed and as the variety and size of vehicles multiplied, many other important uses of the transportation service were introduced. With the advent of smaller (six to fifteen passengers) and more specialized vehicles, moving particular children to special schools, i.e., handicapped, gifted, etc., became economically feasible. The use of buses as mobile classrooms and as learning laboratories also was introduced. More recently, cities and newly emerged suburbs have come to depend upon transportation services for a number of tasks, among them the basic one of moving children from home to school and back, but also for special tasks such as field trips, extracurricular trips, special functions, and transporting students to specialized schools.

Even more recently, the use of transportation services to effect legally mandated student mixes has been a source of confrontation in many urban school systems. School administrators, faced with federal mandates to end segregation by race are increasingly utilizing the transportation system to enable student bodies to be desegregated. While such use of the transportation system acquires a bad connotation in most communities and while the term *busing* has become a "no-no" in most cities, the fact remains that until and unless residential patterns are changed dramatically, the transportation system will have to be utilized as a primary tool for desegregation.

Thus the task of the school business administrator as he plans to meet the transportation needs of a school system becomes a complex, often frustrating, endeavor. Not only must the primary function of moving children to and from school be attended to, but also the very important tasks of moving children for purposes of educational quality and educational equality must be addressed. Since the planning and implementation of transportation programs is neither a very exotic nor desirable chore when compared to the spectrum of duties normally assigned the school business office, the service dimension must be emphasized and rewarded. There are many considerations involved in planning for the transportation of pupils. Following is a brief discussion of some of the more basic planning considerations that must be resolved in order to implement a transportation program.

Policy Planning

Crucial decisions as to what kinds of transportation systems are important to the educational program of a school district must be handled at the policy planning stage. Questions to be addressed include:

1. Is the transportation system to be used only for moving children to and from school?
2. What are other legitimate uses of the transportation system?
3. What are the constraints (legal and otherwise) on the transportation system?
4. What benefits can accrue to the students through expanded use of the transportation system?
5. What state and/or local regulations affect the transportation system?
6. How do children qualify for transportation services? Is distance the only criteria, or are physical and traffic concerns also important?
7. What portion of the educational resource is most profitably invested in the transportation system?

Out of decisions made concerning these and other questions should evolve the transportation policy of a school system. As the policy questions are resolved, operating rules, regulations, and procedures are developed. Periodic, systematic review of transportation policy must be a part of the planning-implementation cycle, for as variables change so must policy dealing with variables change. As policy shifts are made necessary by changing conditions and/or new educational goals, so must rules, regulations, and procedures for implementing policy be modified. The overriding concern must always be that the transportation must provide the best possible support and service to the learner and to the educational goals of the school system.

Contract Versus District-Owned Equipment

One of the early planning decisions to be made is the resolution of the question of contract versus district-owned equipment. There are many advantages and disadvantages to either approach to pupil transportation, and the decision is often one of convenience rather than one based on careful planning and analysis of alternatives. There are a great many considerations to be assessed in reaching a decision on the contract versus district-owned equipment, not the least of which is the capital equipment expenditure. Rolling stock is not an inexpensive investment with the more elaborate and larger buses costing many thousands of dollars.

Convenience to the learner is another important criterion for deciding on the contract versus district-owned issue. If, for example, there exists a well-developed public transportation system that has the capacity to service the needs of the school system while meeting the health, safety, and convenience criteria established for students, the decision to contract is relatively simple. But, if use of the public transit system places a burden on either the system or the clients, then other alternatives must be explored. In many instances, the use of the public transit system provides for optimum use of that system while, at the same time, meeting the educational needs of the school district. In such cases, it is to the advantage of both the school and the transit authority to enter into a cooperative effort and ensure that total utilization of community resources is being implemented.

In other locales there is no public transit system and the decision is more difficult. Contract opportunities with private carriers are alternatives to district-owned equipment. Once again, health and safety needs, convenience, and cost benefits must be assessed before a decision is made. Among the advantages the private carrier offers to the school business administrator are:

1. No large investment is required.
2. A large administrative-management task is eliminated.
3. The school district is not in competition with private business.
4. The onerous tasks of maintaining and operating a bus fleet are not the school district's.
5. Transportation personnel are not added to the complement of school district employees.
6. Many of the criticisms can be directed to the contractor rather than to the school administration.

Conversely, there are advantages inherent in school district-owned transportation systems. These include:

1. Operating costs are usually less than with private contractors.
2. Buses are available for use for other aspects of the school program.
3. There is greater control over matters of health, safety, and convenience.

4. The transportation program can be planned as an integral part of the total educational experience for the learner (as in the use of school buses for field trips).
5. In many states, state subsidy is available to assist the local district in the capital expenditure.
6. Transportation personnel can be selected and trained to ensure an appropriate level of both driving and educational competency. (Bus drivers are considered to have instructional roles as they can influence children in areas of citizenship, human relations, good manners, responsibility, cooperation, and so forth.)
7. There is far greater flexibility inherent in a district-owned and -operated transportation system.

While there are many contract agreements in operation across the country, well over 80 percent of the school transportation systems are district owned and operated.

Routing and Scheduling

Without question, one of the more demanding and frustrating aspects of transportation system planning is the development of routes and schedules. Techniques ranging from maps identifying each student to be served (required by law in many states) to computer programming of routes and schedules are used, sometimes with questionable results. The difficulty in programming the variables of human behavior and the problems encountered when dealing with weather conditions and machinery make the development of routes and schedules additionally sensitive. Problems of routing and scheduling are compounded by population sparseness or density, traffic conditions, road quality and conditions, school schedules, and the variables of weather. Planning decisions on routes and schedules involve determinations as to appropriate roads to travel, what distance youngsters may walk to converge on a pick-up point, services provided the handicapped, effects on property owners of pupils congregating at a certain point, traffic flow and congestion, safety of pupils, time constraints, size of buses, geography of the route, and so on. Another important consideration is how to make the most efficient use of vehicles, i.e., should routes be planned so that buses can make more than one trip, and if so should age ranges of pupils play a major part in the route development.

As transportation systems become a more important component of the educational program, the problems of scheduling for educational use become more complex. Field trips of every description are valuable educational experiences, and the meshing of these activities with the primary home-to-school-to-home obligation presents severe logistical problems. The routing and scheduling of a fleet of buses to provide safe, economical transportation, as well as to support the variety of educational experience possible with extended use of vehicles, requires thoughtful, resourceful, sensitive planning.

Inspection and Maintenance

School bus accidents, while very rare, are tragic specters for school personnel. Accidents due to mechanical failures are especially tragic and often are due to negligence on the part of those responsible for transportation systems. When a school district commits itself to the purchase of a transportation fleet, it at the same time commits itself to a planned, systematic inspection and maintenance program.

It is unfortunate that many maintenance programs are of an emergency nature, when the use of orderly, periodic inspection procedures can lead to a preventive maintenance program that will not only provide greater safety and service to users but also reflect a savings to the school district. Typically the school system finds itself with a growing fleet of school vehicles, but with little or no equipment to use in the care of these vehicles, and with no trained personnel to assign to the maintenance of moving stock. The care of the transportation fleet is contracted to local garages and/or filling stations who attend to simple (e.g., gas, oil, etc.) needs on a regular basis and to other needs as they are requested. Because of the harsh reality of school budgets, vehicular maintenance is usually on an emergency basis and typically only upon major breakdown of the vehicle. This is, in fact, false economy and leads to inconvenience to the user in terms of breakdown of transportation services. Occasionally, this method of operation can lead to mechanical failures that result in tragic and avoidable accidents.

Regular inspection and planned maintenance are crucial to the health and safety of users and permit the optimum utilization of the transportation system to the advantage of the educational program. Inspection and maintenance are closely interrelated and mutually dependent. Inspection is accomplished daily, weekly, monthly, quarterly, and annually, depending on the need of the vehicle. Maintenance, too, is accomplished according to a short- and long-term schedule. Inspection checklists filled out by the driver, mechanic, supervisor, and other personnel give information relative to maintenance needs. Daily inspections, usually performed by the vehicle driver, are mostly visual and are intended to act as safety checks on the vehicle. Examination of tires, testing of turn indicators, checking of braking power, testing of lights, engine warm-up, review of gauge readings, and examination of fuel levels are routine and perfunctory inspection tasks for the driver. Scheduled inspections by mechanics become more minute and intense as use time of the vehicle grows. Periodic lubrication efforts and minor engine tune-ups are performed on a regular basis. Annual inspections involve major repairs and replacement of worn and/or used parts. Certain maintenance tasks are the result of seasonal weather changes and may differ according to geographic location. Certainly, in the northern regions winterizing of vehicles must be planned and accomplished well in advance of winter weather conditions.

The realization of an adequate vehicular maintenance program is the result of careful planning and resource allocation. Equipment, space, and personnel must be provided for such a program to succeed. It is not unusual for school transportation fleets of from fifty to eighty vehicles to employ four to six full-time mechanics and to have garage facilities that will provide indoor work stations for at least six to ten buses. In addition, the stocking of sufficient parts, tires, tools, and equipment calls for an investment of thousands of dollars. It must be recognized that the typical fleet of fifty to one hundred buses represents an investment of from $500,000 to over $1,000,000 and an annual operating expenditure of significant size. If supply and equipment stocking is based on sensible prediction of need and the advantages inherent in volume purchase, great benefits can accrue to the school district. Most important, of course, is the savings involved with curtailment of vehicle downtime. While actual dollar savings cannot be computed in terms of downtime, the fact that the transportation system can meet its obligation in terms of service to the user is of tremendous importance. In addition, the dollars saved by district-performed maintenance will enable the expenditure for transportation to be a high-benefit expenditure.

An important part of the inspection and maintenance program is the keeping of adequate records on each vehicle. Routine and periodic maintenance operations depend on records. Records can also provide the basis for ordering equipment, parts, and supplies on an annual basis to encourage additional savings. Annual bids on fuel, oil, and other consumable materials will add to the savings. The annual bidding on fuel alone can result in enough savings to enable the cost of fuel pumps and storage tanks to be amortized over a very short time. Certain regional accommodations are also appropriate to realize optimum return on investments. For example, the use of antifreeze additives in fuel is desirable in northern climates. It can also be a direct savings if head bolt heaters are installed in subfreezing climates. Installation of such devices will guarantee cold morning starts and save countless hours of driver and mechanic time. One school district known to the authors calculated that the use of head bolt heaters on its fleet of eighty buses saved over $15,000 per year in driver and mechanic overtime, all for an initial expenditure of $2,700.

To conclude, if a school district determines that the transportation system should be school district owned and operated, then plans for adequate inspection and maintenance procedures must also be formulated. Such a program must include adequate provision for regular inspection and preventive maintenance conducted by trained personnel backed by appropriate equipment, space, and supplies. Such planning will not only provide safe, timely service, but will also be reflected in significant savings to the school system.

Staff Supervision and Training

The supervision and training of transportation personnel is another of the difficult tasks facing the school business administrator. Since the number of persons involved in a transportation system can range from very few to upwards of several hundred, general statements can be misleading. Generally, large bus fleets are under the direction of a director of transportation who is responsible to the chief school business administrator. In smaller systems the school business administrator assumes direct control of the transportation system, sometimes with the help of a supervisor or the head mechanic. However the system is organized, some office must assume training and supervisory responsibilities.

The training of drivers is an important task and a demanding one. Not only must school vehicle drivers have driving ability and the capacity to exercise good judgment, they must also have those personal characteristics and qualities that make them positive influences on children—qualities such as tolerance of noise, firmness, fairness, and love and understanding of children are as important as reaction time, driving ability, physical stamina, and good eyesight. The training of drivers must reflect the need for transportation personnel to relate well with young people. Many districts have developed longitudinal programs that couple classroom instruction with on-the-road training with experienced drivers. Classroom instruction covers such items as child growth and development, safety, psychology, vehicular law, negligence, district demography and geography, and driving regulations. Aptitude and personality tests designed to measure adaptive capacity and stability are also used. Over-the-road driving first with the supervisor and/or mechanic is used to develop appropriate driving habits and to learn the handling of large vehicles. As the neophyte gains in ability and confidence he is permitted to accompany other drivers on trips and allowed to actually drive the loaded vehicle. After a series of such experiences, the novice is given certain "short" route responsibilities prior to assignment as a regular. Periodic ratings and test drives are part of the training sequence for drivers.

Many school systems encourage and even require transportation personnel to participate in periodic in-service programs where safety procedures, driving techniques, child psychology, and so on, are reviewed. In addition, periodic physical examinations are required for personnel to retain their positions.

Utilization and Evaluation of Services

As one examines school districts, one often finds beautifully developed auxiliary services divisions that are so underutilized that it is difficult to justify their existence. This is true in the case of many school-owned and -operated transportation systems. Vehicles are used for pupil transportation to school in the morning and to home in the afternoon and then lie idle the remainder of the time. In addition, routes are often planned so that vehicles must cover an area a number of times to accomplish what could have been done more efficiently in a single trip. Low utilization of transportation services not only makes its continuance questionable but, more importantly, negates one of the more compelling rationales for the value of a highly developed vehicular capacity: the availability of buses for use as educational tools for the classroom teacher.

Highly skilled and creative curriculum developers plan cooperatively with the school transportation administrators to incorporate the use of the bus fleet into the continuing educational experience of the student. Regularly scheduled field trips, ranging from visits to the farm or dairy or fire station at the primary level to the high school level visits to the museum or library or art institute and the specialized visits to the university or architectural firm or machine shop, are important components of the program and cannot be left to individual whim or chance. Many sophisticated and innovative school systems provide a series of such trips at each grade level and, in addition, allow individual teachers the opportunity to plan further experiences calling for transportation.

In addition to field trips, appropriate uses for the transportation system include the movement of students between schools for particular programs to encourage optimum use of particular equipment and talent, e.g., a planetarium located in one school, an advanced math program, a technical offering, etc. Also, the use of vehicles for extracurricular and cocurricular activities further optimizes the transportation system. It is important for the transportation division of the school system to recognize that as a service arm of the school it must stand ready to provide transportation services as the demands for such services are generated.

Although pupil transportation costs vary greatly from district to district depending on a great many factors, extended use of vehicles to provide additional educational benefits invariably reduces the pupil-mile cost ratio. This is because the added service provided is most efficient in terms of load factor and single destination. The gains in terms of educational enrichment are not as easily evaluated, but all indications point to greatly expanded opportunities for the learner.

Standards and Specifications

The setting of standards and specifications for school vehicles is very closely related to the purposes and aims of the transportation program as well as the demography and geography of the school district. Minimal standards of safety and health are often prescribed by the state department of education. If not, the local district can call on the U.S. Office of Education for assistance in determining such standards. Because of the minimal nature of the typical state- and/or federal-inspired standards, many local school systems developed their own specifications to incorporate particular standards they deem necessary. Given the ease with which seemingly innocent specifications can eliminate desirable and reputable manufacturers of vehicles, great care must be exercised in their development.

National standards of safety must be made an important part of any specification, but beyond that there are a variety of considerations which must be faced. These include such items as:

1. What size vehicle is appropriate for the kind of use envisioned? If basic uses involve transporting children short distances, and if density of population is such that large numbers of riders are gathered in a short time, then the larger capacity vehicle is most appropriate. If, however, the travel distance is great and children are quite scattered, then a smaller vehicle might be more feasible.

2. What kinds of road conditions exist in the area to be served? The type of vehicle to be specified must enable optimum satisfaction to the user. Excellent four-lane highways and fully developed, paved secondary roads warrant different usage than do gravel roads and rutted, ungraveled trails found in some locales.

3. What is the geography of the area? Level, flat terrain calls for different vehicles than does uneven, mountainous territory. The type of bus, its engine, its capacity, and size will depend on the kind of terrain it must negotiate. Decisions on power equipment, engine capacity and horsepower, tires, gear system, and suspension system are all somewhat dependent upon geography.

4. What is the climate of the area? Heating and/or cooling capacity of the vehicle, types of extra equipment needed, engine size and power, and vehicle configuration are all related to weather conditions.

Answers to these concerns coupled with strict attention to national safety standards can lead to specifications suited to the needs of the particular school system. While it is important not to underestimate the need of a transportation system it is equally important not to overestimate the need. Judgment and careful planning are crucial to the development of standards and specifications.

FOOD SERVICES

Another of the auxiliary services that is fast becoming one of the important support services of the school system is the food services operation. Realization that the hungry child has severe learning impediments and that for many children the only balanced meal of the day is the school breakfast and/or lunch has served to emphasize the importance of the food services program. Federal support has grown steadily first from the provision of surplus foods at minimal (storage) costs to recent aid in the form of direct grants to provide hot meals to needy children. In many of our urban centers, one-third to one-half of the public school children qualify for the subsidized food program. Increasingly the press of an urbanized society with its demands upon the family and the continued expansion of the work force to include more and more women have generated greatly expanded demands for school food services. What was once a phenomenon unique to school districts that served consolidated areas that had to provide food services because of the distance traveled by the students has become a common service extending to many of the neighborhood schools of the country. Originally a means to utilize surplus foods, the food service program has become recognized as a most valuable component of the school system. Increasingly, school systems are using the food service operation as an important sector of the educational program. Health, diet, consumer economics, ecology, nutrition, aesthetic development, chemistry, and the introduction to the service industry are all important contributions that the food services program can make to the curricular efforts of the school. However, the primary role of the food services operation is that of providing tasty, tempting, balanced meals at reasonable cost to the students.

Planning the food services operation is often a terrifying experience to the average school business official who has little knowledge or appreciation of the complexity of such an effort. Often such planning is left to a local woman who, because of some culinary skills, has been named head cook. While such people are experts in providing excellent meals for a family, the mass feeding of hundreds and even thousands of children requires skills far beyond those of persons responsible for food preparation in the home. The food service operation is as complex as that of the largest restaurant chain with split-second demands for service. Such an operation must be carefully planned and developed according to the food needs of the school system. Among the areas of concern to be addressed as the planning for food services continues are the following.

Policies, Rules, Regulations, and Procedures

Policies, as established by the board of education, become the guidelines for the development of rules, regulations, and procedures for the operation of the food service program. Food service policies attempt to establish broad parameters for the operation and include determinations of such questions as:

1. Is the school food program to be available to all children or just to those who meet certain specified criteria?
2. Is the school food service program to be a system-wide centralized operation or is it to be a building-by-building procedure with each building principal, in effect, administering a lunch program?
3. Is the program to be a hot foods program or a sack lunch?
4. If the program is system-wide, should *à la carte* menus be available, or should all children be expected to participate in "type A" programs? What about snacks? What provisions are made for children who carry sack lunches?
5. What provisions are to be made for feeding indigent children?
6. Is food to be prepared at each building or is central preparation with "hot cart" delivery more desirable?
7. Shall the schools observe "open" or "closed" lunch periods? If closed, what about requests for children living close to school to be allowed to go home for lunch?
8. Shall breakfast programs be initiated?
9. What educational benefits can accrue from the food program?
10. What is the line-staff relationship between food service personnel and building principals?

The development of rules, regulations, and procedures as a result of policy statements leads to an operating manual for day-to-day operations of the food service division. Standards and expectations of personnel and methods of operation are defined. Procedures for collection of monies, use of children as helpers, serving of food, dining room regulations, special food service capability, use of lunch facilities by outside groups, amortization and replacement of equipment, etc., are important planning functions. Increasingly, contracts with various school employee groups, i.e., teachers, clerks, custodians, and lunch personnel, become important in the development of rules and procedures. The use of the dining room as an educational resource and its effectiveness depends upon the availability of staff during the dining hours. Minimum standards of health, cleanliness, and decorum are important to the food service operation and must be well defined.

Because of the severe time constraints imposed by the school day, operating procedures have very real logistic implications. Delivery schedules, serving schedules, preparation schedules, and efficiency are very important for the food service program that must quickly accommodate large numbers of children during a short time span. Delays and confusion must be minimized in order to provide optimum service to children. Rules, regulations, and procedures must be explicit and direct while allowing sufficient flexibility to meet unique and unforeseen needs (for example, certain groups may periodically need picnic lunches provided or may have to eat early or late on a particular day or may invite a group from a different city for lunch, etc.).

Staffing and Supervision

Planning for the staffing and supervision of the food services operation requires that close attention be given educational considerations as well as culinary qualifications of aspirants. Compatibility with children, health standards, temperament, adaptability, personal habits, energy level, and general appearance all contribute to the desirability of prospective staff members.

In districts numbering several thousands of students housed in a number of buildings, it is desirable to engage a school food service director (and, if size and volume warrant, several persons) to administer and supervise the food service program. This person is generally trained as a dietician and/or mass-feeding specialist and brings a background in food service work to the school system. Sometimes a certificated teacher trained in food service (home economics) is available and with appropriate support develops the capacity to administer the program. It is a great relief and of great assistance to the school business administrator to have such a person available to handle the day-to-day administration of the food service program.

The determination of the type and size of food service staff needed depends on a number of variables. Immediate concerns are:

1. Is the program to be centralized with central food preparation, or is each building to have its own preparation capacity?
2. What is the projected number of meals to be prepared either centrally or by building?
3. Is the "type A" lunch to be the only meal served?
4. Are silverware and dishes (plastic or china) used or are throw-away utensils and dishes to be used?

If, for example, a centralized food preparation system is projected with "hot cart" delivery to individual buildings, the staffing of the preparation center is very different from the staffing of preparation kitchens in every building. In centralized preparation, specialization in terms of salad chef, meat chef, vegetable cook, baker, dessert chef, etc., might be in order, while in decentralized preparation categories such as head cook, assistant cook, cook's helper, etc., are more common.

In centralized food service operations, provisions for trucking hot food on a very rigid time schedule are most important. Additionally, there must be personnel provided at the receiving schools to serve and distribute the food, to handle the clean-up and dish return or disposal chore, and to supervise the dining room operation. While centralized food preparation is generally considered to be more efficient and while quality is more easily controlled in such a schema, other considerations also enter into decisions of centralized versus decentralized food preparation. Obviously, quality control and administration are easiest in the central food preparation arrangement. Other advantages include savings in capital equipment and space costs; lower unit costs due to quantity preparation; the potential for specialization in tasks; the capacity to develop special foods production (i.e., baking, butchering, salads, etc.), the capacity to accomplish long-range planning and savings that accrue from volume purchasing and storage; and so forth. However, certain disadvantages are also present. These include the loss of the food service operation as a component of the educational program, rigidity in terms of schedules and timing, loss of jobs to neighborhood people, loss of food service resources to community groups, dependence on transportation systems for delivery of foods, limited capacity to meet local food service needs and tastes.

There usually arises another difficulty, especially in decentralized food service operations. This is the conflict over who has line responsibility over kitchen personnel—the principal or the school lunch administrator. Generally, this is resolved by the decision that although the food service administrator sets rules and procedures that pertain to food preparation, menus, distribution, etc., the principal has line responsibility as it pertains to the ongoing program of the school. In this sense, the principal determines serving schedules, collection procedure, dining room expectations, etc. As a service to the teaching-learning process the food program must meet the overall educational needs of the school as established.

Menus, Prices, and Portion Control

School lunch menus are the result of careful long-range planning efforts. Seasonal harvests, market fluctuations, government surplus offerings, unique tastes, ethnic and racial group preferences, talents of preparation personnel, regionality—all play a part in menu planning. Most menu planning is based on cyclical rotation of a basic number of meals so that daily, weekly, and even monthly variety is provided. Past experience and records as to what menus are most accepted are also valuable planning tools. Generally menus are planned for the entire system, or at least subsystems of the total school district. If the basic lunch is "type A" there is little deviation from the menu. If, however, in addition to "type A" lunches there is to be provided an *à la carte* menu and perhaps snack or sandwich opportunities, the planning task is more complex. Usually such questions are resolved by insisting that the one basic meal menu be adhered to at the elementary school level with variety and flexibility allowed at the secondary school.

Prices can and do vary greatly from area to area. The main objective of the food service program is to provide balanced, tasty meals at the lowest possible costs. Labor cost and food price differentials cause variances in prices from place to place. Urban centers tend to reflect higher costs because of the highly unionized labor market and because fewer foods are grown locally. In spite of this, it is often possible to provide food at lower unit costs because of savings realized through mass production of foods.

It is important that the food service operation be a nonprofit operation in order to provide the greatest service at lowest possible cost to the user. It is equally important that the food service division consider such expenses as amortization of capital equipment, replacement of equipment, utilities costs, custodial costs, and overhead when determining the real cost of the program in order to establish a price structure.

Portion controls are usually established by regulation with USDA minimum standards used for determining the amount and variety of food to be served. Differences in age level should be reflected in both the size of the portion and in the price charged. Portion control is relatively easy in centralized operations that prepackage the meals. It becomes more difficult as food is served cafeteria style. Many systems use scales to weigh meat portions and sized serving utensils to determine vegetable portions. It is important that adequacy of portions and consistency of portions be maintained.

An Educational Facilities Laboratories publication provides an important local planning tool for the business administrator as he prepares initial cost calculations which are necessary in order to make decisions related to menus, prices, and portion control. The procedure involves four sequential steps:

I. MARKET ANALYSIS
   A simplified market analysis can be done with the information that each school administrator has in his files or in his permanent records. This simple survey will serve to determine the numerical market for meals in a school lunch program.
   A. Student population _____
   B. Adult population (teachers, staff employees) _____
   C. Total potential market _____
   D. Estimated % participation (It is not necessary to have precise figures. These figures can be based on a school survey, which could be a simple questionnaire sent to all students or parents, or using the Department of Agriculture's estimate of 50% of the total school population.) _____ %
   E. Total potential participation _____

F. Number of school days _____

G. Total number of meals per school _____

II. ABILITY TO PAY

While it is impossible to pinpoint specifically the amount of money that students can pay for meals, an educated guess based upon the neighborhood from which the school draws its students can lead to meaningful estimates. For reference it should be noted that the average charge for a Type A meal across the nation is 35¢.

	No.	¢ / meal	$ total / meal
A. Students from underprivileged or low-income families—who need a main meal supplying the bulk of their nutritional intake	____	_____	_____
B. Students from moderate-income families—who need a healthful supplement to their nutritional intake.	____	_____	_____
C. Students from high-income families—who need a healthful supplement to their nutritional intake.	____	_____	_____
D. Faculty, staff, employees	____	_____	_____
E. Total per meal period	(a) ____	(b) _____	
F. Average payment per meal	$(b \div a)$ ____	_____	
G. Total yearly income (II-F × I-G)		_____	

III. SUBSIDY AVAILABLE

In order to determine the subsidies available to an individual school or school district, the school food service administrator should contact his state board of education. Once again, these statistics will not be of pinpoint accuracy but will serve as a general guide to the administrator in evaluating or planning his food service program.

A. Cash subsidy available from participation in National School Lunch Program—determined by state board of education. _____

B. $ value of surplus commodities available through National School Lunch Program—estimate in consultation with state board of education. _____

C. Total subsidies from NSLP _____

D. Subsidies from other sources _____

E. Total all subsidies _____

IV. TOTAL INCOME POTENTIAL
   A. Within NSLP (III-C + II-G)   ————
   B. Outside NSLP (III-D + II-G)   ————

    With these basic considerations defined, it is possible to make some preliminary decisions about participation in the National School Lunch Program. It is also possible to estimate the fixed and operating costs. From this, prices can be set, and it is possible to determine the amount that can be spent on food.[1]

Purchasing

    Analysis of food purchasing practices among the school districts of the United States reveals that a complete spectrum of purchasing practices is used. This spectrum covers a wide range starting with the practice of the cook calling the corner grocer to place an order for the day's food needs to very sophisticated bidding procedures that involve the cooperative efforts of forty to fifty school systems. The use of the corner grocer to supply all the food needs of the neighborhood school is fast becoming a thing of the past. Food service has simply become too big an operation to neglect the development of sophisticated purchasing procedures. For example, the medium-sized school district that feeds an average of 10,000 students per day will generate a total operating budget of from $600,000 to $700,000. This is quite apt to be the single largest departmental budget in the entire school system and will demand that careful planning be utilized in its expenditure. Since food costs, supply costs, and other purchases will typically involve 50 to 75 percent of the total budget (depending upon the current availability of federal surplus foods), and since there is a wide variety of different items needed in the food service operation, purchasing is fast becoming recognized as an important function in the administration of the food services program.

    The purchasing procedure applicable for school food services is illustrated in figure 13.1. It contains the essential elements of a general purchasing procedure, but it also highlights certain relevant features of school food service purchasing.

    The development of bid procedures and the standards and specifications requirements for food services purchasing is a highly specialized task to be performed by one well versed in the mass-feeding area. Decisions as to canned foods versus fresh and/or

[1] *Twenty Million for Lunch* (New York: Educational Facilities Laboratories, 1968), pp. 13–14.

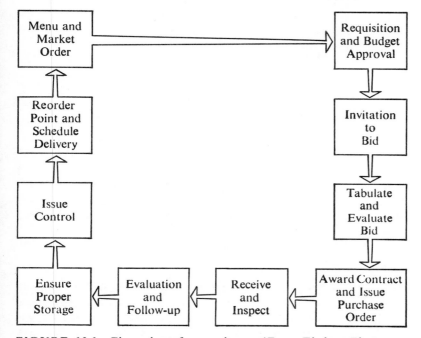

FIGURE 13.1 Flow chart for purchases. (From Thelma Flanagan, School Food Purchasing Guide [Evanston, Ill.: Association of School Business Officials, 1968], p. 120; reprinted with permission.)

frozen foods involve such variables as freezer/refrigerator space, cold storage capacity, dry storage capacity, seasonal variance in food stuff availability, market conditions, and other difficult-to-predict conditions. In addition, the determination of quality standards, container and lot size, quality control procedures, and delivery schedules are for highly skilled food service personnel. Because savings of significant proportions can accrue to the school district through intelligent purchasing practices, the school business administrator must provide the support and talent needed to initiate such an effort. Examples of specific techniques include the purchase of paper goods in carload lots, the timing of bid requests to correspond to seasonal production of specific foods, realistic appraisal of quality (fancy labeled canned goods are premium priced and often not essential to high-quality food service), development of sufficient storage space to enable volume purchasing, contract purchasing of perishable foods to ensure price stability (milk products, baked goods, etc.), cooperative purchasing plans involving a number of school districts to provide volume, and many other creative and money-saving ideas.

Purchasing is an important component of the planning effort of the food services operation. Menu planning, projections of numbers to be serviced, and prediction of items needed all contribute to the purchasing process. Initiation of the purchase is only the start, however. Delivery schedules must be established to ensure that supplies and materials are available when needed. In addition, quality control procedures must be a continuing effort to ensure that standards and specifications are maintained at expected high levels. Skill in purchasing often determines how successful the food service operation will be, for the savings effected here will make possible the stabilization of costs to the user at a reasonable level.

Food Preparation Systems

The nature of food service needs and the nature of the policies of the school system to meet these needs will dictate the specifications of food preparation areas. There are several alternative systems to serve individual situations, as in the Educational Facilities Laboratories publication quoted earlier:

> There are four major types of kitchens, only three of which are actually used for the preparation of food.
> 1. Central Kitchen
>   In a central kitchen operation, food is prepared in a centralized kitchen building and distributed to a number of schools for service.
> 2. Independent/Individual Kitchen
>   This is the most common type of school kitchen where food is prepared and served in a single building.
> 3. Manufacturing Kitchen
>   In a manufacturing kitchen, bulk food products are processed and dispatched to individual kitchens for final preparation.
> 4. Satellite Kitchen
>   The satellite kitchen is primarily an area that receives food from a central kitchen and holds it until it is ready for serving.

The Central Kitchen

The use of a central kitchen is particularly practical in districts where no food service facilities presently exist and in those new districts where building programs are contemplated.

The concept of a conveniently located central kitchen applies not only to a large school district, but to any number of schools—even as few as two. There are successful operations where a kitchen in an elementary school serves only one other school, and there are others where the central kitchen in a secondary school prepares food for as many as eight outlying locations.

The existence of individual school kitchens does not preclude consideration of a central program. It is sometimes economical to remodel the kitchens, utilizing much of the existing equipment.

In order to determine whether or not a central kitchen is practical in a particular situation, the following factors should be carefully considered.

1. The over-all size of the school district.
2. The number and types (elementary and secondary) of schools involved.
3. Estimated percentage of participation in each school.
4. Existing food service facilities.
5. Whether or not the existing (if any) school kitchens are operating efficiently.
6. The type of menu desired.
7. The possible location of a central kitchen.
8. The possible transportation problems between the central kitchen and the participating schools.

In some instances, a central kitchen can be impractical. If the district is in a region having severe weather, transportation of the foods can be unreliable. The terrain of an area may present transportation problems. If the grades on any route between the schools exceed $7\frac{1}{2}$ percent, delivery of bulk food is impractical because of spillage. Heavy traffic and distance must be given consideration in any centralized program, although it should be noted that both Detroit and New York City utilize the central kitchen concept for a large portion of their food service programs.

Also important is the physical access to the premises at both the central and receiving kitchens. Adequate driveways, backing and turning space, docking facilities, and noninterference with playgrounds or pedestrian areas are necessities.

Individual/Independent Kitchens

An individual/independent kitchen which is capable of producing a plate lunch efficiently must be a complete kitchen that includes receiving, refrigerated and dry storage, production, serving, and dishwashing areas.

The kitchen should be arranged in a logical operational sequence from the time food is received until the last dish is washed and placed in storage. Beginning with the delivery entrance, physical organization should be in a line progressing from the entrance to receiving, dry and refrigerated storage, scaling, rough preparation (any food preparation prior to cooking), cooking, finishing, portioning, and serving.

Manufacturing Kitchens

In the manufacturing kitchen, bulk food products are purchased, processed, manufactured, and stored in one location for distribution to satellite kitchens where final preparation takes place.

This type of kitchen is utilized in the Los Angeles City School District. Here, less than 20 employees prepare all meat products (beef patties, meat loaf, Salisbury steak, etc.), meat sauces, dry mixes, cookie and pie doughs, and many other bulk food items for use in over 490 cafeterias. Assembly line production methods and specialized equipment have saved the school district over 800 man-hours per day. Some food service consultants feel that a manufacturing kitchen for fewer than 20 schools is uneconomical.

Satellite Kitchens

There are various methods of satellite school feeding:

1. Where there is no kitchen facility in a school, serving may take place in a corridor. Loaded hot and cold food carts from the central kitchen are wheeled into the corridor and electrical connections established to maintain food temperatures. Accompanying the food carts are eating utensils and a cart containing compartmented trays.

    At the time of service, the server removes a compartmented tray from the cart, dishes the foods from the hot and cold cart, adds the tableware, and hands the assembled lunch tray to the child. From a milk cabinet stationed in the corridor, the child then picks up milk and proceeds to an adjacent area designated as a lunch room.

    Following the serving period, the tray cart and a garbage receptacle are placed at the exit of the lunch room. After eating, the children scrape their trays into the garbage receptacle and place the soiled tray and tableware in the tray cart. The food and tray carts are then returned to the central kitchen for washing and subsequent reuse.

2. Another approach can be taken in which only the hot and cold food carts are sent from the central kitchen. The tray carts and tableware are maintained in the receiving schools. The carts are arranged and the lunch is served in the same manner as described above.

    Following the lunch period, the food carts are returned to the central kitchen, but all other sanitizing is done in the receiving schools. Each satellite is equipped with a garbage disposal, a dishwashing machine, and a small storage area for the tray carts.

3. A third method is to have part of the menu (generally hot foods) sent from the central kitchen and part prepared in the satellite kitchen. Here, just the carts are returned to the central kitchen for sanitizing.

4. A fourth method permits *à la carte* service. Various carts containing hot foods, salads, sandwiches, desserts, etc. are sent from the central kitchen. The food selections are removed from the carts and arranged on a scramble service line in the satellite kitchen. All sanitizing, except of the carts, takes place in the satellite.

These methods can be combined to meet the particular requirements of individual school districts.

It should be stated that the type of kitchen selected does not limit the school administrator to a specific meal type or food preparation method. All four of these basic kitchen types can be used to prepare meals from basic commodities or tailored to use the latest in frozen prepared foods.[2]

Accounting, Reporting, and Cost Analysis

The amount of discretionary tolerance in terms of resource utilization is so slight in the food service operation that very careful and minute accounting, reporting, and cost analysis procedures must be followed. Because in most school systems the food service operation is self-supporting and because unit costs must be kept to a level that will encourage participation by all clients, the record keeping, planning, and implementation tasks are crucial to success.

Many states have well-established accounting manuals for the food service operation. Most recommend a modified encumbrance system that greatly assists in the planning effort. Because of the unique daily cash flow process found in the food service operation, daily income accounting procedures are desired. Records showing number of meals served, income received, food and usable supplies consumed, man-hours of labor required, and peripheral costs incurred are usually required for each cafeteria. Forms indicating these and other data along with bank deposit slips are collected each day from each unit. The reconciliation of bank deposit slips and statements with the daily, weekly, and

[2] *Twenty Million for Lunch,* pp. 22–24.

monthly report forms is a task of utmost importance to the person charged with responsibility for the food service program. Encumbrance of wages, food costs, supplies, utilities, and so on, will enable the reporting system to be meaningful and current. Because most income is on a cash basis (except for billing procedures for special functions and/or organizations) and because all expenditures are in the form of salary vouchers or payment of invoices submitted for goods and services, the use of daily records, purchase orders, and work orders is most important to the accounting process. Periodic audits, both internal performed by the business office and external by an audit firm, require accurate data. Responsible management also requires that recognized accounting practices be followed.

The use of daily, weekly, and monthly records and accounting practices to generate needed reports to a variety of persons is recommended. Reports indicating the overall status of the food services division along with building-by-building breakdowns are important information to be shared with personnel of the food service program as well as with principals and central office personnel. Data such as number of meals served, percentage ·of student· participation, variance of participation with menu, special food services provided, etc., are important items to be reported. Reports including the above and additional interpretive cost data, e.g., unit costs, labor charges, food costs, etc., are useful in the cost analysis requirement and can provide valuable planning data. Many states require reports for participation in state and federal programs. Such reports can be the basis for generating a variety of in-house reports providing specific data of interest to specific groups. It would seem that certain informative data (participation, menu implications, labor and material use, etc.) must be reported on a daily basis while other more interpretive reports should be on a weekly and monthly cycle. It is also important (mandated by law and/or board policy in most districts) that an annual report and audit be submitted to the board of education.

Constant analysis of income and expenditures is most important to the continued health of the food service operation. Decisions and plans developed as a result of careful cost analysis will encourage optimization of the food service program. Given regional labor cost differences and the fluctuations in costs of foods and supplies, the analysis of food services operations must be a continuing effort to ensure maximum benefits for the user.

Comparative cost data will provide for determination of the most efficient and well-operated components of the food service division. If, for example, elementary school A is consistently averaging out to a 10¢ per plate cost for labor as compared to 15¢ per plate for elementary school B and if the total number of meals served in each school are comparable with each school offering the same menu, then it is probable that school B needs some help in organizing its food service operation in order that more efficient operation can occur. Similarly, cost data can provide information leading to a reduction of waste or to an improvement in menus or give clues to deficiencies in certain units. Careful cost analysis should lead to increased benefits for the children of the school system in terms of tastier foods prepared in the most efficient, economical manner possible.

Remembering that the goal of the food service operation is to provide attractive, tasty, well-balanced meals to students at the most economical rate possible leads to full utilization of sophisticated accounting and reporting procedures as means of generating data upon which to base cost analysis.

In-Service Training and Coordination with Educational Program

As in most school-related activities, there is continuing need for staff training and in-service development. Typically, the majority of food service personnel are successful homemakers who for one reason or another are attracted to the school as a source of employment. These women, while usually very fine family cooks, are not attuned to mass feeding and therefore must be encouraged to learn the techniques appropriate to such an endeavor. In addition, the use of the food service program as an important component of the educational program suggests other special talents that must be present and highly developed in food service personnel. The planning for, preparation, and serving of food to several hundred persons each meal is very different from the preparation of a family meal. In-service activities include such items as recipe preparation and use, food display, health standards, reporting procedures, youth culture and preferences, actual preparation and seasoning of new recipes, ordering techniques, storage techniques, cleanliness standards and objectives, staff relations, student relations, and so on. Operating rules, regulations, and procedures are reviewed and adjusted to meet current needs and expectations. Objectives and goals of the good service program are emphasized as part of in-service activity.

Also related to in-service efforts is the coordination of the food service program with the educational program. There exist certain constraints and time obligations that must be met if the food service program is to operate in a school. Children must eat at an appropriate time and they must be fed quickly and efficiently so that the program of education is not unduly interrupted or disrupted. Additionally, the food service program has a great opportunity to become an important part of the educational program and can complement and support curricular efforts at every grade level. Health, safety, nutrition, food chemistry, economics, service vocations, and aesthetics are but a few of the potential areas to be supported by the food service division. Opportunities to provide such fringe services must be nurtured and expanded by making available the total food service resource to the educational staff.

SUMMARY

As two auxiliary services most commonly under the direction of the business administrator, the transportation and food service divisions of the school system perform tasks very important to the primary teaching-learning task. Each of these divisions are specialized activities requiring very talented and highly trained personnel. The staffs of the two divisions not only must possess abilities in the specialized activities involved (e.g., vehicular or food service), but also need to have added talents and strengths in working with children. It is therefore very important that ongoing in-service programs be provided in each of these areas. Success in each of these areas rests upon the development of adequate policies leading to rules, regulations, and procedures governing the day-to-day activities of the two divisions. Supervision and administration of the two divisions often require specialized personnel and are considered full-time activities. The school business administrator must adequately and carefully plan for auxiliary services and recruit well-trained supervisory personnel for the routine operating tasks involved, for each of the services described are highly specialized, demanding activities. As the chief business planner, the school business administrator must have a working knowledge of each service, but he cannot hope to assume the actual operating responsibility of such diverse activities. Planning decisions, in order to be effective, must be made with some detachment from the ongoing operations of an activity.

SUGGESTED ACTIVITIES

1. Design a pupil transportation survey in a school system having such a program. Try to find such things as number of pupils transported, number of pupil miles traveled per day, number of miles traveled by each bus, the amount of driving time each day, etc.

2. Determine the state requirements for your school system to provide pupil transportation. To what extent are these requirements exceeded by local policy enacted by your school system? What is the nature of the local policy which enables this?

3. Using the planning form for food services as it appears on pages 324–26, calculate a food services program for a particular school system. If there are differences in the planned and actual programs, how do you account for them?

4. Test the feasibility of each of the alternative school food service systems as described on pages 328–31 in your own or another school system.

SUGGESTED READINGS

Educational Facilities Laboratories. 1968. *Twenty Million for Lunch.* New York: The Laboratories, 1968.

Featherstone, E. Glenn, and Murray, John B. *State School Bus Standards.* Washington, D.C.: U.S. Department of Health, Education, and Welfare, 1962.

Flanagan, Thelma. *School Food Purchasing Guide.* Evanston, Ill.: Association of School Business Officials, 1968.

Kotschevar, Lendal H., and Terrell, M. E. *Food Service Planning, Layout and Equipment.* New York: John Wiley & Sons, Inc., 1961.

National Education Association. *Minimum Standards for School Buses.* Washington, D.C.: The Association, 1959.

PLANNING OF CAPITAL OUTLAY

The investment in plant facilities for elementary, secondary, and higher education is immense. The trend toward additional investment continues to increase rapidly. This is further complicated by breaks in the traditional concept of school plant utilization. Needs for additional facilities are suggested by the mounting interest in preschool programs, the re-emphasis upon the community school concept, the increasing breadth of the formal educational program (nursery through junior college), the increasing interest in adult education both for enrichment and retraining, and the continuing increase in undergraduate and graduate enrollments in higher education. Because of these rapid advances, facilities will require better planning and greater flexibility. Advances in educational technology will also greatly influence educational facilities.

The Challenge of Planning

During recent years many cultural, social, and technological changes have tended to push education into another new area. These progressive changes are the result of a concerted effort by educators to substitute a substantial portion of traditional classroom instruction with individual pupil instruction, team teaching, independent study, remedial programs, and other forms of educational software.

However, at the same time we must not become so enthralled with educational innovations that they are our sole considerations when planning buildings. A review of current writing would tend to support this view. Educators must take a more comprehensive view of educational facility planning. Basic learning principles must be fundamental and underlie the planning of every instructional element of school buildings.

Many social forces impinge upon the planning of new facilities. The delegation to the schools of the responsibility for social and legal integration will have a tremendous impact upon future facility planning. Employers are complaining that the schools are not instilling the middle-class conservative values that are so fundamental to our industrial economy. The international competition for productive intelligence with its sharp focus on educational excellence, speed, and breadth of learning still exists. The increasing demand for individual freedom in and for learning in contrast to the need for closer supervision to prevent the increasing vandalism of school property create complications for planning facilities. Society seems to be developing greater compassion for the unique educational needs of students of diverse ethnic groups.

For many large urban centers school facility needs may be transient in nature. Neighborhoods may move through land use patterns which may require school facilities for certain pupil populations. At other times, the area may shift to business or industrial needs. Because of this shifting need, the concept of disposable buildings or short-use facilities may be viable. Shared space or leased space might be a possible answer. Some apartment facilities may allot space for school facility needs which as needs shift can be utilized for other purposes. Multiuse facilities may be appropriate; that is, the same buildings may be utilized for schools, community centers, or other community needs.

Concurrently, with society's desire for greater utilization of educational technology and the related increase in cost of facilities the taxpayers are showing resistance to additional taxes to support and house the expanding technology. In many urban areas a more urgent problem may be the remodeling and renovation of existing facilities to implement opportunity for all students to progress at rates appropriate to their backgrounds, cultural levels, and abilities.

The principle of adaptability is another challenging dimension of school plant planning. Educational practices that seem promising when a school is designed may prove to be ineffective or inappropriate later. Flexibility must expedite movement in a desired direction but must also permit movement in alternative ways as educational planning and development dictate. Flexibility and the adaptability to change should be a basic premise of all new school facilities.

Planning Resources

The planning of a physical facility for educational use is a complex process that requires attention to political, social, fiscal, and technical/professional components. This requires concentration on the part of all interested parties. These various parties include: students; the local school board and its superintendent and staff; local voters and taxpayers; the architect; the state education department; planning groups; local municipal agencies; manpower groups and other agencies.

Evaluations of the present educational program and facilities cause much apprehension in many school districts. Everyone has an opinion, but the fundamental question (What is the quality of our local educational system?) is very difficult to evaluate. The comprehensive survey may be the best tool presently for answering the question. In order to emphasize the importance of the future rather than a picture of the present the authors have used the term comprehensive planning. This denotes a more futuristic approach to the concept.

Comprehensive Planning

The principal purpose of most comprehensive planning surveys is to develop an educational plan of action for the future based upon an objective and systematic study of needs, resources, and educational goals of the school system. A document incorporating findings, conclusions, and recommendations is presented to the board of education and to others designated by the board.

To be effective the document must also include alternative plans for consideration by the board and employers.

Castaldi has listed the following as considerations fundamental to comprehensive planning surveys:

1. The comprehensive planning survey creates a favorable psychological climate for making an objective study of the educational affairs of a school district.
2. The comprehensive planning survey offers an effective process for systematically assembling and analyzing data.
3. The comprehensive planning survey is an application of the scientific method of inquiry to educational problems.
4. The recommended long-range program resulting from a comprehensive planning survey is built almost entirely upon facts and logic.
5. The comprehensive planning survey looks toward the future.
6. The comprehensive planning survey views all parts of the educational enterprise in proper perspective.
7. The comprehensive planning survey may reveal inequalities of educational opportunity within a school district.
8. The comprehensive planning survey enables boards of education to plan on the basis of facts.
9. The comprehensive planning survey represents a sound, businesslike approach to school operation.[1]

Components basic to a comprehensive planning survey are projections of the community and pupil populations, finance and business management studies, educational program diagnoses, school facility reviews, personnel appraisals, and recommendations that are realistic, educationally practicable, and financially feasible. The survey may be conducted by local staff, outside experts, citizens, state or regional planning personnel, or a combination of the above. It is the responsibility of the board of education to instigate the survey, determine the dissemination of the survey, and act upon its recommendations. Implementation of any major building program is usually contingent upon public understanding and support. It is imperative that the citizens be fully informed of the identified needs and of plans to meet these needs. While some of the public may not wish to read the report

[1] Basil Castaldi, *Creative Planning of Educational Facilities* (Chicago: Rand McNally & Company, © 1969), pp. 20–21.

in its entirety, there is often wide interest in the major findings, conclusions, and recommendations. Wide distribution of a digest of the survey is one useful public information technique, particularly if community meetings are held to discuss the survey.

Comprehensive planning in the urban centers must involve:

1. Community leaders and neighborhood types
2. Exhaustive demographic study to discuss population trends
3. Identification of indigenous resources (facilities, people, business, etc.)
4. Repeated and continuous progress reports to community groups
5. Capacity to change to meet evolving community goals and wishes.

Communication in Planning

The degree of participation in planning by qualified, competent individuals has a direct relationship with the successful educational facilities acquisition program.

The Council of Educational Facility Planners has suggested that:

> Effective communication is an essential part of any successful design. It is necessary for the educational planners, the governing board, and the design professionals to be in continuous, thorough, frank, sympathetic communication if they would create an outstanding educational facility. A good school building is not the product of an architect working in seclusion; it is not the product of a citizens' committee; it is not the result of petty checking by a maintenance department; it is not the result of standardized plans drafted by a school architect or engineer; it is not the product of a well-written educational specification; it is not the product of a good superintendent of schools. An outstanding educational facility is the result of an effective team effort, the product of carefully planned, coordinated activity of the planner, educator, designer, builder, and user.[2]

Communication is the coordinating media for the above. Along with communication, timing and scheduling are important

[2] *Guide for Planning Educational Facilities* (Columbus, O.: Council of Educational Facility Planners, 1969), pp. 17–18.

ingredients to effective planning. Throughout the planning, many resource persons will assist with specific problems. Communication will facilitate the input of each. Communications must be two way and must include community and students.

Involvement in Planning

Resource personnel from the local, state, and national level plus professional staff, students, and community leaders will be involved in any major capital outlay project. The board of education is a key group because it must ratify suggestions of others to legalize the proceedings. The involvement of the board of education will necessitate the involvement of the superintendent and his staff. The degree of involvement and specialization will depend upon the size and personal expertise of individual members of the superintendency. Others involved in the process are the instructional staff; students; administrative and supervisory construction personnel; planners of equipment and furniture; legal counsel and land agent; auxiliary service personnel; architects (both system and private firm); engineers; contractors (specifically the general contractor); lay citizens; local planning commissions and other city-county agencies; commercial representatives; educational consultants; technical consultants; metropolitan and urban planners; state department of education personnel and state safety inspectors; and appropriate national agencies.

The architect plays a very important role and the board must exercise extreme caution in selection. Some possible criteria for selection include: recommendations of other school districts; quantity and quality of experience of the architectural and engineering staff; nature and extent of previous school design experience; nature of the facility to be designed; current workload and financial status; accessibility of the architect's office; and provision for adequate communication and supervision. The architect should represent the school board rather than the general contractor. See figure 14.1 for a copy of the standard form of questionnaire for selection of architects for school building projects.

Planning the Facility

The educational specifications serve as the formal communications media between the professional educators and the architect. If the educational facility is to be planned for a specific

THE AMERICAN INSTITUTE OF ARCHITECTS

AIA Document B431

Standard Form of Questionnaire for the Selection of Architects for Educational Facilities

*PREPARED JOINTLY BY THE COUNCIL OF EDUCATIONAL FACILITY PLANNERS
AND THE AMERICAN INSTITUTE OF ARCHITECTS*

A. INFORMATION BY THE OWNER TO THE ARCHITECT:

1. Name and address of Owner:
2. Name and address of person to whom questionnaire should be returned:
3. Description of proposed projects:
4. Approximate timetable for design and construction periods:

B. ARCHITECT'S QUESTIONNAIRE:

1. Firm name:
2. Business address:
3. Telephone number:
4. Type of organization (check one):
   - ☐ Individual or sole proprietorship
   - ☐ Partnership
   - ☐ Corporation
   - ☐ Other (describe)
5. Names of principals, professional history, professional affiliations, key personnel, staff organizations (attach information if you prefer):

6. Qualifications for this specific project:

7. Persons whom the Owner may contact for reference:

8. Attach any material which might assist the Owner in giving proper consideration:

AIA DOCUMENT B431 ● STANDARD FORM OF QUESTIONNAIRE FOR THE SELECTION OF ARCHITECTS FOR EDUCA-
TIONAL FACILITIES ● JANUARY 1972 EDITION ● AIA® ● © 1972 ● THE AMERICAN INSTITUTE OF ARCHITECTS, 1735
NEW YORK AVE., NW, WASHINGTON, D.C. 20006

*FIGURE 14.1 Standard questionnaire for the American Institute of
Architects. (This document has been reproduced with the permission of
The American Institute of Architects. Further reproduction is not au-
thorized. Users of this form should ascertain the latest edition when using
AIA forms.)*

educational program educational specifications are a must. Otherwise the architect is forced to plan the facility in a virtual vacuum and will be prone to reply upon his past experience and personal concept of the local educational program. Architects that become stereotyped as to design of educational facilities cannot be faulted entirely. Many times they are working in the absence of guidance by the professional educator.

The educational specifications include the educational program not only as it relates to curriculum, but also as it relates to different types of learning experiences and the spaces that will be devoted to each. Basic to the educational specifications are: number and types of spaces, suggested size of each space, persons to be accommodated, equipment to be housed, special environmental treatment, and the relative space relationship. They are useful in selecting a site as well as in determining the building configuration. The role of the architect is to interpret educational specifications graphically. These educational specifications are essential and should involve staff, specialists, community, students, and other agencies.

Many school systems have come to realize that before the design of a building is undertaken, a set of educational specifications should be developed. Educational specifications are invaluable to the architect and educational leaders since they have come to realize that a school facility must be designed to house and implement the educational program. Since the program is changing, the building of the future must be designed in a way that the physical elements or parts of the facility do not get in the way of the performance of students and teachers. All blocks and barriers to optimum performance must be removed. In the past, school officials and teachers have had very little to say about planning, and the resulting facility was less acceptable to the staff. When educational specifications are developed, teachers have a part in the planning. By being allowed a part in the planning, teachers are more receptive to new ideas and innovations; thus the program potential of the building is more fully realized. Who knows more about how much and what kind of space is needed than the teachers? When teachers have determined the kind of equipment needed, the architect finds it much easier to design a building that will facilitate the program. Gone are the days when a new structure is built without involvement of students, teachers, and laymen. Today's teachers, administrators, boards of education, architects, and laymen must work together in bringing about a functional school building. If schools are to fulfill an important mission, consideration must be given to the best possible means of enhancing the learning environment. Careful planning, imagination, and farsighted vision on the part of all concerned can do much toward producing a healthful and productive learning environment. A dedication to this task is absolutely essential.

Architectural Services

Whether a school building project is large or small, the architect's normal services are similar. It should be noted, however, that special services are often contracted for by special arrangement. The following are normal services of architects:

1. The architect *assumes responsibility* for the implementation for the project in all phases.
2. The architect prepares all contractual arrangements between architect-owner and owner-contractor. The legal complications of any construction project can only be appreciated by one who has been involved in producing a school plant from start to finish. The problems involve code requirements, controls by public agencies, real estate legalities, bonding, inspection reports, progress payments, preparation, administration and enforcement of contract documents, lien laws, recording of all project accounts, certification of construction personnel and the determination of the degree of acceptability of all work performed.
3. The architect aids the client in programming and analyzing his needs. This consultation phase involves administrators, curriculum personnel, teachers, consultants, planners, and engineers. In the interest of expediting the project, site surveys and soil testing may be completed during this phase. These surveys and tests are not normally covered by the architect's fee.
4. The architect, after thorough study of the program, the site, the financial limitations, and the predilections of owners and boards, prepares tentative design studies for review. Generally these are revised several times as review teams make their evaluations. Preliminary drawings usually require detailed illustration of conceptual ideas.
5. The architect develops his schematic work by refining all drawings and preparing illustrations in detail of the plans, site development, features of construction and equipment. Usually he prepares outline specifications for materials, de-

termines the type of construction, and prepares a statement of probable construction costs. Work completed at this point constitutes the preliminary phase. Normally, one-quarter of the architect's fee is paid at this time.

6. The architect develops the construction documents including working drawings, specifications, general conditions, bidding information, and contract forms, and covering in detail the general construction, site development, the structure, mechanical systems, materials, workmanship, and the responsibilities of all parties. The technical knowledge and experience required to coordinate the architectural details with electrical engineers, mechanical engineers, and structural engineers is today one of the most complex skills of any profession. Professional competency in these areas not only has direct influence on costs, but determines almost totally the degree of performance of the completed buildings.

7. The architect obtains approvals for proposed construction from all agencies, including the bureau of school planning, the division of architecture, the state fire marshal, local and regional planning boards and other controlling agencies such as the highway department, flood control agencies, the health department, and so forth.

8. The architect guides the client in the selection of contractors and in the drafting of their contracts. He gives general administration and supervises the work of the contractor. He must keep project accounts, issue certificates of payment due contractors, and expedite all change orders in the contracts as needed. He verifies acceptability of shop drawings submitted by various subcontractors and manufacturers and maintains standards for workmanship, materials, and appliances. He must make periodic inspections at the site and review progress and workmanship with the inspector and the construction superintendent. He must pass on and certify the satisfactory completion of all work.

Architects furnish many special services. Most school building projects require some type of special architectural service. These special services include: civil engineering services beyond site surveys and soil testing; acoustical engineering; landscape consultants and color consultants. If theaters or kitchens are included in a building project, special services should include stage design, rigging, and kitchen layout specialists.

Architectural services also are required in many instances when community-wide population projections and land utilization studies are made, master-planning a total district's site needs.

All applications made by school districts for funds under a state school building aid law usually require architectural services.

Other special services involve extra work on the architect's part which was not anticipated at the time his contract with a school district was signed. Such services would include:

1. Revising previously approved drawings and specifications at the written request of the owner.
2. Preparing documents for alternative bids or change orders at the written request of the owner.
3. Consultation and professional services concerning replacement of any work damaged by fire or other cause during construction.
4. Arranging for work to proceed in case of default or insolvency of a contractor.
5. Administration of a prolonged contract in excess of 25 percent of the stipulated time.

Fees for Architectural Services

Historically the fee schedule for architectural school work in several states has been 8 percent of the construction price. Some districts today use a sliding scale based on the size and complications of the project. Architects sometimes ask for an additional fee beyond the normal 8 percent when they are required to provide special services.

Construction of a typical secondary school from initial work with the client to completion requires about three years. Typical complete elementary school projects can be completed in approximately eighteen months from beginning to occupancy. Smaller projects take less time. During this period the architect attempts to conduct his business in such a way that it will show a profit. This requires a high degree of managerial skill. He must not only maintain his office and all the accompanying overhead of normal business expenses but must pay for a wide variety of skilled personnel.

Normally he must contract for other professional services. Structural engineering services generally run about 1.5 percent of the construction price. Electrical and mechanical engineering services generally each take about 0.75 percent to 1 percent of the construction price. (This percentage is increasing today as a greater percentage of the total cost of school buildings is going into electrical and mechanical work.) Thus the architect's fee is initially reduced from 8 percent to about 5 percent, or less.

With the money that remains, the architect maintains his office staff. This may include an office manager, designers, architectural draftsmen, specification writers, project coordinators, and nontechnical clerical workers. Usually lawyers' fees and accountants' services add to the overhead.

One fundamental fact about fees should remain clear. The architect as a businessman will attempt to maintain a profit for services rendered even when the fees are reduced. He can do this only by gearing his whole operation to a particular fee and setting his time schedules and services accordingly. Cutting time means cutting services with assured lamentable architectural results.

Problems

The following are problems associated with architectual services:

1. One problem is how to assure that a district is securing maximum *total* service. The most critical phase in planning a school is the initial programming, determining needs based on educational specifications, and a proper interpretation of these needs into preliminary designs. This work requires a great deal of time and energy by many specialists if the final school plant is to reflect superior planning. Unfortunately, this initial work is the phase that suffers if fees are reduced. It is very difficult for the architect to reduce the fees paid to engineering consultants or to reduce the production costs of his office incurred in the preparation of working drawings, specifications, or the other contract documents.

2. Another problem is how to relate proper compensation for total architectural service to a fee that is based on a percentage of the bid price of a project. Much of the blurred image the general public has of the architectural profession is based upon this problem. Since the cost of a school building is determined to a large degree by the "bidding climate" existing at the time a project is put out for construction bids, the actual monetary compensation for an architect's services can be only an intelligent guess until after he has performed approximately three-fourths of his services. This uncertainty, in many instances, compels the architect to work from an unbalanced time and money budget. It increases his tendency to come to

quick, and sometimes expensive, solutions to design problems that could have been better solved if he had been able to budget more time to explore various possible answers. The fact, too, that his fee will be greater if more expensive materials are used, makes him suspect sometimes when he recommends the quality of material and/or workmanship that will give the district better value for its money.

Probably the greatest inconsistency in the current fee practice is that often poor architectural service is rewarded more than good service. Construction contractors tend to bid with a sharper pencil when they are building a bid from a good set of plans and specifications than when they are making material and labor take-offs from a poorly prepared set. When meticulously described details are shown in plans and specifications, contractors can tell exactly what they must do to build a project. They do not need to protect themselves against various interpretations of plans and specifications which might add to the cost of the project or delay the construction timetable. Therefore, the architect who prepares hurried, sloppy, indefinite plans and specifications may well cause the bid price to be higher than would have been the case if more professional care had been taken and more time and money spent on plans and specifications. Thus, the less professional architect is paid a higher fee based on a percentage of the higher cost he created by preparing poor plans and specifications. The more professional and competent architect, conversely, is penalized when his well-prepared plans and specifications cause sharper, closer bidding, reducing the estimated construction cost of the project and hence his fee.

Planning the Educational Program

Both the professional and paraprofessional staffs as well as students and community personnel need to be involved in planning the educational program. Each through his diversified interests, skills, and knowledge may make vital input into the educational program. The educational program involves school philosophy and objectives, administrative policy and practice, characteristics of the proposed school, nature and depth of curriculum offerings, requirements in terms of capacity and occupancy, types of administrative organization, and general requirements for special programs.

Planning for the Site

The factors of shifting capacity requirements, the need for facilities to keep up with modern instructional methods, and the obvious impracticability of razing inadequate and outmoded structures before replacement accommodations are constructed indicate that few, if any, school administrators can neglect the constant review of their periodic projections of facility and site need. Long-range site operating and maintenance costs can be avoided by looking ahead at the time of site selection. Admittedly, it is difficult to arouse interest in spending time and money years in advance of actual needs. Planning requires that long-range projections be made of site needs, that these projections be constantly revised and updated, that the highway commission, urban renewal administrator, city government officials, utility companies, and all others whose work affects future site be contacted. Without information about the building's education program, the vehicular and pedestrian traffic anticipated, the rules and regulations concerning student and staff use of vehicles, in addition to other pertinent information, the architects will be unable to provide a facility that lends itself to efficient operation.

The following criteria are useful in site selection. The site must (1) be large enough to meet all needs for instructional, recreational, parking, and play areas, (2) be accessible both for pupils and as a community center, (3) have efficient and economical access to utilities, (4) have elevation and contour which ensure good drainage and turf, (5) have a type of geological formation which provides a good base for footways and foundations, (6) have proximity to public recreational, educational, and cultural facilities, (7) have as pleasant and beautiful a natural environment as possible that lends itself to landscaping, (8) be remote from traffic hazards, disturbing noises, smoke, dust, and odors, (9) have proximity to safety facilities, and (10) have a reasonable cost. It is also desirable that land be optioned well in advance of need. This will require the joint planning of: city and county planners, landscape architect, civil engineer, test laboratory engineer, real estate appraiser, legal consultant, state department personnel, educational consultants, and members of the local educational establishment. The Council of Educational Facility Planners guidelines for size are:

1. Elementary school — 10 acres + 1 acre for each 100 pupils
2. Junior high school — 20 acres + 1 acre for each 100 pupils
3. Senior high school — 30 acres + 1 acre for each 100 pupils

These cannot be applied in urban centers where site costs are prohibitive. Therefore, urban schools are usually multistory to preserve as much site as possible. Some urban schools have roof-top playgrounds, some have razed first stories to provide play space, others have buildings built in conjunction with park areas for multiple use of site area.

Flexibility

School building design is changing. Today's school planners and architects, with the aid of the teaching staff, are planning buildings around the program to be carried out in the facility. Special concern is focused on the role of flexibility in school planning, especially as an important element of the learner's physical environment. Webster defines flexibility as something capable of being bent; susceptible to modification or adaptation; willing or disposed to yield or change. A flexible facility is adaptable, serviceable, changeable, functional, and mutable in the area of education. Flexibility, which by definition exemplifies adaptability, hits at the heart of one of the barriers to providing proper conditions for learning. Flexibility also makes it possible to adapt to conditions not already existing in a facility. To obtain the greatest return on the educational investment, individuals concerned with the educational well-being of people need to be cognizant of the potential of flexible school facilities.

Flexibility of spaces dictates the use of serviceable walls or visual dividers which may be in the form of movable bulletin boards, tack boards, chalk boards, and storage cabinets. The use of these dividers may permit total utilization of the area to provide a desirable teaching and learning environment. Open spaces, wedge-shaped rooms, highly utilized spaces, operable interior walls, and furniture that is adaptable are no longer dreams but realities for students throughout the country. The very nature of changing society requires built-in flexibility in schools. A school building is flexible, serviceable, adaptable, and functional only when the total school program is implemented, thus providing for optimum conditions for teaching and learning.

Media, Machines, and Teachers

The utilization of educational media in schools across the nation is coming to mean far more than such familiar teaching aids as audio-visual equipment, programmed texts, and computers. Perhaps the most promising aspect of the utilization of various media is that the promise of new technology more effectively matches teaching to the individual student. Instead of lock-step education with the teacher leading one class at a time through the curriculum, devices and techniques that facilitate self-instruction could turn the teacher into a manager of learning resources for each student.

In order to maintain high-quality education, programs utilizing new and varied approaches to education must be encouraged. Increased enrollment, the information explosion, and the new emphasis on quality teaching, among others, have placed renewed importance on the need to plan new facilities. Large rooms, small rooms, medium-size rooms, individual electronic carrels, special screens and lighting effects to accommodate audio and visual media are all needed to accomplish good conditions for learning.

This is not to imply that machines will ever replace the teacher. The technological developments in education have greatly increased the need for the teacher to serve as an engineer of learning. The teacher must put these new tools of learning in their proper perspective, which is the improvement of the educational program. The proper use of media and machines by the teacher improves the learning opportunities of the student, which is the sole purpose of the educational program.

Planning Learning Spaces

The goal of planning is to design learning spaces to facilitate the implementation of the desired educational program and commensurate learning activities. This is doubly difficult because one cannot plan for a static program but one must plan for an evolving program process. Educators have found that the traditional classroom is unsatisfactory for self-instruction, team teaching, nongraded programs, and developing forms of educational software. Learning involves not only the mental functions but also possesses a physical dimension. The learner must be protected through careful consideration of the visual, thermal, sonic, and other environmental conditions. Air conditioning and carpeting are now common. Flexibility of space is the key. Nonload-bearing walls and temporary (movable) walls are being used to enhance the flexibility.

Selecting Furniture and Equipment

Planning for furniture and equipment must be an integral part of the educational program planning. Furniture and equipment must be selected on the basis of their contribution to and compatibility with the total educational program. The unit should be designed to harmonize with the architectural surroundings. It is truly a successful environment when all functional requirements are met, yet overall beauty and design emerge as a final touch to the educational complex. New types of modular furniture are being used. Plastic cubes, individual carrels (dry and wet), plus other new materials are being introduced. For selection and development of bidding specifications, see Chapter 10.

Planning for School Modernization

Age is not the sole criterion for obsolescence. New buildings can be obsolete the day they are accepted from the general contractor if proper planning has not taken place. Decisions as to whether a building should be modernized or razed have often been based upon little or no research. Linn related his writing to economic aspects and ignored other factors. He suggested that the decision to modernize a building was questionable if the cost of modernization exceeded 50 percent of the cost of a new project. He suggested that a 40 percent figure would be more realistic.[3]

Building experts, generally, have suggested that the modernization decision should be questioned if any two of the following items are required. The items include major replacement of plumbing and heating; total replacement of electrical wiring; basic structural changes involving space arrangements; complete replacement of roofing; or complete revamping of the fenestration pattern. Again this emphasizes economic consideration and

---

[3] Henry Linn. "Modernizing School Buildings." *American School and University* 24 (1952), p. 401.

ignores educational adequacy. Many buildings are structurally sound but educationally obsolete. School planners may need to consider planned obsolescence.

Castaldi has developed a mathematical expression that more adequately covers school modernization. This formula:

1. Separates, insofar as possible, the total cost of modernization into its major component parts, namely, cost for educational improvements, cost for improvements in healthfulness, and cost for improvements in safety.
2. Takes into account the educational adequacy of the modernized school, which also includes the school site.
3. Clearly indicates whether or not modernization would be of a financial advantage to the school district over an extended period of time.
4. Places replacement costs and modernization cost on a comparable basis.

   The general formula is stated below.

   If

$$\frac{(C_E + C_H + C_S)}{(L_M)\,(I_A)} < \frac{R}{L_R},$$

where

C_E = Total cost of educational improvement
C_H = Total cost for improvements in healthfulness (physical, esthetic, and psychological)
C_S = Total cost for improvement in safety
I_A = Estimated index of educational adequacy (0–1)
L_M = Estimated useful life of the modernized school
R = Cost of replacement of school considered for modernization
L_R = Estimated life of new building

Modernization is justifiable.[4]

The Council of Educational Facility Planners have made the suggestions for an ongoing school modernization program:

1. An old building properly updated does not mean more maintenance than a new building.
2. Sometimes there is a public relations value to moderniza-

---

[4] Castaldi, *Creative Planning of Educational Facilities*, p. 317.

tion as opposed to replacement. There are many cases where a community insisted the school be kept because of a sentimental attachment.

3. In any school there is a public relations value to doing something with the exterior as well as the interior at the time of modernization. Remember, the outside is all the majority of the people ever see.

4. Interior lighting, rather than exterior lighting, seems to be reducing vandalism in many schools where it is being tried.

5. When you decrease the window area of an existing building, you must take a good look at the interior lighting. It is important to remember everything relates.

6. Building evaluation forms can be helpful, but they should be used as a guide with a team of educators, architects and engineers, and maintenance personnel.

7. Creative planning of additions can eliminate the unfortunate mistake of an addition that causes more problems, both esthetically and educationally, than it solves.[5]

Planning for Fiscal Consideration

The traditional method of financing school facilities has been through the utilization of general obligation bonds which are guaranteed by the full faith and credit of the school district. Other methods utilized by the local district are as follows: pay-as-you-go plan, accumulation from a building and site fund, borrowing on short-term or long-term notes, or a combination of the above.

Unless the financing of a school facility is properly managed, a school district may lose thousands of dollars in interest money that could be an added saving to taxpayers, equip the building being financed, or underwrite other school costs. Factors that can be controlled through planning include: the legality of issues in relation to authorization; insurance; advertising; structuring and selling of bonds; presenting evidence of long-range community planning; giving evidence of financial stability; providing evidence of local fiscal managerial efficiency; and giving an indication of knowledge and willingness to prepare a proper prospectus.

During periods when the money market is "tight" and the corresponding condition of very high interest rates exists, many

[5] *Guide for Planning Educational Facilities*, p. 155.

larger districts should seriously consider pay-as-you-go as the most economical way of financing new facilities. Very substantial expenditures for interest can be avoided if this method is used. It is an especially advantageous procedure for a school district with a broad tax base that is growing so rapidly that capital outlay expenditure is an annual experience. It enables the community to conserve credit for hardcore emergencies.

The majority of school construction is financed by borrowing, and this is largely accomplished by issuance of municipal bonds. Attention should be given to factors which can help determine the availability of funds and the cost of utilizing this method of financing.

Voter Approval

Methods of approval of bond sales vary among the states. There is greater degree of uniformity on voter approval than any other phase of bond sales. All states except Alabama, Indiana, and Tennessee require a referendum for the sale of school construction bonds. Tennessee retains the authority to require voter approval for bond sales if the city or county governmental body decides an election is necessary.

Thirty-two states require only a simple majority for approval of bond issues; fourteen states require a favorable vote in excess of 50 percent. Several states have litigation pending concerning the constitutionality of requiring more than a majority for bond issue approval.

Planning Bond Issue

Several basic decisions must be made relative to the specific bonds. The denominations may have a very important impact upon the ease of marketing an issue. Generally, the large banks, trust funds, and other large-lot purchasers desire large denominations. Conversely, individuals and buyers for small institutions desire small denominations. A wide range in denomination size can enhance the bond sale.

Interest rates on municipal bonds are determined largely by the character and the financial capacity of the issuer, length of term of issue, and the relative availability of investment funds at the time of the sale. Many school districts, through past experience, issue bonds with the maximum maturities allowed by the state. This is very expensive for the district that has a relatively constant school facility need. Bond maturities should be kept as short as feasible. If longer maturities are utilized, call features may allow earlier retirement if economic conditions permit.

Serial bonds (bonds maturing annually or semiannually from year of issue to termination date are self-administering and require little management by the local fiscal agent. Because of their popularity these bonds may not command the low interest rate that may be available for term bonds (bonds paid at the end of the bonding period with only interest paid during the intervening period). If state statutes permit the utilization of term bonds and the district has the fiscal acumen for handling such a bond, the term bond may be an alternative that deserves careful consideration.

Retaining a Bond Attorney

In order to consummate a bond sale, a bond attorney whose decision is recognized by the ultimate buyer must be retained and give favorable legal opinion. His service can be invaluable when planning and administering a bonding program. The bond attorney will and should draft the original bond resolution or ordinance, as well as the notice of bond election and the form of the ballot if an election is required under local law. Once voters have approved the issue, he will review preparation of the prospectus, notice of sale, other financial advertisements, and all materials presented to underwriters for bidding purposes. After the bonds have been sold, printed, paid for, and delivered, he will render a final legal opinion (see figure 14.2 for sample legal opinion).

Advertising Sale

Recent widespread rejection of bond issues by school patrons emphasizes the importance of good public relations for the entire bond issue procedure. Assuming passage of the bond issue by the electorate a notice of sale will be required by state statute. Legal requirements can be usually met by advertising in a newspaper of general circulation throughout the district. Bids on school bonds will be encouraged by advertising in the

Gentlemen:

We have examined a Certified Transcript of Proceedings preliminary to and in connection with an issue of the _____ School District, _____ County, school improvement bonds issued for the purpose of acquisition of real estate, construction of fireproof buildings, furnishing and equipping the same and improving the site thereof, being a series of bonds numbered from _____ to _____, both inclusive, in the denomination of $_____ each, aggregating principal amount $_____, dated the _____ day of _____, 19__, bearing interest from the date thereof at the rate of _____ percent per annum, payable on the _____ day of _____, 19__, and semi-annually thereafter on the _____ days of _____ and _____ of each year until the principal sum is paid, and maturing $_____ on the _____ day of _____ in each of the years 19__ to 19__, both inclusive.

We have also examined the law under authority of which said bonds have been issued and executed Bond Number 1 of said issue and find the same to be in due form of law. From this examination we are of the opinion that said bonds, to the amount named, constitute valid and legally binding general obligations of the Board of Education of said _____ School District and, unless paid from other sources, are payable from ad valorem taxes to be levied on all the taxable property in said school district, which taxes are unlimited as to rate or amount.

The interest on the aforesaid bonds, in our opinion, is exempt from federal income taxes under the existing statutes, regulations and court decisions.

Respectively,

FIGURE 14.2 Sample legal opinion. (Courtesy Bricker, Evatt, Barton, and Eckler, Attorneys, Columbus, Ohio; reprinted with permission.)

Daily Bond Buyer or the *Wall Street Journal.* Pertinent data regarding the issue and community should be forwarded to underwriters and potential investors. See Dewey H. Stollar's *Managing School Indebtedness* for a detailed account of steps to follow in marketing municipal bonds.[6]

Bond Rating

A borrower who obtains an AAA rating has the most coveted but most carefully granted financial rating it is possible to acquire. Since secondary market bond buyers accept these ratings religiously, a borrower with a high rating can attract more investors, pay lower interest rates, and profit generally from the esteem bestowed in the business world upon such a rating. Dun and Bradstreet, Moody's, and Standard & Poor's are the major raters of school bonds. Once a favorable rating is obtained, the local district must meet an annual financial records requirement for continuation of the favorable rating. Failure to complete forms will automatically discontinue rated status, which can be detrimental to the future sale of bonds.

Postsale Planning

Almost all school districts face the necessity of future capital outlay expenditure. Because of this, it is obviously important to earn and retain the good will of the financial community by performing properly all required services after the sale is accomplished. Prompt payment of principal and interest is essential, and it is highly desirable to keep bond owners, rating agencies, and underwriters informed of the financial status and progress of the school system and the community.

Planning the Capital Outlay Budget

Inherent to capital outlay budgeting, whether long-range, short-range, and/or individual capital project budget, is the budget calendar. Without a budget calendar, planning will become hurried and usually will not follow the proper sequence. It is important to remember that the capital improvement budget is nothing more

---

[6] Dewey H. Stollar. *Managing School Indebtedness* (Danville. Ill.: The Interstate Printers & Publishers. Inc.. 1967).

than a written expression of educational facility needs, followed by a financial translation of these needs into costs, and closing with an exact statement of how the needed expenditures will be financed. Budget making usually proceeds through four phases: the formulation stage, review and adoption phase, implementation phase, and the appraisal or evaluation phase. Capital outlay budgets should extend for a period of five to ten years, depending upon the growth patterns of the local district and the condition of existing facilities.

The individual capital project budget gives a portrayal of the individual facility construction program. The important consideration is to include each item of expense which will accrue to the school district during the total construction program. Although the budget format will vary from school system to school system, it should include every expense from initiating early study and planning to dedicating the totally completed facility. Items to be included in the budget are as follows: the comprehensive planning survey; educational specifications; acquisition of land and related costs; architectural fees and planning costs; the cost of general and subconstruction contract; site preparation and development; educational media, furnishings, and equipment; supplies and other materials; administrative and legal costs; and contingencies and other costs. It cannot be overstressed that effective budgeting of both annual and long-range commitments, combined with accurately planned project budgets for individual capital needs, is basic to the overall success of the total capital program. It is imperative that those responsible for capital facility planning be keenly aware of the budgeting process and the possible alternative available for financing facility improvement, because good budgeting practices and good fiscal planning lead to economics in financing facility improvement debt.

Planning for Occupancy

The people associated with school construction attach considerable importance to the physical act of turning the building over to the school board by the general contractor. This is usually done at a rather formal ceremony usually referred to as the dedication of the building. Many patrons are less aware of the many details that must be performed before a building is truly ready for occupancy. Service personnel must be trained to perform operational and maintenance chores such as waxing floors, and servicing and operating the various equipment. These should be accomplished through formal training programs.

Although we assume that the general staff was involved in planning the facility, many will not be transferred to the new facility. Hopefully, the new facility will be planned for new programs and educational innovations. If this is to be an effective program the staff will need intensive in-service training as well as psychological acclimation to the new facilities, particularly if there have been major changes in teaching techniques or major technological breakthroughs in educational software.

Normally, construction contracts provide for fixed equipment only, with other equipment and materials being purchased and installed by the local school district. Some districts will not include drives, sidewalks, and landscaping and these become an overburden for the maintenance crew and usually lead to an overtaxing of the maintenance budget. School districts can save money when they purchase movable equipment and furniture because they do not have to pay architects fees for these items. When this approach is used, personnel in the school business office must assume responsibility for preparing specifications, advertising for and receiving bids, receiving equipment and furniture, assembling and installing equipment and furniture, and supervising the placement of the items in the proper rooms. Furniture and equipment specifications must be as carefully prepared and with as much involvement as educational specifications. After all, the building is worthless without proper furniture and equipment. The principal should be employed at the initial stage of planning and follow the project through to completion.

Postplanning and Evaluation

If the district is to benefit from present construction in planning for future construction, postplanning and evaluation is a necessity. Evaluation of a new facility, without diplomacy, can be very threatening. The primary goal of the evaluation is to assess the ability of the new facility to enhance and facilitate good teaching and learning, thus helping to ensure the continued excellence of the ongoing program of school facility planning and construction. The Council of Educational Facility Planners has listed the following guidelines for planning evaluation.

1. The evaluation plan must lead to continued self-evaluation on the parts of planners and other educational leaders.
2. Evaluation must encompass and promote the valued objectives of education and culture. It must consistently and honestly assess the relationship between community needs and educational facilities to meet these needs.
3. Evaluation plans must be developed in a manner which will produce information appropriate for a continued drive toward educational excellence.
4. Evaluation must provide continuing feedback into the larger questions of policy and the relationship of policy to the techniques of planning.
5. Evaluation must facilitate effective planning.[7]

These guidelines can serve as a point of departure in developing evaluation instruments or outlines appropriate for new facilities.

SUMMARY

Of all the activities in which American people engage while living and working together, perhaps none expresses in material form so many aspects of our culture as school construction. The growing national concern for the improvement of education is undoubtedly one of the most pronounced phenomena of our time. Dimensions of education—purposes and content, methods and materials, as well as financial support and status—have been dramatically influenced during the past decade by forces inherent in rapid cultural change. Educators in every corner of the nation have examined the educational process with the full realization that the future of this nation and of the free world depends in large measure on the excellence of education.

One cannot help feeling a change in the tempo of our educational programming. Perhaps the most distinguishing characteristic of any living thing is that it is forever changing. A school facility that never changes gives a good indication that the program within is dead, or was never alive. Therefore, in order to provide for a living, dynamic, and effective educational program, a flexible plant containing the kinds of teaching areas needed to implement the

[7] *Guide for Planning Educational Facilities*, p. 193.

program must be arranged. The educational program must change; therefore, the facility housing the program must be flexible in order to implement this change. The ferment of ideas in education affects every feature of the school plant, namely, flexibility, furniture, equipment, thermal control, acoustical control, and visual and color control. Since buildings are of such a permanent nature and have such a direct and definite influence on the educational process, educational leaders are very much concerned about designing buildings to meet educational needs.

SUGGESTED ACTIVITIES

1. Prepare a PERT network for the planning of a capital outlay project of your choosing. In doing this, proceed through the following steps:
      a. Identify the activities involved in the project.
      b. Draw the PERT network, showing the sequence of the activities.
      c. Estimate the time required to complete each activity.
      d. Compute the time required to complete the entire project and the times at which each activity must be completed in order for the entire project to be completed on time.

2. Outline steps to follow in preparing educational specifications for a particular phase of a building program with which you are familiar.

3. Develop an overview of what should be included in a prospectus for both the primary and secondary bond markets.

4. You have marketed your bonds for a new construction project. The project has been delayed for sometime. Indicate procedures you would follow in reinvesting funds in order to keep the district's loss in interest to a minimum.

5. Prepare a plan for staff, student, and community involvement in planning educational facilities.

SUGGESTED READINGS

American Association of School Administrators. *Planning America's School Buildings.* Washington, D.C.: The Association, 1960.

Boles, Harold. *Step by Step to Better School Facilities.* New York: Holt, Rinehart and Winston, Inc., 1965.

Castaldi, Basil. *Creative Planning of Educational Facilities.* Chicago: Rand McNally & Company, 1969.

Council of Educational Facility Planners. *Guide for Planning Educational Facilities.* Columbus, O.: The Council, 1969.

McClurkin, W. D. *School Building Planning.* New York: The Macmillan Company, 1964.

Meekley, Richard F. *Planning Facilities for Occupational Education Programs.* Columbus, O.: Charles E. Merrill Publishing Company, 1972.

School Planning Laboratory, University of Tennessee. *Profile of a Significant School* (a series of publications, each describing a significant school). Knoxville: Southern Regional Center, Educational Facilities Laboratories, Inc., 1970.

Stollar, Dewey H. *Managing School Indebtedness.* Danville, Ill.: The Interstate Printers & Publishers, Inc., 1967.

PART

IV

THE SCHOOL BUSINESS ADMINISTRATOR AND THE JOB

THE POSITION
OF THE SCHOOL BUSINESS
ADMINISTRATOR

Much of the effort of this book has been directed at presenting a different and expanded role for the school business administrator. As the title implies, the planning approach is, in the authors' view, the future focus of the top-level administration of the school system; and the school business administrator is a key person in the planning component of the school system. Consistent with the authors' bias that the administration of large school systems is no longer a one-person job, this book has addressed itself to the planning tasks faced by one key member of the superintendent's cabinet: the school business administrator. Recent developments in the evolution of the American school systems have emphasized the need for the superintendency team to be developed as the leadership-planning cadre for school systems. As the pressures on educational systems grow, as diverse variables continue to operate, as resource procurement and allocation becomes more complex, as America enters into the era of complete urbanization, educational leaders are forced into a consideration of the importance of planning. While day-to-day operations will continue to be of great importance and probably will continue to require great expenditure of time and resources, the planning role and its potential for the exercise of leadership will grow and dominate.

Therefore, it seems logical to the authors to predict that the success model for educational leadership in the coming decades will include two new components. These are (1) the leadership team composed of personnel who provide complementary and supplementary skills and talents and (2) a planning approach to educational leadership.

A recent publication of the American Association of School Administration, entitled *Profiles of the Administration Team*, reinforces the leadership team notion by stating:

> So complicated and demanding has the superintendency become that those who hold the position have been obliged to depend upon a wide variety of expert assistants in meeting their leadership responsibilities. A cluster of supportive administrative positions has gradually been created to enable the superintendent to amplify his efforts. When referring to the superintendency today, therefore, it is more realistic to consider it as a leadership team than as a unitary position.[1]

The team leadership concept, coupled with recent advances in the area of systems planning, PPBES, and the use of behavioral objectives to determine educational priorities, has served to emphasize the crucial role of the school business administrator as a key member of the leadership team.

VARYING TITLES, RESPONSIBILITIES, ORGANIZATIONAL POSITIONS, AND COMPENSATION DATA

The aforementioned AASA publication is the most recent source dealing with questions of titles, responsibilities, and so forth. It appears that the function, role, position, and title of the school business administrator varies greatly from district to district. Recent trends, however, clearly show that this position is among the two or three most frequently categorized as being of cabinet-level importance.

Titles of persons charged with the responsibility of school business affairs include the following:

1. Deputy, Associate, or Assistant Superintendent
2. Administrative Assistant to the Superintendent

[1] American Association of School Administration. *Profiles of the Administrative Team* (Washington, D.C.: The Association. 1971). p. 11.

3. Business Superintendent
4. Business Manager
5. Controller
6. Director of Business Services
7. Purchasing Agent
8. Clerk-Treasurer of the Board of Education
9. Financial Secretary

As the list implies, the status and responsibility of the school business administrator ranges from that of glorified clerk to that of a top-level administrator. Results of the AASA survey mentioned earlier indicate that if the top business administrator of the school system is not at the top level of management, either the superintendent himself or another top assistant possesses skills in the financial domain and one of these, in effect, is the primary financial advisor to the school system.

One suspects that in many cases the degree of responsibility placed in the school business office depends a great deal on the capacity, skill, and leadership abilities of the incumbents. However, as the titles imply, responsibilities can and do vary from routine purchasing types of activities to accounting-bookkeeping duties, to financial policy setting and implementation. Typically, in smaller school systems the superintendent of schools acts in a dual capacity performing as both the educational leader and the chief business official of the school system. This is usually a role dictated by circumstance rather than preference, for most superintendents have neither the time nor the inclination to devote a major portion of their energy to the business administration function. Quite normally, as the rationale grows for addition of central office personnel, the superintendent is faced with a dilemma: what area of responsibility can he most logically shift to an added person. Usually the decision is based upon the strengths and preferences of the superintendent and will often result in the addition of either a person to assume business responsibility or a person to handle the instructional responsibility. In any case, responsibility for the business activities of the school system is separated from responsibility for those ongoing instructional activities. Organizationally, such a system might evolve as shown in figure 15.1.

It is not uncommon in middle-sized school systems (5,000 to 20,000 students) to find greatly expanded responsibilities vested

TRADITIONAL SMALL SCHOOL SYSTEM ORGANIZATION

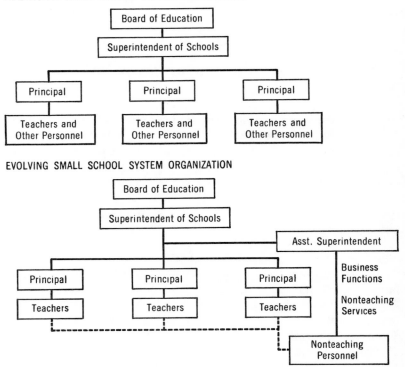

FIGURE 15.1   Organizational evolution of small school systems.

in the school business office. These may range from the typical duties of purchasing and accounting to responsibility for all non-teaching support services, e.g., food services, custodial and maintenance services, transportation services, and so forth. In addition, school business administrators often are charged with responsibility in such activities as personnel negotiations and in school design and construction. In such systems the school business administrator serves in both a line and a staff capacity, and the organizational structure can be similar to that shown in figure 15.2.

Typically, in the middle-sized school system the superintendent and his cabinet develop very close working relationships, and certain responsibilities are shared or assumed by the

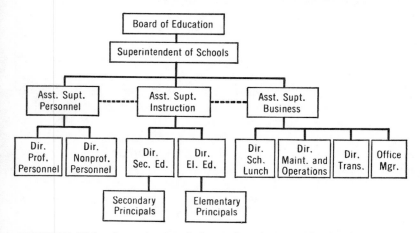

FIGURE 15.2   Organizational chart of medium-sized school system.

administrator with greatest expertise in a particular area. Therefore, it is not unusual in such a system to find that while the assistant superintendent for personnel has direct responsibility for
staff negotiations, he draws heavily upon the assistant superintendent for business in resolving issues relating to economic
questions and upon the assistant superintendent for instruction in
resolving issues pertaining to the educational program. Because
many negotiation issues involve the system's economic situation,
the assistant superintendent for business often finds himself very
much immersed in the negotiations process.

As school systems become larger and more cumbersome, the
responsibilities of the school business administrator become much
more specialized and confined to the basic financial concerns of
the school system. It is not unusual for large, complex educational
bureaucracies to employ several assistant superintendents with
primary responsibilities in specific areas commonly grouped under
the heading of school business administration. Such specific task
areas and titles might include:

1. Assistant superintendent for purchasing
2. Assistant superintendent for data processing
3. Assistant superintendent for operations
4. Assistant superintendent for maintenance

5. Assistant superintendent for plant planning
6. Assistant superintendent for budget and finance.

Where such specialization develops, these positions usually are responsible to a deputy or associate superintendent who, in fact, is the chief school business official for the system. Recent shifts in emphasis in urban school systems to an acceptance of the planning role and toward decentralization of administrative responsibility have changed the duties of the school business administrator. Figure 15.3 represents a typical urban school system organizational pattern in the traditional scheme while figure 15.4 presents an evolving model of school system organization.

As figure 15.3 indicates, the superintendent's cabinet is composed of associate superintendents, each with a specific specialized area of concern and responsibility. In such a centralized, unitary model of organization, the various cabinet-level administrators tend to develop subcabinets with personnel even more highly specialized and isolated from the *gestalt* of the school system. Systems such as this tend to become closed and very difficult to change from the highly routinized status quo. In addi-

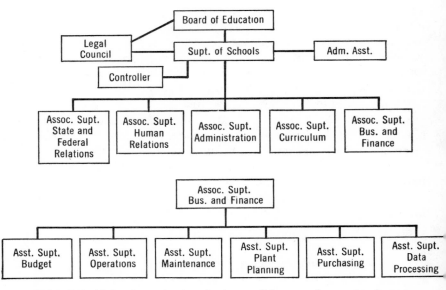

FIGURE 15.3 Organizational chart of large urban school system (traditional model).

tion, it becomes increasingly difficult for such organizations to react to unique and particular demands because of the levels of bureaucracy between policy making and implementation. This very inability to act and/or react to pressures has forced changes leading to organizational structures similar to that shown in figure 15.4.

In figure 15.4 the top-level cabinet is a planning cabinet and does not assume primary responsibility for operation of the school system. This is the task of the deputy superintendent and his staff

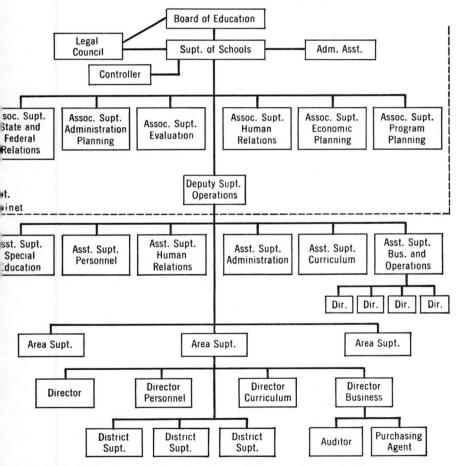

FIGURE 15.4 Organizational chart of large urban school system (decentralization, or evolving, model).

of assistants. Actual operating decisions are further decentralized to the area and district levels in order that decisions be made as close to the source as possible. At each level there exists need for school business expertise with a series of responsibilities appropriate to the situation. The various tasks of the school business office must be performed at each level with appropriate autonomy given to each level. Some tasks, e.g., data processing, payroll, certain purchasing, etc., are best done on a highly centralized basis while others should be performed at the district level. Such flexibility is possible in the model shown in figure 15.4. In addition, the fact that the superintendent's cabinet is a planning staff with little line responsibility further enhances the planning capability and potential of the school system. While traditionally it has been the operating decisions that tended to determine long- and short-range plans, the above model augurs just the opposite.

To summarize, the responsibilities and status of the school business administrator vary with the size of the district, the capacity of the individual, and the organizational model of the school system. Generally, the chief school business administrator is one of the top-level personnel of the school system and holds the responsibility for all matters financial. In a publication entitled *The School Business Administrator*, by Frederick W. Hill, the following major areas of responsibility were identified:

1. Budgeting and Financial Planning
2. Purchasing and Supply Management
3. Plant Planning and Construction
4. School-Community Relations
5. Personnel Management
6. In-Service Training
7. Operation and Maintenance of Plant
8. Transportation
9. Food Services
10. Accounting and Reporting
11. Office Management[2]

The authors propose the addition of two responsibilities to the above list. These are:

[2] Frederick W. Hill. *The School Business Administrator* (Chicago: Association of School Business Officials, 1970), pp. 16–18.

12. Planning
13. Negotiations

Compensation Data

The 1960s saw a dramatic improvement in the salary structure of the educational systems of America. Predictably, salaries and compensation for school business administrators have kept pace with the general improvement experienced by all educational professionals. As the status and responsibilities of school business administrators have shifted to a more expanded and crucial role in the top-level management team of the school system, so have the compensatory benefits exhibited a corresponding rise.

An analysis of salaries in school systems with over 12,000 students indicates the marked increase in salaries paid public school professional employees during the period 1962–63 through 1968–69.[3] During this time, teachers' average salaries rose from $6,263 to $8,520 per annum for a 36 percent increase. Principals' average salaries at the elementary level rose from $9,901 to $13,945 per annum for a 40.8 percent boost, while high school principals enjoyed a 43.9 percent increase, moving from an average salary of $11,042 to $15,890.

Corresponding increases are noted at the central office level. Again, in districts enrolling 12,000 or more students superintendents' salaries rose from an average of $18,911 in 1962 to $25,794 in 1969 for a percentage increase of 36.4. During the same time span, salaries of deputy and/or associate superintendents grew from $17,230 to $22,167, while salaries of assistant superintendents increased from $14,257 to $19,459 or 36.5 percent. In every case administrative salaries have grown more rapidly both in dollars as well as in percent of increase than have salaries of teaching personnel.

In examining the salary improvements provided school business personnel below the assistant superintendent level, similar increases are noted. In the area of general finance and business, the average salary rose from $10,664 in 1962 to $15,045 in 1969 for a 41.1 percent increase. In the area of purchasing a 36.4 percent increase was noted during the same time span,

---

[3]"Salaries Paid Public School Professional Employees," National Education Association, *Research Bulletin*, vol., 47, no. 3 (October 1969), pp. 77–81.

while in the accounting and auditing area salaries grew from $7,912 in 1962 to $11,916 in 1969 for a 50.6 percent increase.

Major gains in the fringe benefit packages given administrators are also evident. School systems quite commonly provide hospitalization and medical benefits, life insurance, liberal sick-leave provisions, paid vacations, driving allowances, and expense and travel budgets for professional growth. Such benefits not only add dollar value to the administrator's contract but more importantly provide the psychological support necessary in difficult, taxing positions.

With the advent of formalized professional staff–board of education negotiations, still larger gains in the compensation data are forecast. In many school systems, salaries of administrators are closely linked to teachers' salaries by ratios developed over time. Such ratios typically project the assistant superintendent at 1.4 or 1.45 the maximum teachers' salary figured on a twelve-month basis. In other districts, administrative salaries are based upon a percentage of the superintendent's salary, while in others a form of merit pay is used whereby each administrator in effect negotiates his own salary.

In summary, all compensation data point to major gains made over the past decade by school personnel in general and school administrators in particular. Predictions are that additional gains will be forthcoming and that the compensation provided school business administrators will be consistent with that provided other professional educational personnel.

JOB SPECIFICATIONS, QUALIFICATIONS

Although job specifications for school business officials vary widely from district to district, a listing of typical duties as compiled by Frederick W. Hill in *The School Business Administrator,* includes the following:

    I. Financial Planning
        A. Budget compilation, in coordination with educational planning
        B. Long-term fiscal planning, operating budget
        C. Receipt estimates

    D. Budget control
    E. Fiscal relationships with other governmental units
    F. Use of systems analysis and PPBES

II. Accounting
    A. General fund
    B. Capital reserve funds and trust funds
    C. Construction funds
    D. Internal accounts
    E. Student activity funds
    F. Voucher and payroll preparation
    G. Inventory
    H. Attendance accounting
    I. Government tax and pension accounting
    J. Special trust funds
    K. Cost accounting
    L. Student stores, bookstores

III. Debt Service and Capital Fund Management
    A. Long- and short-term financing
    B. Maturities and debt payments
    C. Long-range capital programs
    D. Investments
    E. Reporting
    F. Bond and note register
    G. Debt service payment procedures
    H. Short-term debt management

IV. Auditing
    A. Preaudit, or internal, procedures
    B. Determination that prepared statements present fairly the financial position
    C. Propriety, legality, and accuracy of financial transactions
    D. Proper recording of all financial transactions
    E. Postaudit procedures
    F. External audits
    G. Reconciliation of internal and external audits

V. Purchasing and Supply Management
    A. Official purchasing agent
    B. Purchase methods
    C. Stock requisition

      D.   Standards and specifications

      E.   Purchase bids

      F.   Purchase contracts

      G.   Purchase of supplies and equipment

      H.   Storage, delivery, trucking services

      I.   Inventory control

VI.   School Plant Planning and Construction

      A.   Assists in the establishment of educational standards for sites, buildings, and equipment

      B.   Plant utilization studies

      C.   Projections of facility needs

      D.   Design, construction, and equipment of plant

      E.   Safety standards

      F.   Contracts management

      G.   Architect selection

VII.   Operation of Plant—Custodial, Gardening, Engineering Services

      A.   Standards and frequency of work

      B.   Manpower allocations

      C.   Scheduling

      D.   Inspection and evaluation of service

      E.   Relationship with educational staff

      F.   Operating of related school-community facilities, such as recreation, park, museum, library programs, etc.

      G.   Community use of facilities

      H.   Protection of plant and property

      I.   Security and police forces

VIII.   Maintenance of Plant

      A.   Repair of buildings and equipment

      B.   Upkeep of grounds

      C.   Maintenance policies, standards, and frequency of maintenance

      D.   Scheduling and allocation of funds and manpower

      E.   Modernization and rehabilitation versus replacement

IX.   Real Estate Management

      A.   Site acquisition and sales

      B.   Rentals, leases

      C.   Rights-of-way and easements

      D.   Assessments and taxes

       E. After school use of buildings

       F. Dormitories, student unions, concessions

X. Personnel Management

    A. Records

       1. Probationary and tenure status of employees

       2. Sick leave and leave of absence

       3. Official notices of appointment and salaries

       4. Retirement data and deductions

       5. Salary schedules and payments

       6. Individual earning records

       7. Withholding, tax and group insurance or fringe benefits

       8. Civil Service and Social Security

       9. Substitute and part-time employees

     10. Dues checkoffs

    B. Supervision of noninstructional staff

       1. Recruitment

       2. Selection

       3. Placement

       4. Training

       5. Advancement

       6. Working conditions

       7. Disciplinary action

       8. Termination of Services

    C. Relationship to instructional staff

       1. Good will and service concept

       2. Cooperation in procurement

       3. Cooperation in budget preparation

       4. Information on pay and retirement

       5. Personnel records and reports

XI. Permanent Property Records and Custody of Legal Papers

    A. Security and preservation of records

    B. Maintenance of storage files

    C. Purging of records no longer legally required

XII. Transportation of Pupils

    A. Policies, rules, regulations, and procedures

    B. Contract versus district-owned equipment

    C. Routing and scheduling

    D. Inspection and maintenance

      E. Staff supervision and training
      F. Utilization and evaluation of services
      G. Standards and specifications

XIII. Food Service Operations
      A. Policies, rules, regulations, and procedures
      B. Staffing and supervision
      C. Menus, prices, and portion controls
      D. Purchasing
      E. Accounting, reporting, and cost analysis
      F. In-service training
      G. Coordination with educational program

XIV. Insurance
      A. Insurance policies
      B. Insurable values — buildings and contents
      C. Coverages to be provided
      D. Claims and reporting
      E. Insurance procurement procedures
      F. Insurance and claims record
      G. Distribution of insurance to companies, agents, and brokers

XV. Cost Analysis
      A. Unit costs
      B. Comparative costs
      C. Costs distribution studies

XVI. Reporting
      A. Local financial and statistical reports
      B. State financial and statistical reports
      C. Federal financial and statistical reports
      D. Miscellaneous reports
      E. Required legal advertising
      F. Relationships with public information media

XVII. Collective Negotiations
      A. Service on management team when required
      B. Preparation of pertinent fiscal data for management team
      C. Development of techniques and strategies for collective negotiation
      D. Sharing of proper information with employee units
      E. Use of outside negotiators, agencies
      F. Mediation, arbitration, grievances

XVIII. Data Processing
- A. Selection of system
- B. Programming
- C. Utilization of systems analysis
- D. Forms preparation
- E. Broad use of equipment for all pertinent applications

XIX. Board Policies and Administrative Procedures as Related to Fiscal and Noninstructional Matters

XX. Responsibilities for Elections and Bond Referenda

XXI. Responsibilities for School Assessment, Levy and Tax Collection Procedure as May be Set by Law.[4]

In addition to those direct duties as defined above, the school business administrator has an increasing role to play in the expanding communications arena. Relationships with other agencies and with community organizations and the general public are becoming more important to the school system, and the school business administrator must play a vital role in the establishment of appropriate lines of communications with the various publics found in the school district. The preparation and provision of information dealing with school business operations is important to overall school system success in working with the community.

Increasingly, school officials are recognizing that the school, as one institution of many in a community, must actively participate in the total thrust of life goals for members of the community. Therefore, school system goals must be consistent with the larger goals of the community and must support and complement these goals.

A typical job specification and vacancy announcement might be similar to the following one provided by a midwestern urban school system.

School District, City of _____

(date)

ANNOUNCEMENT OF ADMINISTRATIVE VACANCY

TITLE OF POSITION: Assistant Superintendent in Charge of Business and Finance

---

[4] Hill, *The School Business Administrator*, p. 13–29.

SALARY: $24,104 to $29,204 as per administrative salary schedule

QUALIFICATIONS: *Education*—Candidates for this position must be able to satisfy the legal requirements necessary for teaching in the State of _____, and must possess a minimum of a Master's Degree from an accredited institution. Additional graduate work beyond the Master's Degree is desirable. Professional preparation should include systematic study in most of the following areas:

a) Public School Administration
b) Public School Finance
c) Maintenance, operation, and construction of schools
d) Personnel administration

Experience—Candidates must be able to present evidence of experience in most of the following areas:

a) Successful teaching experience in public schools
b) At least three years of experience in central office administration
c) Preparation and administration of school budgets
d) Purchasing and management of school equipment and supplies
e) Maintenance, repair, and operations of school buildings and grounds
f) Administration of school lunch and school transportation programs
g) Supervision of school building programs
h) Personnel administration for classified and nonclassified employees

Personal-Professional—In addition to the education and experiential requirements, the candidate should possess:

a) Interest in and appreciation of the total school program

    b) Intellectual curiosity and knowledge about research and development in the various areas of primary responsibility

    c) Ability to participate actively in local, state, and national professional organizations

    d) Skill in creating and maintaining good human relations with staff, administrators, parents, community agencies, and organizations

DUTIES AND RESPONSIBILITIES: As a member of the Central Administrative Staff, the Assistant Superintendent in Charge of Business and Finance will assume the following duties and responsibilities:

1. Business and Finance
   a. Budget preparation
   b. Accounting of funds
   c. Purchasing
   d. Supervision and control of stock
   e. Food services
   f. Central office management
   g. Data processing coordination
   h. Transportation
   i. Other duties as may be assigned

2. Maintenance and Operation
   a. Supervision of maintenance and operational personnel
   b. Plan long-range maintenance and custodial programs
   c. In-service training programs
   d. Security of buildings
   e. Other duties as may be assigned

3. Building Construction and Renovation
   a. Work with architects and staff in building development. Rec-

ommend architects to superintendent

b. Supervision of construction programs

c. Write specifications, advertise, and summarize bids on contract projects

d. Such other duties as may be required in building construction and renovation

4. Personnel Administration

a. Personnel accounting

b. Research of staff needs

c. Personnel recruiting

d. Staff development, orientation of new personnel

e. Assist in development of in-service programs

f. Administration of, development of, conditions of employment

g. Administration of salary schedules

h. Personnel records

5. Such other duties as may be assigned by the Superintendent of Schools

REPORTS TO: Reports directly to the Superintendent of Schools

METHOD OF
APPLICATION: Candidates meeting the qualifications and wishing to accept the duties and responsibilities outlined should file a letter of application to Dr. _____, _____. Application forms and other related information will be mailed to those who apply.

Personal Characteristics of a School Business Administrator

A recognition of the school business administrator's role as a motivator of others who directs the planning and operations efforts of the school business office is reflected in the listing of personal characteristics compiled by Dr. Frederick Hill. These personal characteristics are:

1. *He should possess plenty of directed drive.* The true leader has more drive than his peers. He has more energy, more staying power, more confidence. His drive is directed toward achieving goals in which he believes.

2. *He should like people and show it.* A good administrator really likes people. A sincere liking for people as unique personalities, coupled with a bright faith in the future, make a winning combination.

3. *He should be able to get along well with others.* Without this characteristic it would be difficult for him to function effectively and for the group he leads to function effectively.

4. *He should be a good listener.* One of the best instruments of the administrator is a pair of good ears.

5. *He should be a person of integrity.* Honesty, sincerity, and truthfulness still win respect and encourage similar traits in others.

6. *He should be fair in his dealings with all.* The administrative menu offers a steady diet of "hot potatoes." The good administrator does not pass the buck but accepts the blame, and he builds a reputation for fairness and deserves it.

7. *He should be a self-starter.* A leader sets the pace for new ideas. He picks up the ball and runs.

8. *He should possess a high threshold of annoyance and a sense of values.* The wise one rarely "blows off steam." He is no victim of his own emotions. He is bigger than the problem that confronts him. His perspective prevents him from taking himself too seriously and gives him inner resources in time of stress.

9. *He should develop high articulation and writing skills and watch his language.* The ability to draw persuasive "word pictures" will help others to see and to accept group objectives. His language should be above reproach, and he should carefully avoid offending anyone.

10. *He should possess the ability to make problems of others his own.* The staff will come to the business manager if they can get help when they ask for it. The willingness to accept the problems of others and to share in the solution is an evidence of leadership.

11. *He should be willing to accept criticism.* He needs to guard against creating a "yes" man attitude on the part of his associates. A good administrator knows how to take criticism and how to use it constructively.

12. *He should be able to render decisions.* Frequently, more grief is created by no decision among staff members than by a poor one. If his batting average is high, he will still remain in the line-up.

13. *He should be willing to bask in reflected glory.* The real business manager sees himself as a member of a team rather than the star player. The good leader sees that good work is recognized and proper credit given to all who have shared in it.

14. *He should be ready to take quick action.* If he sees a situation that could become a crisis, he must deal with it properly. The good administrator is one who can recognize and deal with a small problem before it becomes a big one.

15. *He is, first of all, a good person.*

16. *He wants to be a part of a strong team rather than a strong man standing alone.* He selects able and creative persons as his co-workers, cooperates with them in a give-and-take relationship and desires the efficiency and broad viewpoint that is possible when several first-rate minds are analyzing a situation.

17. *He has respect for all those with whom he deals.* He respects them, first, because he believes in the fundamental dignity and worth of every human being and, second, because he believes that a person should be treated with consideration, not only for what he is, but for what he might become.

18. *He selects qualified assistants.* He delegates as much routine to them as possible.

19. *He is compassionate.*

20. *He never forgets that his power is delegated to him by others.* It is his to exercise only so long as he makes use of it in the spirit and for the purposes behind its bestowal into his hands. His authority is limited on every hand by the objectives he is seeking and the interests and desires of those who are affected by his actions.[5]

It goes without saying that the school business administrator must have a better than average intellect, which, when coupled with good common sense, will lead to an inquisitive, critical analysis of problems and procedures. A capacity to plan and to coordinate the planning effort of others will enable the school business administrator to discover improved ways of anticipating and resolving school issues.

[5] Hill, *The School Business Administrator*, pp. 45–48.

TRAINING PROGRAM

Professional training requirements for school business administrators vary widely from state to state and school system to school system. In most cases where the title of assistant superintendent is used, requirements include the holding of a valid administrative certificate, usually based upon the same standards and certification procedures as provided for the superintendent's certificate. In states where the school business administrator does not have the title of assistant superintendent, certification is not generally required and noneducationally trained persons often occupy the position. Very few colleges and universities provide sufficient course work leading to a degree in school business administration, but most provide work in school business administration as an integral part of the degree programs in school administration.

Degrees

As noted, selected curricular activities are available in most graduate programs. There are a few universities providing sufficient programs to warrant advanced degrees in school business administration, usually at the post-master's or specialist levels. Typically, the student wishing to specialize in school business administration works with a college staff to develop a specialized program that provides experiences in educational administration, business administration, finance, economics, administrative sciences, and law. Such programs are made possible by cutting across departmental lines at large institutions that have such disciplines represented. In addition, many specialist and doctoral candidates focus on school business administration in the conduct of their research leading to the dissertation.

Courses

Courses in school business administration are found in nearly every graduate school of education which awards advanced degrees in school administration. Related topics such as school finance, plant planning, economics of education, school law, systems analysis, and personnel administration are also provided in most schools of education. In addition, a number of universities provide opportunity for short-term workshop activities and seminars that focus on school business administration or a subtopic such as accounting, school planning, maintenance and operations, and so forth. These short courses usually carry graduate credit and can be applied toward advanced degrees.

Professional organizations

The major professional organization for school business administrators is the Association of School Business Officials of the United States and Canada, or ASBO, as it is known. ASBO has for a number of years advocated certification for school business administrators and has actively solicited cooperation from colleges and universities in the development of formal degree programs in the field. In 1967 the ASBO board of directors approved a statement of requirements for a Registered School Business Administrator. ASBO issues a certificate to those applicants meeting the requirements. The certificate indicates the holder to be a Registered School Business Administrator. This certification effort was revised in 1970 and now includes the following criteria:

1. Current membership in ASBO along with evidence of five continuous years of membership.
2. Applicant must be a practicing school or college business administrator or have college teaching responsibilities in school business administration. Applicant must have charge of three out of the five major categories of school business administration, which are: (1) Buildings and grounds, (2) Financial affairs, (3) Transportation, (4) School lunch, and (5) Noncertificated personnel.
3. Applicant must have a minimum of a master's degree from an accredited college or university in an area of school business management or in educational administration.
4. Applicant shall have completed a minimum of five years of satisfactory demonstrated administrative experience in the specific field of school business administration.
5. Applicant must have spent a minimum of three years in one job as proof of professional competency and of job stability.
6. Applicant must submit an administrative organization chart indicating applicant's position as the top school business administrator.

7. Evidence of applicant's participation in the state ASBO organization must be included with the application.[6]

The material presented above indicates the strong desire and continuing effort expended by the ASBO toward certification standards for school business administrators. States are increasingly recognizing such efforts and approximately one-half the states now have some minimum requirements.

Other organizations which have some relevance for school business administrators include: The American Association of School Administrators (AASA), which is basically the highest level organization for school administrators and to which most superintendents and assistant superintendents belong, and The Council of Educational Facility Planners (CEFP), which concentrates its efforts on the facility-planning task of the school business administrator. Both of these organizations provide a variety of programs, seminars, workshops, and conferences that are of high value to the school business administrator.

CONCLUSIONS AND PREDICTIONS

The materials presented in this book are an effort to foresee the changing role of the school business administrator as American school systems undergo change in the current decade. The focus of the book has been upon the planning component of the position of the school business administrator. Planning activities, for so long a peripheral consideration for the school business administrator, are going to become a most important segment of that executive's office. The authors have presented a planners-eye view of school business administration. This is a concept that the authors believe will be the prevailing model in years to come.

Predictions as to the increased importance of the school business office and the school business administrator are easily engendered. One need only be sensitive to the growth of public school systems and to the increased awareness of the public to the use of public monies to recognize the need for top-flight performance in the school business activity. With the recent recognition of the

[6]Hill, *The School Business Administrator*, pp. 107–108.

importance of education to all people, the demand for creative school business administration will increase. The challenge, stimulation, opportunity, and rewards are already available for capable, dedicated, willing school business administrators.

SUMMARY

This chapter reviews the role of the school business administrator and develops a relationship between the nature of the position and the human qualities needed to perform effectively. Organizational placement of the school business administrator in small, medium, and large school systems is reviewed, and responsibilities of the office are outlined. The increasingly attractive benefits and salaries afforded school business officials are presented along with outlines of job responsibilities.

Personal characteristics important to the school business administrator are discussed and analyzed. Preservice and inservice training programs are reviewed and suggestions for expanded training efforts are posed. The efforts of professional organizations, particularly the Association of School Business Officials of the United States and Canada, are recognized as important training and professionalization vehicles. The need for recognition and development of the profession of school business administration is emphasized.

SUGGESTED ACTIVITIES

1. After reading the present chapter and related literature, interview a school business administrator in order to synthesize a job description for him. After completing it, compare it with his present job description. Account for any major differences that seem to appear.

2. In view of the present type of job expectations for school business administrators, how will these be apt to change in the next ten to twenty years? If there are significant changes in present-day expectations, how would you account for them?

3. Given the job description developed in activity number one and the job expectations anticipated in the future, what are

the implications for university-oriented preparation programs of the present and near future?

4. Review the current literature of the American Association of School Administrators and the Association of School Business Officials and determine their positions on in-service education for the professional school business administrator. How do you suggest such activities should best be implemented?

SUGGESTED READINGS

American Association of School Administrators. *Profiles of the Administrative Team.* Washington, D.C.: The Association, 1971.

Association of School Business Officials. *The School Business Administrator.* Evanston, Ill.: The Association, 1960.

Fench, Edwin A., and Wilson, Robert E. *The Superintendency Team.* Columbus, O.: Charles E. Merrill Books, Inc., 1965.

Hill, Frederick W. *The School Business Administrator.* Chicago: Association of School Business Officials, 1970.

Jordan, Forbis K. *School Business Administration.* New York: The Ronald Press Company, 1969.

INDEX